The Evolution of Norman Identity, 911–1154

During the period 911–1154, a newly-constituted people came to control not only a Frankish duchy, but also the kingdoms of England and Sicily. This people, composed of Scandinavian settlers and Frankish natives, came to be known as the Normans. This book examines the growth of the concept of the Norman people (*gens Normannorum*), through the self-perception of group members (*Normanitas* or 'Norman-ness') and the perceptions of 'others'. Using identity models which deal with the interaction of various types of communities, it examines narrative sources (both internally and externally produced) in order to establish what it meant to be a Norman, both to the Normans themselves, and to those with whom they had contact. Beyond these perceptions of self and otherness, examination focuses in particular on the role of the Norman leaders (as the embodiment of Norman identity), the effects of language, the importance of conquest and the sense of homeland, up until the significant change in rulership in both England and Sicily in 1154.

NICK WEBBER is Resources Coordinator for the Department of Media and Communication, University of Central England.

The Evolution of Norman Identity, 911–1154

Nick Webber

THE BOYDELL PRESS

First published 2005
The Boydell Press, Woodbridge

ISBN 1 84383 119 8

The Boydell Press is an imprint of Boydell & Brewer Ltd
PO Box 9, Woodbridge, Suffolk IP12 3DF, UK
and of Boydell & Brewer Inc.
668 Mt Hope Avenue, Rochester, NY 14620, USA
website: www.boydellandbrewer.com

A CIP catalogue record of this publication is available
from the British Library

Library of Congress Cataloging-in-Publication data
Webber, Nick, 1976–
   The evolution of Norman identity, 911–1154 / Nick Webber.
      p. cm.
Summary: "A close examination, through original sources, of the Norman
self-image" – Provided by publisher.
Includes bibliographical references and index.
   ISBN 1–84383–119–8 (hardback : alk. paper)
   1. Normans – Europe.   2. Group identity – Europe – History.
3. Civilization, Medieval.   4. Europe – History – 476–1492.   I. Title.
   D148.W43 2005
   940'.04395–dc22   2004026250

This publication is printed on acid-free paper

Typeset by Pru Harrison, Hacheston, Suffolk
Printed in the United Kingdom at the
University Press, Cambridge

Contents

Acknowledgements

I would like to express my gratitude here to all those individuals who provided me with the motivation to keep going even when it all seemed like the worst idea in the world, not only on this book, but also on the doctoral thesis on which it is based. In particular, I must thank Nicholas Brooks for the help and guidance he has given me over many years, both as student and graduate. Without Nicholas' help, this book would certainly not exist nor, I expect, would the thesis.

Regarding the work itself, I am grateful for the assistance of Eric Christiansen and Graham Loud, both of whom were kind enough to loan me their own translations of sources with which I was having difficulty. I also wish to thank Chris Wickham, David Bates and Emily Albu for their constructive comments on my work, which have helped it achieve its current form. Lastly, I must express my gratitude to Caroline Palmer at Boydell and Brewer, for being kind enough to answer all my naïve questions about publishing.

On a more personal level, I would like to thank Lewis, Aysu and Duncan, and others of Birmingham University medieval history research group, for long conversations about identity and warfare. Also, I am very grateful to the staff of UCE Media and Communication Department, who have been so understanding and helpful.

Finally, I would like to offer special thanks to those people who have helped and motivated me most regularly: Julia; my parents; and my flatmates and friends. Thank you all for your support.

Abbreviations

Adhemar	*Ademari Cabannensis Chronicon*, ed. J. Chavanon (Paris, 1897)
Alexiad	*The Alexiad of Anna Comnena*, tr. E.R.A. Sewter (Harmondsworth, 1969)
Amatus	*Storia de' Normanni di Amato di Montecassino*, ed. Vincenzo de Bartholomaeis, *Fonti per la storia d'Italia* (Rome, 1935)
Apulia	William of Apulia, *La Geste de Robert Guiscard*, ed. & tr. Marguerite Mathieu (Palermo, 1961)
AN	*Annales de Normandie*
ANS	*Anglo-Norman Studies / Proceedings of the Battle Conference*
ASC (C)	*The Anglo-Saxon Chronicle: A Collaborative Edition, vol. 5: MS. C*, ed. Katherine O'Brien O'Keeffe (Cambridge, 2001)
ASC (D)	*The Anglo-Saxon Chronicle: A Collaborative Edition, vol. 6: MS. D*, ed. G.P. Cubbin (Cambridge, 1996)
ASC (E)	*The Peterborough Chronicle 1070–1154*, ed. Cecily Clark, 2nd edn (Oxford, 1970)
ASC (tr.)	*The Anglo-Saxon Chronicle*, tr. Dorothy Whitelock, David C. Douglas and Susie I. Tucker (London, 1961)
Baudri	*Baldricus Burgulianus Carmina*, ed. Karlheinz Hilbert (Heidelberg, 1979)
Carmen (1)	*The Carmen de Hastingae Proelio of Guy, bishop of Amiens*, ed. & tr. Frank Barlow, OMT (Oxford, 1999)
Carmen (2)	*The Carmen de Hastingae Proelio of Guy, bishop of Amiens*, ed. & tr. Catherine Morton and Hope Muntz, OMT (Oxford, 1972)
CMC	*Chronica Monasterii Casinensis*, ed. Harmut Hoffman, *MGH SS*, 34 (1980)
Dudo	*De moribus et actis primorum Normanniae ducum auctore Dudone Sancti Quintini Decano*, ed. Jules Lair, Société des Antiquaires de Normandie (Caen, 1865)
Dudo (tr.)	Dudo of St Quentin, *History of the Normans*, tr. E. Christiansen (Woodbridge, 1998)
Eadmer	*Eadmeri historia novorum in Anglia et opuscula duo de vita santci Anselmi et quibusdam miraculis eius*, ed. Martin Rule (RS, 1884)
Eadmer (tr.)	*Eadmer's History of Recent Events in England*, tr. Geoffrey Bosanquet (London, 1964)
EER	*Encomium Emmae Reginae*, ed. & tr. Alistair Cambell (Cambridge, 1998)
EHR	*English Historical Review*
EME	*Early Medieval Europe*
Falco	*The Chronicle of Falco of Benevento*, tr. G.A. Loud (1990)

Flodoard	*Les Annales de Flodoard*, ed. Ph. Lauer (Paris, 1905)
Gaimar	*Lestorie des Engles, solum la Translacion Maistre Geffrei Gaimar*, ed. T.D. Hardy and C.T. Martin, 2 vols (RS, 1888–9)
GG	*The Gesta Guillelmi of William of Poitiers*, ed. & tr. R.H.C. Davis and Marjorie Chibnall, OMT (Oxford, 1998)
Glaber	*Rodulfi Glabri Historiarum Libri Quinque*, ed. & tr. J. France, RGO
GND	*The Gesta Normannorum Ducum of William of Jumièges, Orderic Vitalis, and Robert of Torigni*, ed. & tr. Elisabeth M.C. van Houts, 2 vols, OMT (Oxford, 1992–5)
GRA	*William of Malmesbury, Gesta Regum Anglorum*, ed. & tr. R.A.B. Mynors, R.M. Thomson and M. Winterbottom, 2 vols, OMT (Oxford, 1998–9)
GRP	*Willelmi Malmesbiriensis monachi gesta pontificum Anglorum*, ed. N.E.S.A. Hamilton (RS, 1870)
GS	*Gesta Stephani*, ed. & tr. K.R. Potter and R.H.C. Davis, OMT (Oxford, 1976)
Hexham	*The Chronicle of Richard, Prior of Hexham*, ed. R. Howlett, *Chronicles of the Reigns of Stephen, Henry II, and Richard I*, vol. III (RS, 1886)
HRE	Flodoard of Reims, *Historia Remensis Ecclesie*, ed. & tr. M. Lejeune (Paris, 1854)
HSJ	*Haskins Society Journal*
Huntingdon	Henry, Archdeacon of Huntingdon, *Historia Anglorum*, ed. & tr. Diana Greenway, OMT (Oxford, 1996)
JMH	*Journal of Medieval History*
LE	*Liber Eliensis*, ed. E.O. Blake, Camden Third Series 92 (London, 1962)
LMH	*Liber Monasterii de Hyda*, ed. Edward Edwards, RS (London, 1866)
Malaterra	*De rebus gestis Rogerii Calabriae et Siciliae Comitis et Roberti Guiscardi Ducis fratris eius Gaufredo Malaterra monacho Benedictino*, ed. Ernesto Pontieri, in *Rerum Italicarum Scriptores* 5.1, ed. L.A. Muratori (Milan, 1927–8)
MGH ES	*Monumenta Germaniae Historica. Epistolae Selectae*
MGH LL	*Monumenta Germaniae Historica. Libelli de Lite Imperatorum et Pontificum, saeculis XI. et XII.*
MGH SS	*Monumenta Germaniae Historica. Scriptores*
Monmouth	*The Historia Regum Britannie of Geoffrey of Monmouth*, ed. Neil Wright, 2 vols (Bern, 1985–8)
NMT	Nelson Medieval Texts
OMT	Oxford Medieval Texts
Orderic	*The Ecclesiastical History of Orderic Vitalis*, ed. & tr. Marjorie Chibnall, 6 vols, OMT (Oxford, 1969–80)
PL	*Patrologiae cursus completus, series latina*, ed. J.P. Migne (Paris, 1844–64)
RGO	*Rodulfus Glaber Opera*, ed. & tr. J. France, N. Bulst and P. Reynolds, OMT (Oxford, 1989)

Richer	Richer of Reims, *Historiarum libri quatuor*, ed. & tr. J. Guadet, 2 vols (1845, repr. New York, 1968)
Regesta	*Regesta Regum Anglo-Normannorum*, i, ed. H.W.C. Davis (Oxford, 1913); ii, ed. C. Johnson and H.A. Cronne (Oxford, 1956)
RRAN	*Regesta Regum Anglo-Normannorum: The Acta of William I (1066–1087)*, ed. David Bates (Oxford, 1998)
RS	Rolls Series (London)
SRG	*Scriptores rerum Germanicarum in usum scholarum ex monumentis Germaniae historicis recusi*
Telese	*The Deeds of King Roger, by Abbot Alexander of Telese*, tr. G.A. Loud
TRHS	*Transactions of the Royal Historical Society*
Vita Ædwardi	*Vita Ædwardi Regis*, ed. & tr. Frank Barlow, OMT (2nd edn, Oxford, 1992)
Vita Willelmi	*Rodulfi Glabri Vita Domni Willelmi Abbatis*, ed. N. Bulst, tr. J. France and P. Reynolds, *RGO*

Introduction

The defeat of the Viking forces at Chartres *c.*911 marked the beginning of an important process in Frankish and, indeed, wider European history. The consequent peace, and settlement of a group of Northmen on an area of land around Rouen, proved to be a momentous decision by the Frankish king of the time, Charles the Simple. The Vikings were given land on the seaboard of Francia, on the condition that they would defend it from their countrymen. This method of dealing with the Scandinavian raiders certainly seemed to be a functional solution to the short-term problems that overwhelmed the Frankish administration. Once matters had settled somewhat, Frankish sovereignty could be restored using military force against these relatively small enclaves, and Francia could be reclaimed. It was, in essence, a risky strategy, but one that was to prove its worth. A similar settlement of the Loire proved short-lived, and the new inhabitants of the Rouennais looked to be following suit. These settlers on the Seine proved more resilient, however, and by the end of the tenth century these raiders, known widely as *Normanni*, had come together as a coherent *gens* settled on a (largely) defined territory.

In the eleventh and twelfth centuries, the Normans, as they came to be known in English, became a people renowned throughout their new, Frankish homeland and, indeed, in an area stretching from Ireland to the Holy Land. In the west, the Normans became the conquerors of England, after their successful invasion of 1066. When Edward the Confessor died with no direct heir, the throne was seized by Harold Godwineson, whose claim was contested by two invading armies. The first of these, under Harald Hardrada of Norway, was defeated at Stamford Bridge; the second, under Duke William of Normandy, was victorious at Hastings, the battle in which King Harold was slain. William became the next king of England, and his sons were to rule after him. From this period date some of the great artefacts of English medieval history – the Domesday Book and the Bayeux Tapestry.

In the south, there was no formal invasion led by the Norman duke. In the area of southern Italy and Sicily, Norman mercenaries were operative from the early eleventh century, fighting on various sides for various reasons. Over time, certain of these men – the sons of Tancred de Hauteville in particular – built up power bases, and the mixture of their increasing strength and the concerns of the existing local powers culminated in a major battle at Civitate, in 1053. On one side stood the Norman mercenary groups, along with some of their Lombard allies; on the other, the papal forces of Pope Leo IX. The Norman forces were victorious and, by the end of the eleventh century, Norman rulers were comfortably installed in the duchies of Apulia and Calabria, and the newly formed kingdom of Sicily.

Some of those Normans who had populated the west and south also had a role to play in the east. In the 1090s, Norman forces were instrumental participants in the First Crusade, both in the journey to and capture of Jerusalem, and in relations with the Byzantine emperor of the time, Alexius Comnenus. Bohemond, the son of Robert Guiscard, and Tancred, his cousin, were particularly distinguished among the contingent from the south; Duke Robert Curthose of Normandy admirably represented the Normans of the west.

By the 1150s, however, the time of Norman expansion had passed. Though the descendants of the Normans lived in all these places still, their membership of any group calling itself Norman can be quite reasonably disputed, with the exception of those people living in Normandy, who remain Normans to this day. However, the widespread influences of the Normans left a distinctive mark on the historical record, not only in terms of voluminous historical writing, but also in the form of various fortresses, mausolea, churches and, of course, a rather famous tapestry. These sources, along with those of the Normans' contemporaries – the Franks / French, the English, the Lombards and the Greeks, to name but a few – allow us insight into the Norman people, or *gens Normannorum*, and provide a means of examining the gradual changes taking place in the way that the Normans saw themselves, and in the way that the world saw the Normans.

Before studying such aspects, however, it is necessary to undertake some discussion of the concepts of identity and identity theory that are currently in use, in both history and the social sciences. It is certainly important, given the vague nature of a lot of writing on the subject, that the evolution of identity ideas be clarified before this study is undertaken. Also, there should be some coverage of the way in which ideas of ethnicity (and also those of nation) relate to identity. As identity is not a phenomenon unique to the medieval period, it proves necessary to employ works both relating to both medieval and modern periods of history.

In the last ten or so years, the study of various forms of identity has graced the pages of an increasing number of scholarly works dealing with both the medieval and modern periods. This decade, though marking a seemingly new field of social historical investigation, is rather the culmination of a slow evolution process in the study of group mentalities, an area that has not long been advanced enough to 'deserve' a badge. Some historians examine the influence of ethnic, territorial, religious and other distinctions on both the internal and external elements of societies, while their colleagues, supported by similar work in anthropology and sociology, pursue investigations in the theoretical context. There is, as yet, little or no consistency among these studies, however, and a divide is particularly evident between identity theorists and those who try to apply identity concepts to their chosen period of study. It is not simply that the two approaches are recognised by writers on identity as different, but more that there seems to be a certain lack of communication between the two groups.

The ideas that form the basis of modern identity writing arose initially in the discipline of anthropology in the last century. The orthodoxy created by the anthropologists was one of simple, concrete definitions: an ethnicity (or *ethnie*) could be recognised through its unique racial, linguistic and cultural profile.[1] Though subsequent work suggested that there was more to an ethnicity, including social values, interaction and communication, the perceived concrete nature remained until the

---

[1] *Ethnie* (the French term for ethnicity) is often used to provide a distinction from the meaning attributed to ethnicity by American sociologists, who have tended to use the noun 'ethnicity' to refer to an ethnic minority.

mid-twentieth century.[2] It is in the post-war period, however, that the study of identity as a complex phenomenon has its roots. After E.R. Leach's study of North Burmese hill tribes (1954) undermined one of the basic precepts of pre-war thinking, the field became open to newer ideas. The existing view had been that cultural features and ethnicity were directly correspondent – namely, if two groups exchanged enough cultural features, then they could be expected to amalgamate into a single ethnic group. Leach challenged this viewpoint, proving that cultural features did not correspond closely enough to ethnicity to make such a generalised statement, and showing that ethnicity was neither simple nor particularly logical.[3]

In the 1960s, more 'modern' theories of identity began to be expressed. Elie Kedourie's book *Nationalism* gave pre-eminence to language in the construction of identity, drawing heavily on J.G. Fichte's *Addresses to the German Nation* of 1807–8, and extending these ideas to the constitution of the nation.[4] It was, however, *Ethnic Groups and Boundaries*, edited by Fredrik Barth, that proved to be the definitive work from this period. This collection of papers advocated a reassessment of the very simplistic model of ethnic identity previously provided. The idea that ethnic identity was an objective reality was no longer considered accurate, and the contributors saw ethnicity as more of a subjective phenomenon. This led them to emphasise the importance of ethnicity as something that was claimed by those within a group, and attributed by those outside it. The focus was, therefore, not on the groups themselves but rather on the boundaries between those groups, and the interactions around and across those boundaries.[5]

The result of this research was the 'instrumentalist' school of thought, which considered ethnicity not as something inherited, but rather something taken on voluntarily – it was a rational choice, and a situational construct. Of course, not everyone agreed with this interpretation, and the strongest reaction against this school of thought is known as 'primordialism'. From the primordialist perspective, ethnic identity is an almost subconscious phenomenon, and one which acts beyond the rationality of thought. Individuals can be inclined to act in a certain manner, based on their affiliation to a group identity / *ethnie*. Sometimes, such actions will go against the dictates of 'material calculation' because the individual's freedom of action is constrained by the membership of the group.[6] As the former of the two lines of research is based on the study of the group, and the latter on the study of individuals, it seems likely that the solution lies somewhere in between – one's ethnic identity is not a wholly voluntary choice, but is manipulable in some circumstances, and will exercise a more or less powerful hold depending on the context.

As one might expect, the differences of opinion do not end there. In discussions of identity, as applied to both medieval and modern history, few writers are able to agree on what constitutes an *ethnie* or a nation, and how ethnic and national identities

2   Peter Heather, *The Goths* (Oxford, 1996), 3.
3   *Ibid.*, 3–4.
4   J.G. Fichte, *Addresses to the German Nation* (tr. R.F. Jones and G.H. Turnbull, 1922, repr. Westport, CN, 1979); Elie Kedourie, *Nationalism*, 3rd edn (London, 1966; repr. 1979).
5   Fredrik Barth (ed.), *Ethnic Groups and Boundaries. The Social Organisation of Culture Difference* (1969, repr. Illinois, 1998), in particular 13–15. For some further discussion of these ideas, see Heather, *Goths*, 4–5 and John Hutchinson and Anthony D. Smith, *Nationalism* (Oxford, 1994), 141f.
6   Heather, *Goths*, 5.

relate to these communities. An *ethnie* has been defined as a 'community bound together by belief in common descent and actual common interests', an extension of the *idiom of kinship*, a community that attaches import to its difference from others and reflects this in an ethnonym, or a group of people with a shared cultural identity and spoken language.[7] Equally, a nation has been said to be a race with a pure language, a community with a spirit of co-operation, or 'a named human population sharing an historic territory, common myths and historical memories, a mass, public culture, a common economy and common legal rights and duties for all members'.[8] With so little similarity between definitions, one wonders if these scholars are even discussing the same thing.

It is inevitable, then, that with such varied descriptions of the *ethnie* and nation, those identities that are constituted by membership of these should also be portrayed with great variety. Whether such identities are believed to be based on language, or reflected in language, or based on culture, or territory, or any number of other criteria, the only clear conclusion that can be drawn is that identity is very much a subjective concept. Perhaps some of the difficulties arise from historians striving to be objective about subjectivity. The aforementioned lack of communication between theory and application further aggravates the difficulties. Some historians, not realising that identity is just as divisive an issue in anthropology as it is in history, support their particular view of identity with passing theory references. For example, one historian writes of how anthropology bases group identity on the political circumstances of the moment, this being called 'instrumental ethnicity'; this is, however, only one aspect of the debate.[9]

The history of early Normandy is no exception to this 'rule', and is possibly one of the more problematic cases. Initially set aside as a 'myth' or literary motif, Norman ethnic identity, so evident in their literature, has been revitalised by the recent moves towards identity study in the medieval period. Unfortunately, some writers have opted not to approach identity as a phenomenon to be explored and understood, but instead have used it as an excuse to make apparently unfounded statements about the nature of 'Norman consciousness'. While identity, it is true, is conceptual and largely abstract, evidence is still the mainstay of the historian's craft. To draw conclusions about a perceived identity based more upon unsupported opinion than on careful analytical work is perhaps a little speculative.

Of course, this criticism is by no means levelled at all the historians who work on this period. A good deal of exciting and informative work has been produced in recent years, with a variety of approaches, from complex and informed literary analysis to more anthropological studies. Some, such as G.A. Loud, have supported their

[7]   Patrick Amory, 'Names, Ethnic Identity, and Community in Fifth- and Sixth-Century Burgundy', *Viator* 25 (1994), 4; Pierre van den Berghe, cited in Hutchinson and Smith, *Nationalism*, 97; Ernest Gellner, *Encounters with Nationalism* (Oxford, 1994), 35; Adrian Hastings, *The Construction of Nationhood. Ethnicity, Religion and Nationalism* (Cambridge, 1997), 3.
[8]   Fichte in Kedourie, *Nationalism*, 64–7; Ernest Renan, quoted in P.M. Jones, '1789 and all that. Constructing Identity in Modern France', Inaugural Lecture at the University of Birmingham (9th May 1996), 3; Anthony D. Smith, *National Identity* (London, 1991), 14.
[9]   Sarah Foot, 'The Making of *Angelcynn*: English Identity Before the Norman Conquest', *TRHS* 6 (1996), 36.

ideas with reference to contemporary medieval ideas, such as those of the *gens*.[10] In addition, some of the most compelling modern work on medieval societies has used a combination of methods The most recent work in the Norman sphere has provided useful literary analyses of some of the Norman histories, and Hugh Thomas' recent volume, *The English and the Normans*, undertakes a very full examination of Anglo-Norman integration in the years following the conquest.[11] A substantial amount of such work has also been produced for the early medieval period, focusing on, for example, the Goths, the Avars and the Franks.

It is perhaps to such multi-disciplinarians that we should look for an understanding of the meanings of ethnic identity, considering that identity is something that bridges period divides so very easily. Among these writers, there is a general consensus that identities are prone to constant change (and are thus unstable), that ethnicity is not necessarily the only form of community in a society, and that ethnicity need not be the primary form of identity for an individual.[12] The association of identity and cultural features retains currency even in this modern approach, yet it is no longer the simple equivalence denounced by Leach. While Peter Heather views group identity in terms of the historical myth of the group and the group's established social norms, he signals an awareness that these symbols are only an expression of the identity. It is, therefore, not necessarily possible to define identity by reference to these.[13] While these expressions can help to reinforce the boundaries of an identity, therefore, they are not responsible for shaping that identity.[14] Patrick Amory, also, notes that it is not always easy to determine a subjective ethnic identity from the objectively visible culture.[15]

Identity theories in this vein reflect a school of thought within the social sciences that seeks to go further and create 'conceptual frameworks' for the study of identities.[16] Peter Weinrich's 'identity structure analysis' (ISA) is a 'meta-theoretical framework', which integrates a number of perspectives on the development of identity.[17] Weinrich uses psychological, sociological and anthropological tools to take account of both internal (*ego-recognised*) and external (*alter-ascribed*) identity influences,

---

[10] See G.A. Loud, 'The "Gens Normannorum" – Myth or Reality?', *ANS* 4 (1982), 104–16.

[11] Hugh Thomas, *The English and the Normans. Ethnic Hostility, Assimilation, and Identity 1066-c.1220* (Oxford, 2003). For recent literary analyses, see in particular Leah Shopkow, *History and Community. Norman Historical Writing in the Eleventh and Twelfth Centuries* (Washington, D.C., 1997) and Emily Albu, *The Normans in their Histories: Propaganda, Myth and Subversion* (Woodbridge, 2001).

[12] See, for example, Heather, *Goths*, 6; Patrick Amory, *People and Identity in Ostrogothic Italy, 489–554* (Cambridge, 1997), 13, 16 & 317. Notably, Barth suggested that ethnic identity was superordinate to *most* other statuses (Barth, *Ethnic Groups*, 17; my italics).

[13] Heather, *Goths*, 5 & 309.

[14] Thomas draws regular attention to the reinforcement of identity boundaries through such phenomena as religion, culture, stereotypes and history (*English and Normans*, 14, 283, 300–1, 306, 327, 361, 390, 392). Though he reminds us, quite rightly, that identity constructs cannot operate independently of cultural and social realities, he sometimes overstates the case for history, particularly, as a 'shaping' force (*ibid.*, 347–66). The relationship of the historical myth to the creation of ethnicity is also mentioned by Amory (*People and Identity*, 14).

[15] Amory, *People and Identity*, 16.

[16] For the model, see Peter Weinrich, 'The operationalisation of identity theory in racial and ethnic relations', *Theories of Race and Ethnic Relations*, ed. John Rex and David Mason (Cambridge, 1986), 299–320.

[17] *Ibid.*, 306.

allowing his model to respond to the changing nature of identity.[18] The model also creates some understanding of identity conflicts (such as those between migrant groups and their neighbours), the causes and effects of such situations, and their role in identity development and redefinition. Perhaps most significantly of all, however, this framework allows the student to 'sketch in some features of complex societies where a generally "superordinate" ethnic community contains within it different "subordinate" ethnic communities', and to investigate the affinities of 'dual social-ised' and bilingual individuals.[19] The intention behind this model is to create a dialogue between all areas of identity theory, providing an important framework within which different cases of ethnic phenomena can be related and understood.[20]

Unfortunately, given the focus of most social sciences, such models have often only been applied to modern society, and have not been considered in a medieval context (and may not work there). Modern frameworks do not, for example, deal with the tradition of the *gens*, which is so prominent in medieval sources, and have not been produced with medieval societies in mind. The modern world is not a place in which one encounters many large monarchies, many empires or many conquests. As a result, the possibility that the models may prove insufficient for the task is always present; the advances and changes in society may have taken their toll. Equally, the possibility remains that the behaviour of humans has not changed very much, and that the passage of one thousand years has not particularly influenced the pressures, challenges and responsibilities found within group membership.

Historians such as Herwig Wolfram have sought to remedy this problem by trying to examine medieval society in its own terms. As the general conclusion had been drawn that a self-conscious *gens* manifests an ethnic identity, Wolfram investi-gates the meaning of the word *gens* to contemporaries. It seems that *gens* not only came to incorporate a wide spectrum of meanings during the early middle ages, but that it was used in a context similar to our modern *ethnie*.[21] The criterion for membership of a *gens* was the acknowledgement of the tribal tradition, either through birth or admittance – language was not a barrier.[22] Wolfram also notes that, when first formed, a *gens* had no *patria*, but later grew into a *populus*, reflecting Reinhard Wenskus' theory (1961) that a historical ethnicity was a duality of tribal formation and political constitution (*Stammesbildung und Verfassung*).[23] In the long term, the existence of the *gens* was validated by evolution into a *populus*; this was not just the case for Goths, and another example can be seen, by the eighth century, in the Burgundians.[24]

More recent scholarship has returned to the idea of political constitution of the *gens* as a tool to assist in definition and understanding. As *gentes* evidenced a tendency to establish kingdoms – *regna* – they may be considered as political rather than purely 'ethnic' units. In essence, the *gens* was not a simple community of common biological descent or shared tradition, but something more. Certainly, the *origines gentium*

[18] *Ibid.*, 299.
[19] *Ibid.*, 300.
[20] *Ibid.*, 315–16.
[21] Herwig Wolfram, *History of the Goths* (Munich, 1979; tr. Thomas J. Dunlop, Berkeley, 1988), 5–6.
[22] *Ibid.*, 6.
[23] Wenskus, cited in Wolfram, *History*, 11.
[24] Amory, 'Names', 6.

tended to associate their origins with the reign of kings, reinforcing any perception of a political element in the nature of *gentes*.[25] Furthermore, studies on the transformation from *gens* to *regnum* have highlighted the significance of kingship in ethnicity for the early medieval period – the figure of the king, it has been suggested, was a central focus of reference for the people of the *regnum*.[26]

It is worth noting here, however, that these approaches have not met with universal approval. Caution is advised by, for example, Heather, who warns against overestimating the importance that the Amal dynasty played in shaping the ethnogenesis of the Ostrogoths.[27] The significance of kingship, then, cannot be taken as universal. Importantly, also, the lack of clarity implied by *gens* (and, indeed, other antique terms) has prompted concern among a number of historians. The relatively commonplace translation of *gens* as 'tribe' highlights one such problem. The definition of 'tribe' includes the idea of a common descent, but it has been noted that this may be genuinely biological or entirely mythical.[28] Indeed, the uncertainties surrounding terms such as *gens* have prompted Amory to argue against their use in this 'naïve' way. He suggests that modern models are rather more helpful to our understanding, as long as we retain an awareness of their limitations.[29]

These issues are further complicated by the fact that west European *regna* have been analogised to modern nations by a number of historians, owing to their commonality of custom, law and origin myths. Wolfram's thesis supports this, giving the example of Toledo: he comments that the meaning of *gens* changed in this instance to that of a legally constituted 'national people'.[30] This theory is also supported by Susan Reynolds who, observing that 'the fundamental premise of nationalist ideas is that nations are objective realities, existing throughout history', views a comparable ideology in the medieval *regnum* (considered as a people with a permanent and objective reality).[31] But historians of the modern period, writing on the nation and nationalism, could not disagree more. Be it on the provision that nations require such criteria as mass education and media, or a single political culture, modernists are agreed that the nation could not have existed prior to a widely debated date some time between 1600 and 1900.

A number of the modernist arguments against medieval nations can be countered, however. One of the seemingly salient features of the nation is that of territory. It has been said that nation involves a 'named human population sharing an historic territory', and that many nationalisms transfer the focus of their identity from ethnicity to territory.[32] As we have already seen, this is not something that is unique to modern

[25] Hans-Werner Goetz, Jörg Jarnut and Walter Pohl (eds), *Regna and Gentes. The Relationship between Late Antique and Early Medieval Peoples and Kingdoms in the Transformation of the Roman World* (Leiden, 2003), 5 & 623.

[26] *Ibid.*, 624.

[27] Peter Heather, 'Gens and regnum among the Ostrogoths', in Goetz, et al., *Regna and Gentes*, 95.

[28] J.H.W.G. Liebeschuetz, '*Gens* into *regnum*: the Vandals', in Goetz, et al., *Regna and Gentes*, 55.

[29] Amory, *People and Identity*, p. 18, n.11.

[30] Wolfram, *History*, 10.

[31] Susan Reynolds, *Kingdoms and Communities in Western Europe 900–1300* (Oxford, 1984; repr. 1986), 251–2. These ideas of identity and its relation to history are similar to those of the philosopher Immanuel Kant, who cited awareness of existence across time as one of the three bases of formulation of personal identity.

[32] Smith, *National Identity*, 14; J.J. Breuilly, *Nationalism and the State*, 2nd edn (Manchester, 1993), 6.

states, but something that occurs readily throughout the medieval period during the process of political constitution. The Burgundians were just one of many groups for which this process apparently took place, transferring their ethnonyms to toponyms in the middle ages, two other obvious examples are the Franks (Francia) and Angles (England).

The close relationship of these toponyms to the identities of these peoples can be seen through the titles adopted by their rulers, the importance of whom to ethnic identity has already been mentioned. The ruling family are often the only members of society who can trace a pure line of descent (however mythical) from their heroic forefathers, and they occupy a place at the top of the social hierarchy. During the medieval period, there are numerous changes of title from, for example, the duke of the Normans (*dux Normannorum*) to the duke of Normandy (*dux Normanniae*). This change reflects a change of emphasis for those people involved in the social order of which the duke is head. The same is true with the king of the Franks (changing to the king of France) and so on. The argument for territory as a mainstay of nation is further refuted by reference to France in the eighteenth century. In this alleged period of nation formation, it is interesting to see the king of France, *le roi de France et de Navarre*, retitle himself *le roi des Français* – the king of a people, not of a territory.[33]

The most resounding denunciation of the modernist assertions comes not, however, from a medieval historian, but from a theologian. Adrian Hastings has found evidence for the concept of nation throughout the medieval period, and this not solely in *regna* either. The Latin word *natio* appears throughout the Vulgate in the context of a translation of the Greek *ethnos*. While this shows that at the time of translation, *natio* did not hold the meaning that we attribute to nation today, the fourteenth-century Wycliffite Bible (from the Vulgate) renders this word as *nacioun* (the precursor of our 'nation').[34] As elsewhere in Wycliffite literature the same word is used, in such a context as to indicate a modern interpretation of nation, it seems to indicate awareness of the concept of nation in this period. Further support comes from Richard Rolle's edition of the Psalms, also from the fourteenth century, which uses the same word in a similar manner.[35] Even the typical modernist argument against the use of the word *natio* as evidence for national ideas can be disproved. Though it is often asserted that *natio* only referred to the administrative divisions within medieval universities, evidence from *c.*1140 suggests otherwise, as Bernard, bishop of St David's, described the Welsh to the pope as a *natio*, a people distinguished by their 'language, laws, habits, modes of judgement and customs'.[36] The pope appears again later as a proving ground for the identity of the nation, in context of the 1320 Declaration of Arbroath, addressed 'to the lord supreme pontiff by the community of Scotland'.[37] Hastings further reminds us that, while it is all very well to debate on the applicability of the word nation to Ming China (where it was foreign to society), it is quite another thing to allege that the word was not relevant to people who used it of themselves.[38]

33 Alfred Cobban, quoted in Hutchinson and Smith, *Nationalism*, 249.
34 Hastings, *Construction*, 15.
35 *Ibid.*, 16.
36 *Ibid.*, 17.
37 G.W.S. Barrow, *Robert Bruce*, 2nd edn (Edinburgh, 1976), 425.
38 Hastings, *Construction*, 19.

It seems clear that the study of (ethnic) identity in history is an area riddled with terminological difficulties. The acceptability and application of certain words and ideas seems to vary not just between schools of thought, but also between individual scholars. Yet to avoid using all the group terms that appear in our sources would create rather significant problems during discussion. It is necessary, therefore, to use these terms with a certain element of care, in the manner in which medieval people used them rather than as anthropologically defined elements. However, the aim should be to include not only those practical aspects of identity revealed by the source material, but also a consistent and informed theoretical perspective. Identity is a very informative area of study, but without structured analytical and theoretical guidelines, one can conclude almost anything from a given source. As such, one cannot usefully approach identity from the perspective of a single discipline, but must instead utilise the wide variety of ideas available, in medieval and modern history, in literature, and throughout the social sciences. To do as some have suggested and define our criteria for *ethnos*-based research wholly within a single discipline would be a mistake.[39] It is only through a combination of such approaches and ideas that an effective study of identity, ethnicity, nation, and so on can be performed, and unfounded and unevidenced speculation only muddies the already unclear water.

---

[39] Michael Schmauder, 'The relationship between Frankish *gens* and *regnum*: a proposal based on the archaeological evidence', in Goetz et al., *Regna and Gentes*, 292.

PART I

The Normans in Normandy

1

Sources, 911–1066

The study of Norman identity in the period from 911 to 1066 is a rather problematic one. Tenth-century Normandy is already renowned for its lack of usable source material, and the information provided by the Frankish sources over the same period is hardly voluminous. Though the source base does improve once one reaches the countship of Richard I (942–96), with the appearance of charters and, from the end of his rule, the composition of Dudo of St-Quentin's *Historia Normannorum* (written *c*.994–*c*.1015), there is still a very real shortage. These problems are compounded by the fact that it is necessary to limit ourselves further in the sources that can be employed, particularly at the end of our period, when sources are fortunately more plentiful. Work produced after the conquest of England, for example, is liable to bear a very different mark from that produced beforehand, and consequently such works are not relevant to the identity of the pre-conquest period.

The sources that we have at our disposal, therefore, can be divided into three main sections. Firstly, there are those sources produced internally, i.e. within Normandy, either by native Norman writers or by those writing under Norman auspices. The second grouping covers those works produced externally (elsewhere in Francia / France) that make explicit reference to the Normans in context of this period. Finally, we have charter sources, including those produced both in Normandy and in Francia.

The earliest of the two main Norman writers in this period is Dudo of St-Quentin. Dudo was a Frankish clerk from St-Quentin in the Vermandois, originally sent to Normandy as an emissary by Albert of Vermandois, to secure Albert's return to favour with the newly crowned Hugh Capet. Given that Albert's death occurred in 988, this embassy must have taken place in either 987 or 988. Dudo seems to have been chosen on account of his education in the Carolingian tradition, probably at Liège, and perhaps also of his youth.[1] As already noted, Dudo's history was written between *c*.994 and *c*.1015, in a style that utilises a mix of verse and prose (prosimetric), with a later dedicatory letter to Bishop Adalbero of Laon. In this letter, Dudo discusses his commission, claiming that Richard I, two years prior to his death in 996, had asked him to write the history, and that this commission was renewed by Richard II and by Richard I's brother, Rolf of Ivry (called by Dudo the narrator (*relator*) of his work). The latter date for the history is also extrapolated from the

---

[1]   Leah Shopkow, 'The Carolingian World of Dudo of Saint-Quentin', *JMH* 15 (1989), 25; Shopkow, *History and Community*, 36 & n. 2. Shopkow places Dudo in his early twenties in 989, extrapolating from Dudo's comment that he was five decades old in his closing poem.

dedicatory letter, in which Dudo refers to himself as '*Dudo . . . Sancti Quintini decanus*', a position that he did not hold until 1015 and as a consequence of which he spent a good deal less time at the Norman court.[2] The wording of the letter further implies that the history already exists at this point.

Unfortunately, as a historical source, Dudo has until recently been widely disregarded. Henri Prentout's positivist *Étude critique sur Dudon de St-Quentin et son histoire des premiers ducs normands* of 1916 confirmed fifty years of accrued disregard following the publication of Jules Lair's edition of 1865 (still the most recent Latin edition). This disregard is perpetuated by many modern scholars, who fail to distinguish between considered embellishment and simple inaccuracy or ineptitude. It is true to say, and many have, that propaganda as we understand it was not a feature of this period, but to liken the positive areas of Dudo's work to boasting is not, one would think, an anachronism. It is precisely this manner of expression that makes Dudo such a fundamental source for the study of Norman identity in this period: Dudo was making a statement with a strong motive, just not a political one.

Dudo, of course, only allows a look at Norman identity during the period up to 1015. For the countships of Richard II (996–1026) and III (1026–7), Robert (1027–35) and William (1035–87), it is necessary to employ the *Gesta Normannorum Ducum* of William, a monk of Jumièges (*Gemmethicensis cenobita*), who wrote under Abbot Robert III (1048/9–79).[3] Jumièges had a strong connection with the counts of Rouen, having been refounded, with a grant from William Longsword, in the early 940s after its abandonment shortly after 862 following Viking raids.[4] William used Dudo's work as an historical foundation for the early parts of his history, but drew also on Frankish sources (such as the *Historia Francorum Senonensis*, covered below) and various works of hagiography.[5] William was probably born *c*.1000, and wrote most of his work in the 1050s, returning later to make additions concerning the Norman conquest of England (the whole being completed *c*.1070–1).[6]

The later section of William's work clearly shows the importance of this history. We know that he was witness to events from Richard III's countship onwards, and in his dedicatory preface he states that he had eyewitness accounts 'related by many persons trustworthy on account equally of their age and experience'.[7] He certainly displays specific knowledge of Évreux, and it is postulated that one of these eyewitnesses may have been John, bishop of Avranches and archbishop of Rouen, the son of Dudo's proclaimed *relator* Rolf of Ivry.[8] Unlike Dudo, however, William does not appear to have been directly commissioned, merely referring to 'the encouraging support of several good friends', although the work is dedicated to Duke William II (the Conqueror).[9]

---

[2] Dudo, 115.

[3] *GND* I, 4–5.

[4] *Ibid.*, xxiii.

[5] Elisabeth M.C. van Houts, 'The *Gesta Normannorum Ducum*: a History Without an End', *ANS* 3 (1981), 108.

[6] Van Houts, 'History', 106 and *GND* I, xxxii.

[7] *GND* I, xxxi, xxxix & 4–6: '*Relatu plurimorum ad corroborandam fidem eque idoneorum annis et rerum experimentis*'.

[8] *Ibid.*, xliv; Dudo, 125.

[9] *GND* II, 182: '*Bonis quibusdam adhortando fauentibus*'.

Though there are a variety of other Norman sources in addition to these two histories, these are by far the most informative and useful for the study of identity, and thus discussion has been restricted largely to these two pieces. Additional sources that may further enhance our understanding of the Norman viewpoint include the anonymous *Lament on the Death of William Longsword*, and the *Inventio et Miracula Sancti Wulfrani*.[10] Originally thought to be a Frankish work, based on the origin of the two extant manuscripts, Elisabeth van Houts has provided a convincing argument for the *Lament*'s production at Jumièges, based on the knowledge of Jumièges evidenced therein (although she notes that this does not preclude the possibility that it may have been written at Poitiers).[11] As the poem mentions that William III of Aquitaine is still alive, it must have been written before his death in 963, and obviously after that of William Longsword (most likely on 20th December 942), making it the earliest Norman source at our disposal.[12] Although far shorter than our histories and consequently less informative, the *Lament* still provides a useful insight into the time at which it was written. The *Inventio* was a rather later work, written in 1053–4 at St-Wandrille, shortly after the transfer of relics to Rouen (25–31 May 1053); the lack of mention of the Battle of Mortemer (February, 1054) and the rebellion of Count William of Arques (1053) support an early date for most of the text.[13]

In order to balance the perspectives provided by these Norman sources, it is necessary to employ a range of external material. Firstly, we have Flodoard of Reims, whose *Annals* provide us with some Frankish opinions of the Normans. Flodoard's focus, in his coverage of the events of 919–66 (the year in which he died), is the Carolingian royal court and its relations with the major Frankish principalities. As a consequence of the minority of Richard I, Normandy plays a significant role in the *Annals*, as there was a great deal of royal concern with Norman problems. This is not the case in Flodoard's other well-known work, the *Historia Remensis Ecclesiae*, whose concern is restricted to the locality of Reims, reflecting the intense regionalism of the later Carolingian period. Flodoard's work is well-founded: we know that he was a canon of Notre-Dame de Reims, and it seems probable that he was the archivist there; he was certainly held prisoner for dissension by Herbert of Vermandois in 940.[14] His writing style is considerably less passionate than such as Dudo, and this has led historians to consider him to be a very accurate source, although he does have a tendency to stress the royal viewpoint, reflecting the tradition of the *Annales Regni Francorum* and of Hincmar.[15] Overall, though, he evidences a lack of any particular favouritism, and as a result, he gives away little about his opinion of the Normans as a people.

[10] Editions of the *Lament* can be found in J. Lair, *Bibliothèque de l'École des Chartes* xxxi (1870), 389–406; J. Lair, *Étude sur la vie et la mort de Guillaume Longue-Épée* (1893); Ph. Lauer, *Le Règne de Louis IV* (1900), 319–23; P.A. Becker, 'Der planctus auf den Normannenherzog Wilhelm Langschwert (942)', *Zeitschrift für französische Sprache und Literatur* lxiii (1939), 190–7. The Lauer edition is used here.
[11] *GND* I, xxix.
[12] See *GND* I, p. 95, n. 2 for the date of William's death.
[13] Elisabeth M.C. van Houts, 'Historiography and Hagiography at Saint-Wandrille: the "Inventio et miracula sancti Vulfranni" ', *ANS* 12 (1990), 237–8.
[14] Jean-Paul Devroey, *Études sur la grande domaine carolingien* (Aldershot, 1993), II: 81.
[15] *GND* I, pp. 122–3, n. 2.

Richer of Reims, on the other hand, is much more forthcoming about the nature of the Normans (at least as he perceives it). His *Historiarum Libri Quatuor* cover the period from 888 to 995, having been written for Gerbert of Aurillac, the archbishop of Reims, some time in either 995 or 996.[16] Richer seems to have intended to continue the *Annals of the Frankish Kingdom* of Hincmar of Reims, but he had literary ambitions, and attempted to employ styles gleaned from classical writers such as Sallust. Furthermore, the Capetian succession removed the standard preoccupation with the Carolingian kings, and thus Richer uses more varied material. As Flodoard's successor, he made wide, if careless, use of Flodoard's *Annals* for the earlier years of his history, but his carelessness means that this section of his work often proves inaccurate or misleading. However, from 970 the historical quality of the work improves; certainly Richer seems to have been close to political affairs after this point, and we know that he attended Hugh Capet's coronation in 987.[17] Fortunately, Richer is no less opinionated here than in the earlier sections. The work's sudden ending with the events of 995 seems unusual, especially given the presence of notes suggesting the contents of subsequent chapters; it was, however, apparently unconnected with the departure of Richer's patron, Gerbert, who fled to the court of Otto III in 997.[18] Regardless of these flaws, Richer's work is still extremely useful for his free expression of opinion on contemporary rulers and peoples.

Less useful is the *Historia Francorum Senonensis*, written by an anonymous monk of Sens.[19] The author lacked the knowledge of political events of Flodoard or Richer, although he does provide information that we do not have elsewhere. The relatively small size of this work (only five and a half pages of print) quite obviously limits its usefulness in this context, especially as it bears a much greater similarity to Flodoard's *Annals* than Richer's *History*. It seems to have been written *c*.1035 x 40, and has a distinctly military bent; thus, although there is a fair amount of coverage of the activity of the Normans in the context of the stabilisation of Capetian power, the author has little to say concerning their character.[20]

Rodulf Glaber, on the other hand, has a good deal to say about the Normans, related in part to the level of contact he had with them as a consequence of studying under the noted Cluniac William of Volpiano (St William of Dijon). Born *c*.980, Rodulf was a Cluniac monk who produced two works that have value in our context: his *Historiarum Libri Quinque* and *Vita Willelmi*. Similar to Dudo in being a writer of external origin who wrote positively about the Normans, Rodulf was of Burgundian extraction but had connections, via William of Volpiano, with monasteries such as Fécamp, which William reformed in the Cluniac tradition. Rodulf spent his life in the monasteries of Burgundy, and wrote his *Histories* during his time

---

[16] Rosamund McKitterick, *The Frankish Kingdoms under the Carolingians, 751–987* (London, 1983), 306.

[17] Jean Dunbabin, *France in the Making, 843–1180* (Oxford, 1985), 19.

[18] Dudo (tr.), xx; *The Letters of Gerbert*, tr. H.P. Lattin, Records of Civilisation Sources and Studies 60 (New York, 1961), 15.

[19] *Historia Francorum Senonensis*, ed. G.H. Pertz, *MGH SS* IX (1925), 364–9.

[20] The dating of this source had previously only been vaguely set at some time after 1015 (see Dunbabin, *France*, 124), but Elisabeth van Houts has argued for this more precise dating based on information drawn from a paper by J.H. Ehlers (*GND* I, xxxix & n. 96; J.H. Ehlers, 'Die Historia Francorum Senonensis und der Aufstieg des Hauses Capet', *JMH* 4 (1978), 1–25).

at St-Bénigne at Dijon and St-Germain-d'Auxerre (a period beginning before *c.*1030 and ending *c.*1045/6); his *Vita Willelmi* was produced alongside the *Histories*, during a short stint at Cluny between 1031 (the year of William's death at Fécamp) and *c.*1036.[21] Rodulf's work is an ideal source for the study of identity: he is opinionated in his writing (perhaps owing to his apparent lack of patronage), and it has been noted that 'the *Histories* clearly bear the stamp of the age in which they were written'.[22]

Another informative writer is Adhemar of Chabannes. While not as freely spoken as Richer or Rodulf, he maintains a clear stance on the Northmen as a race, associated with their destructive attacks on Aquitaine, his home. He was probably born *c.*988, a date extrapolated from a mention of his age in a letter dating from *c.*1028.[23] Whereas Rodulf would appear to have been an ordinary monk, Adhemar was of noble extraction, and was given to the monastery of St-Cybard at Angoulême as a child: here he passed the greater part of his life. His work, the *Chronicon*, is an excellent source for the history of Aquitaine, but there is at least some mention of the Northmen in the region, as well as some events in Normandy. The *Chronicon* covers the period from the origin of the Franks to 1028, although the first two books (up to the end of the reign of Charlemagne) seem to be little more than a reiteration of earlier works. The third book has a sizeable debt to the *Annales Laurissenses*, which form the bulk of the content of the first fifteen chapters, though the remainder of the work is Adhemar's own.

Finally, we come to the charters. For reasons of convenience (i.e. the limits of time and space), these have been limited to the Norman ducal charters for the period (edited by Marie Fauroux in *Recueil des Actes des Ducs de Normandie, 911–1066*), and their Frankish royal counterparts (published in the series of *Chartes et Diplômes Relatifs à l'Histoire de France*).[24] Although the Norman charters do not actually begin until 965, the first Frankish charter in which they are mentioned (after the settlement) dates from 918, and the charters from this point allow study of the changes in comital / ducal titles. This in turn can present us with something of a picture of Norman prestige throughout the period, and the various donative and foundation charters give us an insight into the Norman attitude to religion.

In summary, this study of Norman identity in the period 911–1066 will focus on a number of historians, and a modest amount of charter evidence. The external sources employed give us an acceptable variety of perspectives from various areas and, while analysis is restricted in the main to only two internal histories, these are both sizeable works that tell us a great deal about the Normans as a people in this period. Charter evidence, also, can include opinion and illustrate power and wealth, and thus we are given access to the documentary information required for a study of Norman and Frankish perceptions of the Norman race in the period 911–1066.

---

[21] *RGO*, xlv.
[22] *Ibid.*, cvi.
[23] Adhemar, v.
[24] On the early Norman charters, see Joseph R. Strayer, 'Recueil des Actes des Ducs de Normandie (Review)', *Speculum* 37 (1962), 607–8.

2

Internal Identity

The name Norman, derived via Old French and recorded in various Latin forms such as *Nordmanni*, *Nortmanni* and *Normanni*, in popularly linked with the medieval conquerors of England, and is synonymous with military prowess and cunning. While both these things are integral to ideas of 'Norman-ness' (*Normanitas*), the name is unlikely to have been the choice of the 'Normans', but rather a title imposed by the other peoples with whom they had dealings (primarily the Franks). Yet, as is evident from the work of chroniclers and historians, such as Dudo of St-Quentin and William of Jumièges, this title became something of which this *gens* were proud and, more, something associated with the aspects of culture and society that the Normans valued. In fact, the name Norman became a label for an identity construct that was no less powerful than that of their contemporaries, and often more clearly evident.

From both an actual and a theoretical viewpoint, this is proof of the adaptability of those people who inhabited the Rouen area during the tenth century. The Scandinavian settlers seem unlikely to have been an overall majority, though there may have been some areas where they were. In Norman culture, however, we see a combination of both Frankish and Scandinavian elements that suggest not simply a 'Scandinavian impact', but a synthesis of cultural ideas, showing both change and evolution in the ideas and identities of all the people inhabiting the area later called Normandy. This is, to an extent, unusual when one considers modern theory. Identity structure analysis suggests that the situation created by this settlement would be one in which identities were threatened, leading to cultural conflict.[1] In such a situation, adaptive identities undergo a process of change (as they alter to reflect the new situation), while other, 'vulnerable' identities are threatened, often as a consequence of their inability to change. The result, therefore, is a change in the nature of one or both of the identities in an area that allows them to coexist; 'vulnerable' identities become 'broken', and will probably not survive.[2]

While this model fits the Norman situation to some degree, it draws heavily upon modern immigrations, and focuses on the power structures as regulators and, in some cases, as instigators of these conflicts. A subordinate (immigrant) community lacks resources with which to combat threats to its integrity and identity, as these are in the hands of the superior community: this lack renders the 'settler' vulnerable to 'racism'.[3] But how does one apply such concepts to a settlement in which the

---

[1] See Weinreich, 'Operationalisation', 299–320.
[2] *Ibid.*, 300.
[3] *Ibid.*, 303.

resources and power at the local level come under the control of the settlers? Logically, this is the case in most subordinate communities to a degree, but the relative scale of the power structures must be considered. The comparison between a small locality in Britain, for example, and the strength of a centralised modern government is very different from that between comital Rouen and the highly fragmented Frankish power structure.

To use a conquest model would be equally inaccurate, as can be seen when one looks at conquests about which we are better informed. The situation of the 'Native Americans' comes readily to mind: they maintained a distinct identity, although the ethnic title seems something of a concession to the white colonists. The strength of their identity has proven itself by the final removal of the ill-conceived 'Red Indian' ethnonym, and their capacity to maintain their culture, but there is no uncertainty about where the power resides in America. In early periods, we see races that are subjugated seemingly disappear from the historical record, only to re-emerge many years later as their conquerors weaken: the Gepids, who had been 'Huns' for a considerable period, were instrumental in the revolt that shattered the Huns after the death of Attila in 453.

The evidence of this sort of subjection persists throughout history: the Normans in England, though having an impact as conquerors, disappeared comparatively rapidly as an independent *ethnie* there; they were absorbed and became 'English'.[4] So, in terms of conquest, one of overwhelming numbers results in the persistence of subordinate identities, while a smaller-scale affair leads to the disappearance of the conquering influence. However, the Normans break the rule again, as Normandy is to this day seen as having its own unique blend of culture, even though it has been controlled by the French for almost 800 years; some of the customs introduced under the settlers remain. If this is the case, however, and the standard models cannot be easily applied, how should we perceive Norman identity?

The answer seems to lie in the way in which the two societies (those of the Vikings and the Franks) interacted. The toponymic evidence that we have suggests that after the settlement, the communities in the area were of various types. There were those composed entirely of Franks, those of mixed ethnicity, and probably a few that were either entirely or primarily Scandinavian. Consequently, a situation was created in the future duchy in which cultural ideas could mingle within the centres of mixed ethnicity. This would naturally result in an exchange of surface cultural features, a process that would have been aided by the fact that a number of Scandinavians had converted to Christianity. However, there were also areas of a single, predominant ethnicity, which functioned as bastions of conservatism and cultural preservation. For the Scandinavians, these were those maritime settlements in which the sea was the primary producer and links to a nautical existence were maintained; for the Franks, it was those areas nearest the borders of other Frankish provinces, and those in which the Carolingian traditions and offices were left unchanged. The resultant cultural confusion, as change pressed outwards and conservatism pressed inwards, was compounded by inconsistency in what we know of the leaders' policies.

If Dudo of St-Quentin is to be believed, Rollo, the first Norman count of Rouen, resisted the Carolingian hierarchy during a meeting with King Charles the Simple,

---

[4]   Below, Part III.

and introduced laws that seem to have caused some confusion among the pre-existing peasantry (or, at the very least, resulted in anecdotal stories).[5] His successor, William Longsword, seems to have acted in precisely the opposite way: Dudo credits the rebel Scandinavian Riulf with the comment that 'our lord William . . . has procured Frankish friends for himself, and is deprived of our counsel', made to 'several of the chiefs of the Northmen'.[6] Furthermore, Dudo reports that a key was found on William's body after his assassination that could be used to open a box containing a monkish habit: William apparently intended to become a monk at Jumièges if he had returned alive from his meeting with Arnulf of Flanders.[7] William of Jumièges records the same tale, probably gleaned from Dudo, but an associated idea was advanced in the *Lament for the Death of William Longsword* before either writer broached the subject.[8] The *Lament* comments that William 'seemed by his manner to serve the life of monks', suggesting that a tradition to this effect may have been present at Jumièges, which perhaps encouraged William of Jumièges to recount the tale that Dudo told.[9]

Finally, Richard I, William's son, was a mix of both the Scandinavian and Frankish worlds, being born of mixed parentage and educated in the customs of both races: both Dudo and William of Jumièges mention that Richard's father had him instructed both in the 'Dacian' (Scandinavian) and 'Roman' (French) tongues.[10] Thus, Richard had cultural ties to both societies, and acted as such. These changes in the approach of the Norman leaders merely added to the confusion, as they were seen to stand first with one side and then with another. The fact that the power structures in the area had been entirely taken over by newcomers, be they Scandinavians or other recruited aristocracy, meant that even the control of power and resources was divided; it was not until later in the period that the dukes extended their power over all others.[11]

It is here that we return to the name 'Norman'. The Old French words *Normant* (sing.), *Normans* (pl.) and *Normanz* (pl.) from which the name comes were unlikely to have been used by the Scandinavians of themselves. Although they are, in essence, reduced forms of *Northmen* (a Teutonic or Scandinavian term), the various forms of *Normanni* that appear in our ninth- and early tenth-century French sources are insultingly general.[12] They provide no real distinction between the different Scandinavian peoples, and certainly do not encapsulate the Frankish inhabitants of the settled area: Orderic Vitalis tells us that the term is a conjunction of 'north' and 'man', hardly descriptive of the inhabitants of the Rouennais.[13] Yet, although the Frankish inhabitants of that area may have considered the Scandinavian settlers as

5   Dudo, 168–9, 171–2; Dudo (tr.), 48–9, 52–3.
6   Dudo (tr.), 64; Dudo, 187: '*Noster senior Willelmus . . . Francigenas amicos acquirit sibi, nostro concilio privatus*'; '*plurimis principum Northmannorum*'.
7   Dudo, 208; Dudo (tr.), 84.
8   For William's version, see *GND* I, 92–4.
9   Lauer, *Louis IV*, 321: '*vita[m] monachorum suo more / videretur deservire*'.
10 Dudo, 221–2; Dudo (tr.), 97; *GND* I, 88.
11 Eleanor Searle, *Predatory Kinship and the Creation of Norman Power, 840–1066* (Berkeley, 1988), 5.
12 For *Northmen*, see *Oxford English Dictionary*, vol. X, 517. For the derivations of *mann* from a common Teutonic root, see vol. IX, 284.
13 Orderic, V, bk IX 24–6.

Northmen, other Franks appear to have made no distinction between the settlers and the pre-existing population: they are all simply *Normanni*.[14] So why did these 'proto-Normans' adopt another people's generalisation in such a proud way?

The root of this problem seems to rest in the cultural confusion in comital Rouen. The maintenance of the pre-existing ethnic groupings was impossible: by their very nature they implied difference, and yet the two cultures had become rapidly intermingled, as Scandinavian custom met Carolingian law, and languages altered accordingly. While identities are essentially fluid constructs, it may be that these exchanges of ideas and concepts occurred too quickly to be met in a simple evolutionary manner; whatever the case, a new way was sought, one that could encompass the identities of both groups while diminishing neither. Unlike the *Alemanni* of the third century, however, neither group was capable of smoothly accommodating the disparities between the two.[15] It was probably simpler, therefore, to adopt a new name than to try and maintain older distinctions, especially if intermarriage was as intense as has been suggested.[16] If this was, however, the case, the complexities and peculiarities of Norman identity are in some way explained. If we are no longer dealing with (at least) two distinct *gentes* in the Norman territory, then we cannot expect the Normans to conform to models that deal with the interaction of antagonistic identities. The Norman identity that we can examine through our sources ceases to be an identity that is simply evolving on ordinary terms; a new *gens* had been created, and its identity was correspondingly new. The adoption of this new ethnonym marked the ethnogenesis of a new people.

Cassandra Potts makes mention of a similar interpretation.[17] She suggests that Normandy was 'the product of a difficult but ultimately successful union between these newcomers and natives', these 'Norman rulers' and 'their Frankish subjects', implying an identity constituted by territory through the process of state formation.[18] Her slightly contradictory consideration that the Normans were 'a new people born of the synthesis of several groups' (and thus not rulers of Frankish subjects, but rulers of Normans), is rather more compelling, but she does not, unfortunately, explore the ethnic ramifications of this idea. That this period saw the creation of 'a new people, a new ethnicity and identity' is not in disagreement; however, to suggest that this was the result of 'the successful incorporation of various peoples from different backgrounds into one community' is to go too far.[19] The newcomers and natives were only a community insofar as they lived in the same area;

---

[14] See below, pp. 40–1.

[15] Hans J. Hummer has examined the apparent peculiarity of the Alemannic identity in the Late Antique period, concluding that Alemannic identity essentially had no ethnic context (being ideologically flexible), and was thus able to accommodate a number of quite different groups ('The Fluidity of Barbarian Identity: the Ethnogenesis of Alemanni and Suebi', *EME* 7 (1998), 6–7).

[16] For considerations on intermarriage, see David Bates, *Normandy Before 1066* (London, 1982), 21 and Lauren Wood Breese, 'The Persistence of Scandinavian Connections in Normandy in the Tenth and Early Eleventh Centuries', *Viator* 8 (1977), 58.

[17] See Cassandra Potts, *Monastic Revival and Regional Identity in Early Normandy* (Woodbridge, 1997), and '*Atque unum et diversis gentibus populum effecit*: Historical Tradition and the Norman Identity', *ANS* 18 (1996), 139–52.

[18] Potts, *Monastic Revival*, p. 2, n. 5; *ANS* 18, 151.

[19] Potts, *Monastic Revival*, 3.

the community of customs and *mores* was the product, not the cause, of the ethnogenesis of the *gens Normannorum* and its correspondingly new identity.

Examination of this fledgling identity is, however, difficult. Norman histories that were actually written within the period 911–1066 are few and far between; of the two most significant, the earliest is Dudo's *Historia Normannorum*, which was not produced until at least the end of the tenth century (*c*.996–*c*.1015). His successor in the Norman historical tradition, William of Jumièges, was writing in the 1050s (though he did add to his work after the conquest of England), and he is generally acknowledged to have drawn heavily on Dudo for the earlier sections of his work.[20] Unfortunately, this leaves us with scant internal evidence for the Normans under the leadership of both Rollo and William Longsword. While Dudo provides coverage of the countship of Richard I, his account of the life of Rollo has been intensively scrutinised by a variety of historians, all of whom are deeply critical of his reliability as a source – David Douglas observes that 'Rollo's biography must be constructed independently of the dean of St. Quentin'.[21] In fact, the rest of Dudo's work is no more highly regarded by many, and recent work by such historians as Eleanor Searle, Felice Lifshitz and Leah Shopkow has in part sought to rehabilitate Dudo as a source.[22] If we are to use Dudo for our examination, however, there remain problems to be resolved, both in the areas of his value as a literary source and as a factual one.

Possibly the most important issue to address when employing Dudo's *Historia Normannorum* is that of veracity. Given the lack of sources for tenth-century Francia, it is tempting to take a great deal of what Dudo claims at face value; however, the inconsistencies in his life of Rollo and elsewhere have led some historians to ignore everything he says unless it can be substantiated elsewhere. For our purposes, however, Dudo can perhaps be considered a 'safer' source. By his own admission, he was in a position to draw on personal experience for the writing of his final book, on the life of Duke Richard I: he refers to a ducal commission, which he received (presumably in 994), and he seems to have known the ducal family personally.[23] We know almost for certain that this was the case later, as two of the Norman charters that survive from the countship of Richard II bear his name, one with reference to a benefice granted to the chapter of St-Quentin by Richard I and the second bearing the legend '*Dudo capellanus Richardi Northmannorum ducis et marchionis hanc cartam composit et scripsit*', declaring Dudo to be playing a clear role within the ducal household.[24] Furthermore, after the death of Richard I, Dudo was exhorted to

---

[20] *GND* I, xxxi.

[21] See Henry H. Howorth, 'A Criticism of the Life of Rollo, as told by Dudo de St. Quentin', *Archaeologia* 45 (1880), 235–50; Henri Prentout, *Étude critique sur Dudon de St-Quentin et son histoire des premiers ducs normands* (1916); David C. Douglas, 'Rollo of Normandy', *EHR* 57 (1942), 418.

[22] See, for example, Eleanor Searle, 'Fact and Pattern in Heroic History: Dudo of Saint-Quentin', *Viator* 15 (1984), 119–37; Felice Lifshitz, 'Dudo's Historical Narrative and the Norman Succession of 996', *JMH* 20 (1994), 101–20; Shopkow, *History and Community*.

[23] Dudo, 119; Dudo (tr.), 6.

[24] *Recueil des Actes des Ducs de Normandie, 911–1066*, ed. M. Fauroux, Mémoires de la Société des Antiquaires de Normandie 36 (1961). The concession appears in charter 18 (pp. 100–2), of 8th Sept. 1015, and the legend in charter 13 (pp. 86–9), of 15th Sept. 1011. We possess original copies of both charters.

complete his work by both Richard II and his uncle, Count Rolf of Ivry (*Insistunt ambo precibus, ut quod memorabilis vitæ dux Ricardus precando præceperat exsequerer*).[25] It seems that from this time onwards Dudo drew on the memories of Rolf, who he refers to as the 'source' (*relator*) of his work in his poem *Versus ad comitem Rodulfum, hujus operis relatorem.*[26]

Therefore, Dudo is perhaps not such a poor source for the countship of Richard, at least. Even in the earlier books, where we know his facts can be muddled or incorrect, his intention was not to mislead. His dedicatory letter to Adalbero of Laon states quite clearly that his purpose for sending his work is so that 'its untruths may be removed'; further, he writes of the wishes of his patrons, Richard and Rolf, that his work 'should not deviate into the vice of ambiguity, nor appear to be blemished by the least stain of falsehood'.[27] Of course, Dudo was by no means the first historian to make professions of truth – most ancient and medieval historians did this – and it must be remembered that truth in this sense did not mean genuine historical fact.[28] It is widely understood that medieval historians never wrote simply to record, but always with a view to influencing the thought and behaviour of their audience, and that it was more important to them to produce an interpretation or directed vision than simply to recount random facts.[29]

The art of historical writing owed a good deal to classical rhetoric, and it was the norm to mingle facts obtained from letters, other histories, verbal testimonies and the like with imaginary input – for example, records of conversations – held in check by a sense of verisimilitude and the expectations of the audience.[30] Even if they did sometimes blur the line between fact and fiction, therefore, we can at least rely on our historians to have avoided conscious deception. If they were sometimes willing to believe uncorroborated, or partially corroborated, testimonies, they did this from a trusting reliance on 'moral truth'.[31] Dudo's protestations of truth were therefore in keeping with the accepted standards of his time; they do not provide us with any certain sense of historical accuracy. However, for the reign of Richard at least, it would appear that he was well-sourced, and the fact that his patrons would be aware of the contents of his history is surely undeniable, especially if they were providing a lot of his information. They would also, no doubt, be aware of Dudo's external contacts, and the fact that he sent a least one copy of his work into Francia suggests that they were happy with what he had written.

From this, we are able to see that Dudo's depiction of the Normans was

---

[25] Dudo, 119–20; Dudo (tr.), 6.

[26] Dudo, 125; Dudo (tr.), 11.

[27] Dudo, 120: '*Ut falsa amputarentur*', '*In bilinguitatis vitium versum, videretur ullo mendacii inquinamento pollui*'; Dudo (tr.), 6.

[28] For truth claims in medieval historical writing, see, for example, Roger Ray, 'Historiography', in F.A.C. Mantello and A.G. Rigg (eds), *Medieval Latin: An Introduction and Bibliographical Guide* (Washington, DC, 1996), 639–49; John O. Ward, 'Classical Rhetoric and the Writing of History in Medieval and Renaissance Culture', in Frank McGregor and Nicholas Wright (eds), *European History and its Historians* (Adelaide, 1977); Nancy F. Partner, *Serious Entertainments. The Writing of History in Twelfth-Century England* (Chicago, 1977); Suzanne Fleischman, 'On the Representation of History and Fiction in the Middle Ages', *History and Theory* 22, no. 3 (1983), 278–310.

[29] Ray, 'Historiography', 641; Ward, 'Classical Rhetoric', 5; Fleischman, 'History and Fiction', 290.

[30] Ray, 'Historiography', 642.

[31] Partner, *Serious Entertainments*, 187.

favourably accepted by them, and he was therefore portraying them in the way that they saw themselves, or were willing to be seen – he was, therefore, expressing their identity. We can make similar statements about the *Gesta Normannorum Ducum* of William of Jumièges, although William was not patronised in the same manner. He does not refer to any grand ducal commission, but merely to 'the encouraging support of several good friends', which seems to have been the driving force behind his writing.[32] The final destination of his work, suggested by his dedication to be Duke William II (the Conqueror), is of less importance in this case than the general popularity of the work. The *Gesta Normannorum Ducum* appears to have been the most widely circulated of all the Norman histories, with 45 extant manuscripts (there are only 15 of Dudo's *Historia Normannorum*).[33] This circulation suggests that it was widely enjoyed, and thus that the Normans who owned and or read it were happy with the picture of themselves within it. This is not, of course, to say that William thought of himself as a 'creative' writer: by his own admission he was very interested in the portrayal of truth, and wrote 'in truthful and straightforward language'.[34]

For the study of Norman self-perception, then, we have two major historical works that both ostensibly provide the truth, but also a record of events that the Normans found believable. As both of these histories were so clearly accepted, and present what is essentially Norman self-opinion (particularly in the case of William of Jumièges, a native Norman), we are left able to extract from these sources information about *Normanitas* and the *gens Normannorum*. These histories, along with other sources from the period (charters, etc.), provide a means for historians to access the structure of social and cultural perceptions that influenced not only the way the Normans behaved, but also the way in which they evolved as a people into a real power in the western European sphere. As these two histories are separated in time by roughly fifty years, it is sometimes necessary to examine them separately, as identity is very much a fluid concept, and fifty years can change it greatly.

It is perhaps fitting that such an examination begins with Rollo's oft-recounted dream, which Dudo reports that he had after the people of one region of 'the English land' had sworn fealty to him.[35] This account is perhaps the single most important passage in the *Historia Normannorum* from the point of view of identity. The dream is riddled with motifs and metaphors, all of which are relevant to the foundation of what would become the duchy of Normandy. While none of these metaphors are original, between them they summarise the Norman attitude to their race:

32 *GND* II, 182: '*Bonis quibusdam adhortando fauentibus*'; Shopkow, *History and Community*, 190.
33 See Gerda Huisman, 'Notes on the Manuscript Tradition of Dudo of St-Quentin's Gesta Normannorum', *ANS* 6 (1984), 124; Van Houts, 'History', 106; Loud, 'Myth or Reality?', 107; Shopkow, *History and Community*, 40–1 for a discussion of this.
34 *GND* II, 182: '*Per ueritatis tramitem directo sermone prosecutus*'.
35 Dudo, 145–6: '*Anglicam terram*'; Dudo (tr.), 29. Notably, the later comment that Dudo records as having been made by the satrap Theobald, that 'the English also submit to him [Richard] obediently' ('*Angli quoque ei obedienter subduntur*': Dudo (tr.), 140; Dudo, 265) is part of a speech designed to rouse the French king against the Norman duke, Richard. It cannot reasonably be considered to be 'a hint that there was more to Anglo-Norman relations than we know' (J. Campbell, 'England, France, Flanders and Germany: some comparisons and connections' in *Ethelred the Unready*, ed. David Hill, B.A.R. British Series 59 (1978), 260), as the next sentence, 'all peoples of all kingdoms attend him and obey him' ('*Omnium . . . regnorum omnes gentes ei famulantur et obediunt*'), might be expected to reveal.

... he seemed to behold himself placed on a mountain, far higher than the highest, in a Frankish dwelling. And on the summit of this mountain he saw a spring of sweet-smelling water flowing, and himself washing in it, and by it made whole from the contagion of leprosy and the itch, with which he was infected; and finally, while he was still staying on top of the mountain, he saw about the base of it many thousands of birds of different kinds and various colours, but with red left wings, extending in such numbers and so far and so wide that he could not catch sight of where they ended, however hard he looked. And they went one after the other in harmonious incoming flights and sought the spring on the mountain, and washed themselves, swimming together as they do when rain is coming; and when they had all been anointed by this miraculous dipping, they all ate together in a suitable place, without being separated into genera or species, and without any disagreement or dispute, as if they were friends sharing food. And they carried off twigs and worked rapidly to build nests; and furthermore, they willing yielded to his command ...[36]

The overtly Christian nature of the dream notwithstanding, it includes one particular piece of symbolism to which many writers have attached importance – that of the birds. The birds signify empire, in this case a unity of many races and cultures in one grouping, and a recognition of the 'polyethnic' nature of the *gens Normannorum*. Unusual as this seems in the context of medieval Europe, in which most peoples emphasised a unifying collective origin, this is not an inexplicable phenomenon when the Norman situation is considered. When Dudo was writing, the settlement around Rouen was still comparatively recent. As a newly formed people, the Normans could not look back centuries for their origins; the new *gens* did not have a semi-mythical past in which to couch an *origo gentis* story to rival that of their neighbours. Consequently, the Normans were alive to the realities of their situation and, more importantly, were accepting of these realities. Dudo's Normans were a race of mixed descent because they could not conceivably be otherwise.[37]

By the time of William of Jumièges and, indeed, that of the author of the *Inventio et miracula sancti Vulfranni*, the essential basis of this tale had changed little. The most significant statement in the *Inventio* deals with the origin of the *gens Normannorum* – how Rollo 'won over people of all origins and different skills, and so made one people from various *gentes*'.[38] This is, quite clearly, a recognition of the

---

[36] Dudo (tr.), 29–30; p. 29, nn. 134–5 for discussion of the metaphorical significance of the mountain, leprosy and the birds. The Latin, from Dudo, 146, reads: '... *videre videbatur præcellentissimis quodam præcelsiore Franciscæ habitationis monte se positum: ejusque montis in cacumine fontem liquidum et odoriferum, seque in eo ablui et ab eo expiari contagione lepræ et prurigine contaminatum; denique illius montis cacumine adhuc superstes, circa basim illius hinc inde et altrinsecus, multa millia avium diversorum generum, varii coloris, sinistras alas quin etiam rubicundas habentium, quarum diffusæ longe lateque multitudinis inexhaustam extremitatem perspicaci et angustato obtutu non poterat comprehendere; cæterum congruenti incessu atque volatu eas sibi alternis vicibus invicem cedentes, fontem montis petere, easque se convenienti natatione sicuti solent tempore futuræ pluviæ abluere, omnibusque mira infusione delibutis, congrua eas statione sine discretione generum et specierum, sine ullo contentionis jurgio, mutuo vicissim pastu quasi amicabiliter comedere; easque deportatis ramusculis festinanti labore nidificare: quin etiam suæ ... imperio voluntarie succumbere ... .*'.

[37] Interestingly, modern theories of ethnogenesis suggest that name-giving peoples who constituted kingdoms originated from syntheses of various population groups (Goetz, et al., *Regna and Gentes*, 610). As the Normans constituted what was, in effect, an ethnically separate duchy, one might expect the same to be true.

[38] This phrase can be found in *Inventio et miracula sancti Vulfranni*, ed. J. Laporte (Rouen, 1938), 21.

same 'polyethnic' nature that had been attributed to the *gens Normannorum* by Dudo, when he wrote of Rollo's dream. If anything, the *Inventio* is even more explicit, and while this evidences the continuation of the *origo* story into the mid-eleventh century, the *Inventio*'s acceptance of this tale sets it at variance with William of Jumièges.

Acknowledged as a 'revision' of Dudo's work, William's major alteration to the origin story was that he was even more careful than Dudo with his terminology.[39] Although Dudo occasionally called the Viking raiders *Normanni* (in the generic sense), William never did this. As such, until the actual arrival of Rollo and his companions, there are Danes and Franks: the Normans are produced in Francia.[40] In the *Gesta Normannorum Ducum*, the Scandinavian settlers of the Rouen area are not first led from 'Scanza' to England, and then to Francia, but rather they journey around in six ships in some kind of collective fashion; Rollo does not become their leader until they land in Francia, when he is chosen 'by lot'.[41] Once Rollo has been selected, William largely follows Dudo's lead, with Rollo aiding Æthelstan of England and so on.[42] However, throughout his history, William lacks the explicit acceptance of a mixed race that is provided by Dudo and the *Inventio*. This is not to say that William asserts that the Normans were pure-blooded; rather, he just seems far less interested in the composition of the Norman *gens* than Dudo and the *Inventio*. Writing in the 1050s (and, at least to some extent, after the author of the *Inventio*), William saw the Normans as a well established and recognisably distinct *ethnie*; his reference to Rollo's marriage as '*more Danico*' is perhaps a recognition of how far he felt they had come.[43] He did not wish, at this late stage, to examine the ramifications of any cultural blending or borrowing: their culture was bred into them, and it was *their* culture.

Thus by the 1050s the Normans seem to have been showing a certain disinterest in the exact composition of their race, though there was still an awareness, perpetuated from the end of the tenth century, that they were descended from a mixed background. The implications of this lack of ethnic unity are vital to our understanding of the Norman thought world. If the Normans had considered themselves a united race of either pure Scandinavians or Franks, there is no way that they could have resisted the attempts of the Franks to destroy or assimilate their newly formed enclave, and they would thus have become indistinguishable from any other Frankish province. They were Scandinavian enough to be separate but Frankish enough not to offend. This suggests that, while racial heterogeneity was a feature of the Norman identity, it was not the foundation on which the *gens* was based: a myth / symbol complex requires a historical myth, and an occurrence almost within living memory can hardly be classed as one.[44] It is arguable that, at this comparatively early stage of

---

See also Potts, 'Historical Tradition', 139 and Elisabeth van Houts, *The Normans in Europe* (Manchester, 2000), 10 & 38.

[39] *GND* I, xxxv; Loud, 'Myth or Reality?', 108–9.

[40] The transition occurs when Rollo is defeated at Chartres: *GND* I, 62.

[41] *Ibid.*, 32 & 52.

[42] *Ibid.*, 58–60.

[43] *Ibid.*, 58. For the Viking marriage, see Elizabeth Eames, 'Mariage et concubinage légal en Norvège à l'époque des Vikings', *AN* 2 (1952), 195–208.

[44] Heather, *Goths*, 5.

ethnogenesis, the historical myth had not yet been devised (Heather suggests that such a myth should be one of the group), but it is more realistic to think that a collective formed under such circumstances required a bonding ideal. This was, in all probability, reflected in the ethos of Norman leadership.

While it is true that the entirety of the Norman people could not consistently trace their descent from anywhere, it was not beyond reason that Dudo could trace a historical line of descent for Rollo and his kin from an external ethnic tradition. In the *Historia Normannorum*, the Danes are referred to as 'descended from Antenor', who was believed to have slipped away from Troy while the Greeks were laying waste to the city.[45] The Danes held descent from Antenor, and Rollo held descent from these *Daci / Danai / Dani*.[46] Although the evidence of later material (such as Orkneyinga Saga and the *Leges Edwardi Confessoris*) suggests that Rollo was of Norwegian descent, we know that the majority of the settlers were of Danish extraction, and Eric Christiansen has suggested that, in light of later Anglo-Norman, Welsh and Icelandic pedigree-makers, a connection with Norway is unlikely.[47]

But the connection with historical myth that Dudo provides is not simply with that of the Danes. Antenor had been claimed as an ancestor of the Franks by both Fredegar and Aimoin of Fleury: it is likely that Dudo was at least aware of the former work, educated as he was in the Carolingian tradition, and Aimoin was writing at around the same time as Dudo (*c*.996–8), showing that this belief was current in

[45] '*ex Antenore progenitos*': Dudo, 130; Dudo (tr.), 16.

[46] Both Christiansen (Dudo (tr.), p. 16, n. 75) and Emily Albu ('Dudo of Saint-Quentin: the Heroic Past Imagined', *HSJ* 6 (1994), 114; *Normans in their Histories*, 14–15) have drawn attention to Dudo's apparent treatment of Antenor as a Greek. The problem arises when Dudo observes that 'the *Daci* call themselves *Danai*, or *Dani*, and boast that they are descended from Antenor' (Dudo, 130; Dudo (tr.), 16). The *Daci* were, as Dudo noted, a tribe living on the Lower Danube (Dudo, 129; Dudo (tr.), 15). Danaus was, in Greek myth, the son of Belus from Egypt, who became king of Argos. His followers, the *Danai*, became the Greeks. Hence Δαναοί / *Danai* is a poetic term for the Greeks in both Greek (Homer) and Latin (Vergil) poetry. Christiansen, noting that Antenor was a Trojan, does acknowledge that he was related to Greeks and sympathetic towards them. Albu sees the apparent inconsistency on Dudo's part as a quiet elision of Antenor with the *Danai*, in order to capitalise on the easy etymological change of *Danai* into *Dani*. Yet according to Dudo, Antenor 'slipped away through the middle of the Greeks', implying that he was on the other side; otherwise it would surely be 'from the Greeks'. Furthermore, Albu's suggestion that Dudo's use of Antenor is a humorous gibe at the expense of the Normans does not ring true. According to Leah Shopkow, it is likely that Dudo knew little Greek: he reproduces only those words used in the *Vita Sancti Germani* (which he knew) (Shopkow, 'Carolingian World', 25). Dudo's tendency to borrow his classical quotes from other Carolingian and Merovingian texts has also been remarked upon (Shopkow, 'Carolingian World', 20), suggesting that his knowledge of the Latin poets of the Trojan War was unlikely (Albu, 'Heroic Past', p. 114, n. 12). By extension, he probably knew only the *Aeneid*'s version of Antenor (who was not depicted as a traitor by Vergil, Albu, 'Heroic Past', 114), rather than the more negative Greek depiction. The use of Antenor as an ancestral figure was also not an innovation, and Flodoard had called the Franks *Antenoridae* (Dudo (tr.), p. 16, n.75). With this, and the concept of a connected Frankish/Danish origin, it seems highly unlikely that Dudo was attempting to give 'a sinister cast to the upstart Normans he was pretending to honour' (Albu, *Normans in their Histories*, 15) unless he intended the same for his own people.

[47] Dudo (tr.), p. 26, n. 114. Orkneyinga Saga refers to one Hrolf or Göngu-Hrolf, the son of Earl Rognvald the Powerful and Ragnhild, daughter of Hrolf Nose, who conquered Normandy (*Orkneyinga Saga: the History of the Earls of Orkney*, tr. Hermann Pálsson and Paul Edwards (Harmondsworth, 1981; repr. 1982, 1984), 26). The *Leges Edwardi Confessoris* states that the ancestors of 'all the barons of Normandy' ('*omnium baronum de Normannia*') came from Norway (Bruce R. O'Brien, *God's Peace and King's Peace: The Laws of Edward The Confessor* (Philadelphia, 1999), 192; Douglas, 'Rollo', 424).

monastic and perhaps princely circles. In addition, the connection of descent between the two races had been alluded to as early as *c.*868 by Ermoldus (*In Honorem Hludovici*).[48] A proud historical tradition was thus created for the descent of the Norman leaders, which drew on both the Frankish and the Scandinavian aspects of their origins.

Dudo could not, however, simply combine the *origines* of both peoples to provide an origin. The Normans were not simply Franks and Danes as it stood, as they incorporated Bretons, Norwegians, Anglo-Saxons and so on, but moreover, such an origin story would exacerbate the divide between peoples, and the primary idea behind an *origo* is its unifying nature. Thus the Normans were unified through a noble ruling dynasty, in which Rollo was the son of a powerful chief among the Danes and the Danes were descended from Antenor.[49] This tradition of leadership could be further reinforced in the event of disunity, as the noble status of the Norman ducal family in context of the Antenoran descent gave them a perceived 'right to rule' that could be believably upheld, Frankish restrictions on power notwithstanding. Furthermore, this focus on leadership is continued by William of Jumièges.

In the *Gesta Normannorum Ducum*, as we have noted, William of Jumièges shows a marked disinterest in the actual ethnicity of the Norman people. Though this can be acknowledged as a move away from an acceptance of the mixed-race *origo* propounded by Dudo, a unifying *gens* origin story is still notable by its absence. Consequently William, too, adopts a strong focus on leadership. In the *Gesta Normannorum Ducum*, however, Rollo is not descended, as he is in Dudo, from Antenor (who was simply a king of Denmark), but rather his is a lineage far more in keeping with William's own understanding of the world, and also with the sensitivities of the time.[50] As will be seen later, William was a writer who was far more interested in religion and morality than Dudo, and his refusal to associate his rulers with heathens from the classics leads him instead to plumb the depths of the Bible for his *origo*. Rollo, as a Dane, was descended from Magog, grandson of Noah, via the Goths (who colonised Denmark, according to William).[51] Here we see the close association of the Norman leaders with religion that seems to have been so important to William, and resulted in his deliberate omission of the life of Rollo as 'neither honourable or edifying'.[52]

Dudo had further added to the strength of his *origo* territorially, and it is from this direction that a territorial element to identity, based on Normandy, began evolution among the *gens Normannorum*. The early involvement of territorial ideas stems to a great extent from the way in which Normandy was created. As rulers, the comital / ducal family did not have a pre-existing set of subjects, but rather their subjects were constituted by the settlement, which in turn was the result of a grant not of power but of land. If the two *gentes* had not interacted, had remained administratively separate,

---

48 Dudo (tr.), xx; p. 16, n. 75.
49 Dudo, 141; Dudo (tr.), 25–6.
50 *GND* I, 14–16. Interestingly, William is clearly aware of the reputation of Antenor as a traitor to his people.
51 *Ibid.*, 14–16.
52 *Ibid.*, 6. Leah Shopkow has misinterpreted van Houts' initial translation of '*nec . . . honesti uel utilis*' appearing in van Houts, 'History', 108 ('neither honest nor useful') as a comment on historical truth (Shopkow, *History and Community*, 191).

then this culture of separation would, in all likelihood, have served to reinforce the boundaries between their existing identities, and the territory would not have been an issue. Yet the newly created *gens Normannorum* was essentially constituted from those people living in the area controlled by the ruling family. Thus, as identity was linked to these rulers, so it was in some way linked to the territory that they controlled. The concepts of the *gens* and the *tellus* were becoming fused in the conception of identity, and in Dudo we see the territorial idea not only applied to help define the Normans as a group, but also to define their relationship to those around them.

The position of the Normans' home, in relation to the rest of Francia, was made explicit by Dudo in the expression *regnum Normanniæ*, and this was not a perception unique to Dudo, but one echoed in a number of ducal charters.[53] The eighth- and ninth-century conception of *regna* as 'non-Frankish territories governed with a Frankish type of administration' would seem quite fitting, but the political structures of the tenth century and onwards were rather more permanent, and the use of *regnum* by Dudo's time was more of an attempt at definition in territorial terms than anything else.[54] The practice of styling principalities as *regna*, though infrequent, was widespread. Whereas, at one time, to be one of those *regna* within the *regnum Francorum* was to support the superior status of the *rex Francorum* (in evidence when Charles the Bald dispensed royal vestments to Erispöe of Britanny, or when Geoffrey Grisegonelle acknowledged that he held Anjou from Hugh Capet), by the eleventh century things had changed.[55] As well as territorial definition, *regnum* implied power, and a certain amount of independence from the monarch, visible in the lack of royal charters relating to Normandy after 1006.[56]

Whether or not such power still required legitimisation is questionable. It had been thought that the king remained the primary source of authority – the ducal charters provide royal names, and often regnal years, and the 'count Richard' who signs his name in a list of *Francie comites* in an act of Robert II can only be Richard II of Normandy.[57] However, the apparent freedom with which the Normans sided with and against the Frankish kings has led Robert Helmerichs to challenge this viewpoint, suggesting instead that the power of the Norman leaders was that which they were able 'to encourage or force others to recognise'.[58] Dudo, certainly, was concerned to maximise the claim to power, and Richard I is referred to as *Northmannorum dux*, though this may or may not have been accurate.[59] According to K.F. Werner, though Richard II was clearly a duke by 1006, it was impossible for the Norman leaders to have held the ducal title prior to 987 and the accession of

[53] *Actes des Ducs*, ed. Fauroux, no. 61, p. 186 ('*regni statum*'), no. 74, p. 215 ('*regni Normannorum*'), no. 92, p. 243 ('*regni Nortmannorum*'), no. 122, p. 289 ('*regnum nostrum*'), no. 158, p. 344 ('*ad gubernandum regnum*').

[54] McKitterick, *Frankish Kingdoms*, 97; David Bates, 'West Francia: the Northern Principalities', *The New Cambridge Medieval History*, vol. III, c.900–c.1024 (Cambridge, 1999), 402.

[55] Janet L. Nelson, *Charles the Bald* (London, 1992), 166; Bates, 'West Francia', 411.

[56] Bates, 'West Francia', 411.

[57] *Ibid.*, 419. *Actes des Ducs*, ed. Fauroux, nos 2, 3, 12 & 13 for examples of regnal years. The text of no. 22 (p. 108) reads, '*Presentibus Francie comitibus et episcopis cum eorum suffragensis, ubi hec carta confirmata est . . . S. Richeri comitis*'; Fauroux's comments on the identity of this *Richer* appear on p. 107.

[58] Robert Helmerichs, '*Princeps, Comes, Dux Normannorum*: Early Rollonid Designators and their Significance', *HSJ* 9 (2001), 70.

[59] Dudo, 254, 263; 250–1, 267.

Hugh Capet to the throne, as he had been a *dux* himself and they were his vassals.[60] It is therefore conceivable that Richard I *may* have taken the ducal title in the years between 987 and his death in 996, though there appears to have been a lack of confidence in the ducal title even into William the Conqueror's dukedom, and *dux Normannorum* was not the sole title in use until the twelfth century, under Henry I of England.[61]

Helmerichs, again, has raised objections to this scheme. He also draws attention to William's failure to use *dux* consistently, but as an indication that this was probably not 'a "promotion" his ancestors had received from *comes*'.[62] Though for Dudo there was apparently no doubt about the Norman *duces*, Helmerichs suggests that the use of titles by the Norman leaders was neither rational, precise, nor based on their relationship to the Robertines.[63] He evidences the loose meaning of the term *comes* in the ducal charters, and proposes a 'genuine confusion . . . or perhaps better a genuine lack of interest' among the Norman leaders with regard to their titles.[64] If this is correct, it lends some credence to Dudo's use of *dux*, and shows that the importance of the ducal title was recognised to at least some extent by the Normans, though not necessarily before the eleventh century.

Territorial identification is continued in the *Gesta Normannorum Ducum*, but in a more refined and advanced state, perhaps because William's leadership motif is rather weaker than that of Dudo. Dudo's Rollo is descended from a chief and born to power, William's is chosen, and this election was likely to be less compelling in the rather undemocratic world of the eleventh century. The Normandy that William's Rollo receives is complete, a single unit, over which he is empowered immediately after his baptism as the Norman duke.[65] All Rollo's successors are dukes in their own right, and there is no apparent mention of the comital title actually held by Rollo, William Longsword and Richard I, and visible in contemporary Frankish annals, histories and charters.[66] Furthermore, Normandy as the settlers find it is slightly different from the Norman land of Dudo's *Historia Normannorum*. In line with the tenth-century acceptance of a mixed-race *gens*, Dudo refers to towns and cities, and an existing population; though 'desolated, bereft of warriors and untilled by the plough', Dudo's Rouennais was clearly inhabited.[67] William's 'Normandy', conversely, 'was everywhere overgrown by forests as a result of the daily raids by heathens, and had not been tilled with coulter and ploughshare'.[68] Again we have a somewhat ambiguous statement from William: he does not explicitly state that the

---

[60] K.F. Werner, 'Quelques observations au sujet des débuts du « duché » de Normandie', *Droit Privé et Institutions Régionales: Etudes historiques offertes à Jean Yver* (Paris, 1976), 698, 700–1; *Actes des Ducs*, ed. Fauroux, no. 9, p. 80, refers to '*Richardus Norhtmannorum dux*'; no. 3, p. 71 is a charter of Richard I, in which he acts '*cum assensu senioris mei Hugonis Francorum principis*'.

[61] Bates, 'West Francia', 412; Werner, 'Quelques observations', 691–2.

[62] Helmerichs, 'Rollonid Designators', 64. Helmerichs notes William's overwhelming preference for *comes* over *dux* or *princeps* before 1050 (*ibid.*, p. 64, n. 26); interestingly, after 1066, the preference is apparently for *princeps* and *dux* (*RRAN*, p. 87).

[63] Helmerichs, 'Rollonid Designators', 70.

[64] *Ibid.*, 75 & 70, and *Actes des Ducs*, ed. Fauroux, no. 4.

[65] *GND* I, 66–8.

[66] Werner, 'Quelques observations', 696 & 698.

[67] Dudo, 153 & 166: '*desolata, militibus privata, aratro non exercita*'; Dudo (tr.), 36 & 47.

[68] *GND* I, 66: '*ob diuturnos paganorum excursus, siluis ubique adultis, a cultro et uomere torpebat inculta*'.

area was uninhabited, but suggests it. It was believable and, by a process of selective common memory, no doubt acceptable.[69] Certainly, the later use of the phrase 'fatherland of Normandy', both by William, and in a number of ducal charters, suggests a very strong tie to the *tellus Normannica*. This is further supported by the evolution of the ideas of regional custom: we find, in charters from the 1030s and later, the idea of *mos patrie* and *mos Normannie* – the customs of a people connected to a land by that people.[70]

Yet, if Normandy held the spirit of *Normanitas* by the 1050s, the Norman leader still personified it for both Dudo and William. The Normans clearly felt that their leaders were important – an early eleventh-century poem described Richard III and Robert the Magnificent as 'the mainstays of the world' – and as the focus of the identity of the *gens Normannorum*, the leader would be expected to be someone who set an example.[71] This tendency slowed the process of definition of *Normanitas*, at least initially, as the leaders seemed undecided about precisely what was to constitute 'Norman' behaviour. As we have noted, Rollo drew more heavily on his Scandinavian heritage, although the figure of Hasting in Dudo's history provides a counteractive, more fully Viking figure for a comparison in Rollo's favour. Hasting was a Dane, but pointedly is never termed a Norman (it must be noted that Dudo was writing after the new ethnonym had been accepted), and thus could not be expected to adopt those features that made the Normans so special. As a Viking, he was a raider, barbaric in the extreme: he raped, plundered and enslaved people; even after he settled in Francia, he did not gain 'Norman' qualities.[72] Rollo, on the contrary, was not a raider: when he fought against the Franks, they attacked him and not the other way around.[73] Even so, Rollo's seafaring ways and his pagan nature could not be reconciled with that of the Franks, and thus his Scandinavian nature was too pronounced.[74]

William Longsword was quite a different ruler. Although he was perhaps more 'Norman' than Rollo, and certainly more cosmopolitan, he became arguably too Frankish. It was his lack of reference to his Scandinavian heritage that triggered the revolt of Riulf against him, who accused him of having 'Frankish kinsmen' and being 'alien to us, and hateful'.[75] As Potts notes, William's identification with the Franks

---

[69] Peter Jones discusses the role of common memory as a socially mediated unifier within an identity (Jones, '1789', 3–4).

[70] *GND* II, 6, 48: '*Normannicam patriam*'; *Actes des Ducs*, ed. Fauroux, no. 120, p. 285 ('*patriam Normannie*') and no. 232, p. 447 ('*Normannie patria*'). Further references to *patria* appear in no. 61, p. 186 ('*patrie salutem*'), no. 85, p. 225 ('*patrie nostre*') and no. 150, p. 335 ('*in tota patria ipsius*'), and the phrase '*Normannorum terra*' can be found in no. 124, p. 294. For regional custom, no. 85, p. 225 ('*morem patrie nostre*') and no. 132, p. 306 ('*morem Normannie*'). On the evolution of Norman custom, see Emily Z. Tabuteau, *Transfers of Property in Eleventh-Century Norman Law* (Chapel Hill, 1988), 223–9.

[71] Warner of Rouen, *Moriuht*, translated in van Houts, *Normans in Europe*, 93. The importance attached to leadership is reminiscent of the role of kingship in early medieval *regna*, where a king would provide a central focus of reference for his people (above, pp. 6–7).

[72] Dudo, 131; Dudo (tr.), 17.

[73] Dudo, 156; Dudo (tr.), 37–8.

[74] Dudo, 161–2; Dudo (tr.), 42–3. A pointed passage here shows how even Frankish peasants hated pagans enough to do battle, and how Rollo reacted by crushing them as he saw this as a personal slight.

[75] Dudo, 189: '*Francos suos parentes*', '*nobis est incongruus et obnoxius*'; Dudo (tr.), 66–7.

had gone too far, and to them he had become something less than Norman; the *Lament* observes that William accepted King Louis' seniority in order to survive his enemies and rule 'in the manner of a king'.[76] The Scandinavian aspects of his character, however, re-emerged when, dealing with those of originally Scandinavian heritage, he received what can only be called a quintessentially Scandinavian insult to his manliness.[77] While this for Dudo is simply a motif by which William's seemingly dormant Scandinavian blood is raised (he does not appear to have dealt philosophically with insults, at least), this style of behaviour also fits a modern model concerning the identity of bilinguals, which William appears to have been.[78]

The model in question provides a system for individual responses from a position of 'dual-socialisation', namely, of mixed cultural background.[79] It suggests that, when someone has interactions with one society in one language, and another society in a second language (with both languages being, in context, the 'first' language), they adopt different identities in relation to the language in use: they have 'dual linguistic-personality systems'. Furthermore, it can be derived from this idea that any equally significant cultural scenario could have this effect. From the sagas, and other Scandinavian literature, it is quite evident that to impugn a warrior's manliness was considered one of the greatest insults, and if we apply the model to William's behaviour, it can be suggested that this insult 'cues' him from a Frankish, more pacific identity into a more aggressive Scandinavian form. Elsewhere, the insult paid to the Normans and, more particularly, to William himself by the Lotharingians and Saxons is understood through William's knowledge of the Scandinavian tongue, again cueing his latent aggression.[80] While it is, of course, highly speculative to apply such models to an anecdote like this, it is nonetheless necessary to consider such ideas as routes through which an understanding of the relationship of the Normans to both Franks and Scandinavians can be achieved during a period in which their identity is, at best, confused.

The leader who perhaps best reflects this model is, however, William Longsword's son, Richard. We know from a passage in Dudo that Richard was bilingual, being educated both in the Frankish (Roman) and Scandinavian (Dacian) tongues, and that he received education under the Normans in general, but also under the more Scandinavian Botho and as a prisoner of the Frankish king Louis IV.[81] As a Norman,

---

[76] Potts, 'Historical Tradition', 144; Lauer, *Louis IV*, 320: '*Hic audacer olim regem Hcludowicum / sibi fecit seniorem regnaturum / ut cum eo suparet hostem suum / regnaretque regum more*'.

[77] Dudo, 190; Dudo (tr.), 67: Bernard the Dane comments that William is 'womanish' (*effeminatus*).

[78] Dudo, 197, Dudo (tr.), 73 for an instance in which William loses his temper with the German king Henry.

[79] Weinreich, 'Operationalisation', 305–6 for the model.

[80] Dudo, 197; Dudo (tr.), 73.

[81] Dudo, 221–2, 229–30; Dudo (tr.), 96–7, 104–5. Dudo reports William Longsword's wishes for Richard's education (Dudo (tr.), 97): 'As the city of Rouen much prefers the use of the Roman tongue rather than Dacian [Danish] eloquence, and Bayeux uses the Dacian more often than the Roman tongue, so I wish that he [Richard] be taken to Bayeux as quickly as possible; and I wish that he be educated with great care under your tutelage, Botho, and should have the benefit of the Dacian talkativeness, and learn it thoroughly by heart, so that in the future he should be able to express himself more fluently to the Dacian-born'; Dudo, 221–2: '*Quoniam quidem Rotomagensis civitas Romana potius quam Dacisca utitur eloquentia, et Bajocensis fruitur frequentius Dacisca lingua quam Romana; volo igitur ut ad Bajocensia deferatur quantocius mœnia et ibi volo ut sit, Botho, sub tua custodia et enutriatur et educetur cum magna*

Richard provided a perfect archetype for identity. As well as being perfectly at home with his own people, he was the ideal synthesis of both Scandinavian and Frankish culture. He could play the Frankish political game, and did with various successes against both the Frankish monarchs and magnates, as a *comes Francie*; he also managed to secure a marriage to the daughter of the powerful Capetian *dux Francorum*, Hugh the Great, which gave the dynasty a tie to the future Frankish kings.[82] In addition, Richard could rely on Scandinavian aid, showing that he was also adept at dealing with Scandinavians in a manner that was not merely acceptable: the Dacians were 'delighted by these embassies'.[83] These aptitudes suggest a dual linguistic-personality system, resulting in Richard being comfortable in both Scandinavian and Frankish contexts and yet, of course, being most comfortable at home, where the Normans provided a unique and by this time less confused synthesis of the two.

Richard's successors also exhibited these cosmopolitan aspects, which were an important aspect of Norman leadership. In the space of book five of the *Gesta Normannorum Ducum*, Richard II deals with Normans, English, Norsemen, Swedes, Bretons and Franks. While Richard III's life is perhaps a little too brief for such things (William of Jumièges devotes only three paragraphs to him), both Robert ('the Fearless') and William ('the Conqueror') have dealings with Normans, Franks, Bretons and the English. All these ruling men are capable of dealing adequately with those cultures around them, and the consistency in their approaches suggests that the Norman identity had become strong and stable: the Normans could interact with other cultures without losing anything of themselves, or being swayed to imitate their neighbours. There was no need here to 'fit in', as the individuality of the *gens Normannorum* had been acknowledged within their local context, and cultural threats to their society were fewer and weaker as a result. This realisation is perhaps evidenced in one of the later pre-conquest charters, in which William ('the Conqueror') expresses an understanding of the perceptions 'others' held of the Normans' greed – he says of the giving of alms that, '*although we are Normans*, we know well that this ought to be done and, if it pleases God, we shall do it'.[84] Thus the actions and capacity of the rulers reflect the consolidation and evolving separateness of *Normanitas*.

Throughout both Dudo's and William's histories, then, we can see that the ruler of the Normans embodies the Norman identity, personifying the *gens Normannorum* and *Normanitas*. The focus of these histories on the Norman leaders is essentially a means of consigning to a written form the perceptions the Normans had of themselves. In addition to this 'record', Dudo's *Historia Normannorum* stands at the head of a historical tradition that was one of the most productive during the medieval period. There is a clear tendency in later writers to draw on earlier writers within the tradition (as in most historical traditions), and Dudo's division of his history into a

---

diligentia, frucus loquacitate Dacisca, eamque discens tenaci memoria, ut queat sermocinari profusius olim contra Dacigenas.'

[82] *Actes des Ducs*, ed. Fauroux, no. 22, p. 108, and above, p. 29; Dudo, 263; Dudo (tr.), 137–8.

[83] Dudo, 239, 276–7: '*His legationibus hilares*'; Dudo (tr.), 114, 150.

[84] *Actes des Ducs*, ed. Fauroux, no. 199, p. 387: '*Licet Normanni simus, bene tamen novimus quia sic oportet fieri, et ita, si Deo placuerit, faciemus*'; my italics.

book-per-ruler format sets the standard for the various successive incarnations of the *Gesta Normannorum Ducum*, which was heavily indebted to his work. If history does become so important to the Normans as one of the symbols in their myth / symbol complex, it is necessary to understand why. To do this, we can examine those factors that motivated Richard I to commission Dudo's work, acknowledged to be the first history of a Frankish province, and what motivated Dudo to write it.

Dudo's motivation has been perhaps even more the subject of recent discussion than his rehabilitation as a source. It is certainly an oddity that this man, who is viewed (by some) as an 'encomiast' of the Norman counts, should not even be a Norman himself. Felice Lifshitz has proposed that a basic political motivation accounted for Dudo's writing, at least to some extent. Referring to manuscript versions of the source that differ from those edited by Lair, she argues for the role of the source in the smoothing of political transition between the countships of Richard I and II. Part of the argument, however, hinges on a postulated scribal error, an incorrect copying of *Ricardus* as *Rollonis*, meant to refer to Richard II.[85] Even conceding her superior knowledge of palaeography, Christiansen's translation, which incorporates the genitive version of Rollo present in the Latin, makes perfect sense as is, and Lifshitz's reference to Richard II would certainly seem forced in the context.[86] Christiansen himself also counters Lifshitz's argument, offering the opinion that a long-winded and prosimetric work of this nature would hardly be likely to ensure the support of Adalbero of Laon, the politically powerful cleric to whom it is addressed, in ensuring the smooth transition of power from Richard I to Richard II in the face of threats from Flanders, King Robert of France and Odo of Blois-Chartres. These threats were, as Christiansen indicates, a thing of the past after 1013.[87]

Other proposed motivations for Dudo stem from the basic function of *gesta*-type works (which record 'deeds'), namely, to provide glory for the patron. In this case, it is accomplished by the glorification of the Norman ducal dynasty. Christiansen has proposed that there was a rivalry in cultural innovation between Dudo and two of his contemporaries, Richer of Reims and Aimoin of Fleury (arising from a political competition between their various patrons). Richer wrote his *History* for Gerbert of Aurillac between 996 and 998, while Aimoin produced his *Historiae Francorum* for Abbot Abbo of Fleury some time between 988 and 1004 (probably 996 × 998). Christiansen's own acknowledgement of the lack of evidence other than 'many points of similarity and empathy' between the works, however, creates a margin of doubt, in the contemporary context.[88] While it is conceivable that the Frankish writers may have been making a concerted, literary attempt to preserve notions of Frankish identity by 'disowning' the Normans, the Normans were not interested in depicting themselves as Franks; such a move by the Frankish intelligentsia could only succeed in legitimising the separate nature of the Normans.

Also, we have noted that leadership was an important part of *Normanitas*, and weak leadership (or kingship) is often reviled in Norman writing. The weakness of

---

85 Lifshitz, 'Historical Narrative', 106.
86 Dudo (tr.), 6.
87 *Ibid.*, xxviii–xxix.
88 *Ibid.*, xx and n. 33.

the Frankish monarchs in this period may have provided further motivation for the Normans to emphasise their separate nature, as well as material for Dudo's derisive commentary (on, for example, Louis IV). Searle's suggestion that Dudo be viewed as 'heroic history', and as part of an aristocratic epic tradition popular in the tenth century could support either side of this argument, but her various suggestions of the 'Norse' nature of the work would remind us that the work's purpose was not, at a base level, dictated by Dudo but by his patrons.[89] As such, although Dudo may have perceived himself as a participant in a cultural competition, the Norman patrons perceived any such competition as already won.

However, in the light of the original commissioning of the source, it may be that historians are perhaps approaching Dudo's writing from the wrong direction. Richard I, when he commissioned Dudo to write his *Historia*, was an old man, with only two years to live. And yet, he had recently reached a landmark of rulership: he had held the countship of Rouen for a little over fifty years. Richard was the product of two cultures, educated in the ways of both of these, and thus capable of understanding those things that either or both social groups respected; he headed a society that was a synthesis of the two. What we see in Dudo are the signifiers of a Scandinavian society where actions, *gesta*, are all portrayed within a contemporary, and learnedly Frankish, literary model. Dudo provides the Normans with a monument to their success, a display of the successful blending of Scandinavian deeds and Carolingian learning, justified in the context of one great ruler who had battled with adversity to become a powerful political figure. Christiansen's translation draws attention to this; Dudo writes that Richard I requested

> that I should describe the customs and deeds of the Norman land, nay, the rights which he [Richard I] established within the land of his great-grandfather Rollo

though a more accurate rendering would be:

> that I should describe the customs and deeds of the homeland, nay also [those] of his forefather Rollo, which he [Richard I] established in the *regnum* as rights.[90]

Thus, Richard wanted a monument, a *Vita Ricardi*, to celebrate his achievements.

If it was, indeed, a monument then by its very nature the *Historia Normannorum* had no active agenda – it was not meant to *do* anything – and this model would provide Dudo with more freedom to express his own ideas, and with a motive for the hagiographical style (see below). Furthermore, the desire to display learning explains the use of poetry, and some Greek vocabulary. Even Dudo's unwillingness and self-professed inadequacy should perhaps be regarded as a learned modesty *topos*. The Normans already understood their greatness, and Dudo's work displayed this in a way that was universally acceptable to the pro-active, to the intellectuals and to the religious. For the Normans, history was ceasing to be simply a means of recording their achievements, and becoming a distinct cultural symbol – the achievements of

---

89 Searle, 'Fact and Pattern', 121–2.
90 Original translation: Dudo (tr.), 6. The Latin, from Dudo, 119 reads: '*ut mores actusque telluris, quin etiam et proavi sui Rollonis, quæ posuit in regno jura describerem*'. Christiansen notes (pp. 178–9, n. 32) that this passage is much disputed, and that, while *proavi* means great-grandfather, it can also have the more general meaning of forefather. I am indebted to Professor Nicholas Brooks for discussion of this particular passage.

the Norman lords were being recorded so that a tradition of greatness could be handed down to subsequent generations, both of Normans and 'others'.

We can see this idea of a tradition of greatness most clearly within the military arena. The Norman rulers, and thus the Normans themselves, in both the *Historia Normannorum* and the *Gesta Normannorum Ducum* (and, in fact, in the majority of subsequent histories) seem to possess some sort of 'innate martial valour', which results in many victories and very few defeats.[91] In the words of William of Jumièges, 'at this time the Normans always used to put their enemies to flight, but fled before none of them'.[92] When Rollo fought the English, 'he charged unhesitatingly into battle against them, and laid many of them low'; after his battle with Riulf and the rebels, 'William inspected the corpse-strewn field and found none of his own men among the dead'.[93] Even the short-lived Richard III is described by William as 'extremely capable in war . . . guiding the throngs of soldiers with a strong and just hand' – he wins the only military engagement in which he is involved.[94] It is such an outlook that explains Dudo's account of Rollo's abdication of power to William Longsword. Rollo did not die for five more years, but the Normans required victory and Rollo was getting older and less useful in war as a result.

The simple fact of victory is not, however, the only aspect of this tradition, as importance is also placed on how the victories were won. Throughout the battles recorded in both the *Historia Normannorum* and the *Gesta Normannorum Ducum*, one can find accounts of tactics used by the Normans in a way that suggests that they are integral to perceptions of military *skill*, rather than courage or heroism. The feigned flight performed during the Battle of Hastings is well known among most Norman historians, but this was by no means the first time that Normans had employed this tactic. King Otto of Germany's 'nephew' found himself on the receiving end of just such a ploy as he approached Rouen with his uncle's vanguard, and the Normans 'experienced in such encounters, feigned flight as if vanquished by the enemy'.[95] King Henry I's army fared no better against Duke William II ('the Conqueror'), when the Normans 'who seemed to be fleeing, turned round and began violently to cut down the French'.[96] Rollo is cited by Dudo on two occasions as concealing the true size of his army so as to surprise and outmanoeuvre his enemies, and the Normans under Richard I are considered to gain considerable defensive advantage from their position in relation to the Seine.[97]

The importance of their military tradition to the Normans is undeniable. They not only gloried in their victories, but saw these successes as reflecting directly upon their *gens*: military victory and prowess were the primary means by which the worthiness of their people was measured. Even William Longsword, seemingly the most

---

[91] R.H.C. Davis, *The Normans and their Myth* (London, 1976), 7.

[92] *GND* II, 34: '*Cuius tempore etatis semper fuerunt assueti hostes fugare Normanni, terga uertere nulli*'.

[93] Dudo, 145: '*Qui more solito ad prælium indubitanter illis occurrit, plurimosque illorum prostravit*'; 191: '*Willelmus, lustrans campum cadaverum, et non inveniens mortuum ullum suorum*'; Dudo (tr.), 28 & 68.

[94] *GND* II, 44: '*in armis bellicis ualde idoneus . . . equo libramine militares turmas moderans*'.

[95] Dudo, 255: '*nepos*'; '*ipsi vero Northmanni talium colluctationem gnari, simulantes fugam quasi hostibus convicti*'; Dudo (tr.), 130. The name of the 'nephew' is not present in the tale, and neither Lair nor Christiansen speculate as to his identity.

[96] *GND* II, 104: '*qui uidebantur fugere, uersa facie, ceperunt eos acriter cedere*'.

[97] Dudo, 150, 156 & 256; Dudo (tr.), 33, 37 & 131.

restrained and peaceful of the Norman counts, could be incited to violence easily and be 'raised up on high by the slaughter and destruction'.[98] Thus, as our writers show us, violence was integral to *Normanitas*, but violence against one's enemies, on the battlefield. Yet even as the stories of continuous victories were central to the symbolic aspects of the *gens Normannorum*, the tale of a defeat was perhaps even more so. At Chartres, shortly before the settlement agreement, Rollo did battle with a mixed force of Franks and Burgundians, and proved equal to the task until a force of clergy and citizens of Chartres attacked his rear, led by Bishop Walter, 'bearing the cross and the tunic of the holy Virgin Mary'.[99] Rollo realised that he was not winning, withdrew defeated and was later drawn to treaty.

It is tales like this that bring out most clearly the importance of religion to the Normans, and thus to *Normanitas*. Rollo is not admonished here as a coward or weakling (or even as a woman), but rather regaled for his common sense. Dudo's *Apostropha ad Rollonem*, which directly follows the battle in the text, reassures:

> No Frank puts you to flight, nor does the Burgundian strike you,
> Nor the gathering of all sorts of people, in double formation;
> No, but the bountiful tunic of the virgin mother of God, also
> The relics, and reliquaries too, and the venerable crucifix
> Which the reverend prelate carries in meritorious hands.[100]

William of Jumièges goes even further than Dudo, and observes that Rollo abandoned the fight 'as a wise man, not as a timid coward'.[101] Even as both writers acknowledged that Rollo was a great warrior, God could defeat him and he was not yet a Norman. As we have already noted, William's use of *Normanni* is consequent upon this battle. Rollo is humbled by the power of the Christian God and undergoes a subtle change, which allows for the creation of the Norman *gens*.

The strong Norman association with Christianity is also apparent from our charter evidence, which provides us with a constant stream of both donative and foundation charters for monasteries throughout Normandy. The comital association with the Catholic faith and, in particular, with the monastic life is equally apparent in the histories. In the *Historia Normannorum*, William Longsword is credited with the refoundation of Jumièges and a very deep interest in religion; his desire to be a monk has already been remarked upon.[102] Richard I, in turn, founded Fécamp, the 'ducal abbey', while under the government of Richard II 'many flocks of monks grew'.[103] The links of the Normans with the Cluniac tradition, through the medium of William of Volpiano, are well known, and it is, no doubt, the Cluniac reform in the duchy that William refers to here; notably, the *Inventio* portrays Richard I and II as 'champions of monastic reform'.[104] In fact, apart from Richard III, who is

---

98 Dudo, 192: '*caede atque ruina sublimiter exaltatus*'; Dudo (tr.), 69.
99 Dudo, 162: '*bajulansque crucem atque tunicam sacrosanctæ Mariæ Virginis*'; Dudo (tr.), 43.
100 Dudo, 163: '*Non te Franco fugat, te nec Burgundio cædit, / Concio multimodæ gentisque utriusque phalangis: / Sed tunica alma Dei genitricis Vriginis, atque / Reliquiæ simul ac philateria cruxque verenda, / Quam vehit in manibus meritis præsul reverendus*'; Dudo (tr.), 43.
101 *GND* I, 62: '*prouido consilio non timida ignauia*'.
102 Dudo, 200–1; Dudo (tr.), 76–7; above, p. 20.
103 Dudo, 291; Dudo (tr.), 165; *GND* II, 6: '*Plurima monachorum adoleuere ouilia*'.
104 Potts, 'Historical Tradition', 151. William of Volpiano (Dijon) was invited to the duchy by Richard II in 1001 (see *RGO*, p. 272, n. 1, and below, p. 51).

excluded on account of the shortness of his life, all the pre-conquest counts are religious devotees, as both Rollo and Robert the Fearless are shown performing overtly
religious acts (Robert's pilgrimage to the east, and Rollo's conversion). There is never
any doubt expressed about the piety of these leaders.[105]

The *gens Normannorum* was therefore a race conceived within Christianity, as its
creation essentially post-dates Rollo's conversion. The Christian faith was thus
innate to the conception of *Normanitas* held by both Dudo and William of Jumièges'
– Normans were Christian and had been since their creation as a *gens*. William's
Gesta Normannorum Ducum even suggests a biblical ideal, as his work is very much
geared towards the 'chosen people' in their 'chosen land', led, at least initially, by a
chosen leader. For the Normans in general, however, religion was simply something
else to do well. They were already the self-proclaimed military superiors of their
neighbours; their intensive support of the monastic movements, and especially
Cluny, suggests that they were attempting to take the religious crown as well. The
fact that William Longsword was ostensibly planning to become a monk at Jumièges
suggests a significant and close connection between the Norman leaders and their
monastic foundations.

In the Norman identity, we can see several elements at work. The *origo* concepts
of the *gens Normannorum*, derived through the leadership structure to provide a
historical myth, grounded themselves firmly in the acceptance of a multi-cultural
race. *Normanitas* was not a simple and static construct, but rather a collection of
tightly held referents and distinguishing symbols, which allowed for the preservation
of cultural ideas in a identity-threatening environment. Its propensity for the adoption of new ideas and universal acceptance of difference were the result of evolution
and change that maintained several core concepts (military prowess, strong leadership, piety, etc.) to which different approaches could be taken based on the particular
social / cultural environment. Thus a Norman could be of many cultures, either
Germanic or Romance, and of one, Norman. However, given the strong focus on
leadership, a short assessment must be made of exactly how far this identity applied
to the majority of society.

It has already been noted that, by the end of this period, territorial identification
was in a fairly advanced state of evolution, with the slow creation of the idea that

---

[105] It should, of course, be noted that Christian observance among the leadership did not necessarily
indicate a similar movement among the people that they ruled, particularly not during the early decades.
It is true to say that the accounts of neither Dudo nor William of Jumièges of the religious practices of the
Normans provide us with a clear understanding of the religious situation among the people, and certainly
do not agree with the external perception of an extremely slow conversion (below, p. 51). Dudo's *Historia* hints, for example, at continued non-Christian practice during the time of William Longsword, in
his reference to Riulf as a 'manifold blasphemer and perjurer' (Dudo, 218: '*multifariam blasphemum et
perjurum*'; Dudo (tr.), 94), implying that the cultural rift between him and William may have contained
a religious element. Yet neither Dudo nor William of Jumièges make any direct reference to paganism
among the Normans after Rollo's conversion. As they were churchmen, by presenting the history of a
gens that had very strong religious ties by the time they were writing, both men clearly had a motivation
to avoid discussion of the Normans' pagan past and good reasons to present the leadership of the
Normans in a very Christian light. Consequently, their religious commentary cannot be assumed to be
'true' in any objective sense. That said, their writing presents a strongly Christian image for *Normanitas*,
and one that appears to have reflected the interests and identity structures of the Normans of their own
days.

Normandy was vacant before the Normans arrived.[106] Certainly, once such an iden-tity was in effect, this can happily be said to apply to all the territory's native inhabit-ants: they were born into *Normanitas* as they were born in Normandy, the *patria Normannorum*. Prior to this, we can still apply the identity structure to those calling themselves 'Normans'. As noted above, this ethnonym had numerous associated cultural meanings; to use it of oneself, therefore, evidenced a willing acceptance of these. Furthermore, the adaptability of the Norman race allowed the acceptance into the Norman fold of those who were not of Scandinavian origin, and this would asso-ciate with the conception that this identity was meant to encompass all those in the settled territory. It therefore seems likely that the identity applied to the majority of people in the Norman areas, as it was far easier to passively accept such change than to actively oppose it. The day-to-day routine, which involved worship in churches built in a 'Norman' style, government by overlords calling themselves Normans and justice provided by the Franco-Scandinavian 'Norman' laws, would result in absorp-tion into *Normanitas* at the lowest social levels.[107]

However, it proves very difficult to make an accurate assessment of such things solely from the internal, i.e. Norman, sources. Identity, as we know, is not purely the result of one's own perceptions, but also those of others, and in the case of ethnic determination, those of other *gentes*. It seems true to say that the Normans perceived themselves as a race held together by great men and heroic victories, all accomplished with God on their side, but it is quite a different matter to claim such perceptions of their neighbours through a study only of their own writings. It therefore proves necessary to examine external views on the Normans, both centrally Frankish and more provincial, in order to gain a fuller idea not only of what it meant to call oneself 'Norman', but also of what it meant for others to do the same.

---

[106] Above, pp. 30–1.

[107] For a useful summary and bibliography of the evolution of pre- and post-conquest religious architec-ture, see Marjorie Chibnall, *Anglo-Norman England, 1066–1166* (Oxford, 1986), 216–18, and p. 216, n. 28. Also helpful are Lucien Musset, *Normandie Romane – 1: La Basse-Normandie*, La Nuit des Temps 25 (La Pierre-qui-Vire, 1975) and *Normandie Romane – 2: La Haute-Normandie*, La Nuit des Temps 41 (La Pierre-qui-Vire, 1975). Recent studies include Maylis Baylé, 'Norman Architecture Around the Year 1000: Its Place in the Art of North-Western Europe', *ANS* 22 (2000), 1–28 and E.C. Fernie, 'Architec-ture and the Effects of the Norman Conquest', in David Bates and Anne Curry (eds), *England and Normandy in the Middle Ages* (London, 1994), 105–16.

3

External Identity

To understand an ethnic identity fully, investigations must be made not only of those things that constitute the people from their own viewpoint, but also those that distinguish that people to the external observer.[1] We have already examined the perceptions held by the Normans and committed to a written form by Dudo of St-Quentin and William of Jumièges, but to obtain the full picture we must also look at the external considerations that affected the creation and continuation of Norman identity. The Frankish central and regional histories provide us with a collection of information, which, while far less concentrated than the Normans' own, is still substantial owing to the larger number of Frankish writers. Although the references to the Normans are often incidental or of limited scope, each one provides some insight into the way in which these 'others' considered the Normans. Based upon their own identities and thus justified in terms of their own social norms, it is the attitude of these writers towards the Normans, be it in terms of war, religion or leadership, that impart information to us. Identity is a distinguishing feature, and the Franks necessarily distinguished the Normans in a different way from the way in which the Normans distinguished themselves.

The name that the Franks gave to the Normans in their histories (and, as already noted, the name that the 'proto-Normans' adopted) was *Normanni* (or variants of this), presumably reflecting an equivalent vernacular form considering that neither of the ethnonym's components are native Latin words. However, this was also the name that the Franks had given to any and all settlers, raiders and others of Scandinavian or perceived Scandinavian origin; they were 'Northmen' and, importantly, not Franks. The widespread usage of this term is borne out by sources throughout the period, and before. The term '*Nor(d)manni*' is present throughout both the ninth-century *Annals of St-Bertin* and *Annals of Fulda*, appearing alongside '*Dani*'; in Fulda, the Danes are mentioned as 'the most powerful people among the Northmen', while in St-Bertin it is apparent that the *Dani* are the 'known' quantity,

---

[1] The perceptions that members of a *gens* hold of themselves, those things that are *ego-recognised*, are beliefs that are far less likely to be held by an 'other', who is not a member of the group. Both the common beliefs of the community in a historical myth and their established norms of behaviour support and define their identity, and neither of these structures is accessible to an outsider. Consequently, the external observer constructs beliefs about a people in a similar manner to those constructed by the people themselves, but based upon a different myth / symbol complex. As identity is a fluid and, to an extent, reactive construct, the interaction between these two (or more) sets of perceptions defines the identity, which in turn alters the perceptions and continues the cycle. Therefore, both internal and external (*alter-ascribed*) aspects of an identity are integral to its study.

and the *Nortmanni* the 'unknown'.[2] Flodoard of Reims speaks '*de Normannorum infestatione*' in his *Historia Remensis Ecclesiae* (fully twenty chapters before he first mentions Rollo), but also titles Richard I '*filius Willelmi Normanni*' in his annal for 961.[3] Rodulf Glaber, writing after 1030, is no exception to this 'tradition'; for Rodulf, Robert the Fearless is '*Robertus, Normannorum dux*'.[4] Elsewhere, we have similar usage: in Richer '*multis Normannorum*'; in Adhemar '*victores Normanni existunt*'; and, in the *Historia Francorum Senonensis*, '*gens incredula Normannorum*'.[5] Non-literary sources provide no different information – we have references to the Normans as *Normanni* in royal charters throughout the tenth century, for example.[6] Yet such usage creates a degree of confusion for the historian. With so general a term in use, it is often impossible to tell the ethnicity of a particular group referred to in the histories, or even to comprehend whether the *Normanni* mentioned are actual Normans, or Scandinavians of one form or another. The associations that the Franks made with this ethnonym require examination.

It cannot be argued that the term 'Northman' is anything other than general. When applied to the Scandinavians, it makes no distinction between the various origins of those groups operating around the coast of Francia throughout the ninth and tenth centuries. Further, its equal application to both of the Scandinavian settlements in Francia is evidence of the truly generic nature of this term, which required any specific group to be referred to by locality and leadership: the charter of Charles III of 14th March 918 refers to 'the Seine Northmen, namely Rollo and his companions'.[7] It is with regard to the settlements in particular that the generalised usage makes the least sense. It is not unreasonable to assume that, although there may have been similarities between the behaviour of some of the settlers and the perceived stereotype of a Northman, the Franks would be aware of the cultural and social changes that the 'Norman' society, at least, underwent. Such a blanket term was not, therefore, one that aided understanding so much as one that aided demonisation: 'Northmen' was a negative term that carried overtones of barbarity and foreignness for the Franks, serving much the same purpose as the term 'Hun' did when employed by the British during the two world wars.

It must not be forgotten, however, that the Frankish society was not forged under the same unusual conditions as the Norman society. By the tenth century, the Franks were happily certain of their origins and their ethnic unity, having long since

[2] *Annales Bertiniani*, ed. G. Waitz, *SRG* (Hannover, 1883), 35 & 55; *The Annals of St-Bertin*, tr. Janet L. Nelson (Manchester, 1991), 65 & 95; *Annales Fuldenses*, ed. F. Kurze, *SRG* (Hannover, 1891), 120; *The Annals of Fulda*, tr. Timothy Reuter (Manchester, 1992), 122.
[3] *HRE*, IV:1, 415; Flodoard, 150.
[4] Glaber, 202.
[5] Richer, I, 2:85, p. 254; Adhemar, 178; *MGH SS* IX (1925), 365.
[6] A charter from the reign of Charles III (the Simple), dated 21st May 907, makes mention of Norman attacks on Notre-Dame de Paris (*Recueil des Actes de Charles III le Simple, Roi de France (893–923)*, ed. Philippe Lauer, Chartes et Diplômes Relatifs à l'Histoire de France (Paris, 1949), no. 57, pp. 123–5). Later references include a so-called original charter of Lothar from 7th February 966, requested by '*Richardus, Nortmannorum marchisus*' (*Recueil des Actes de Lothaire et de Louis V, Rois de France (954–987)*, ed. Louis Halphen, Chartes et Diplômes Relatifs à l'Histoire de France (Paris, 1908), no. 24, pp. 53–7.
[7] *Actes de Charles III*, ed. Lauer, no. 92, pp. 209–12; '. . . *Normannis Sequanensibus, videlicet Rolloni suisque comitibus* . . .' (p. 211).

undergone the difficult process of identity formation – conquest, internal conflict and conversion – that the Normans were only just beginning. Even the alteration of the leadership *origo* prompted by the succession of a new royal dynasty does not appear have significantly affected their outlook. As a strong and relatively stable *ethnie*, it is perhaps more reasonable to expect the Frankish society to fit theoretical models than the Norman, and such models allow some explanation of this broad application of the 'Northman' ethnonym. The identity structure analysis model of ethnic interaction suggests that a common reaction to a contemporary immigrant population is to ascribe a derogatory 'racial' identity to them, and that such a reaction is normally the product of those who consider the immigrants a threat.[8]

While, in a modern context, the threatened groups are generally the 'working class' and 'restrictionist right', the existence of the 'working class' in our period cannot readily be accepted. The existence of the 'restrictionist right', however, is not really in doubt, though its form may be somewhat different. In an age when power was concentrated in the hands of a few, it unlikely that these few would readily accept a new community with pleasure, especially not one that had its own independent army and with which they would logically be forced to share their power. Furthermore, the Church, considered in modern times to be a bastion of conservatism, would certainly react in a negative fashion to an immigrant population who were largely pagan, even if conversions were taking place. Such was the environment in which our Frankish writers were producing their work.

Of course, it is unlikely that the discomfort of a few members of a society could produce such a widespread disinterest in the ethnic composition of these 'Northmen'. The reaction signified by this attribution of a general and indistinct group seems far less defensive and far more dismissive. In fact, the overtones of this affected ignorance are most reminiscent of a social or cultural superiority complex, in the same vein as the one that produced the term 'barbarian' so many years before. The term 'Northman' and 'barbarian' have a definite ring of similarity in their widespread application, and serve to distance the outsiders or 'others' from the 'real people'. In fact, Richer of Reims, who is well known for his attempts to showcase his knowledge of the classics, uses the term 'barbarian' in his description of the settlers, referring to the 'disgraces of the barbarians'.[9] Furthermore, although the term 'Northman' initially presents itself as a geographically influenced ethnic signifier (as 'barbarian' is a cultural one), it may also have held cultural overtones. During the period in which the term *Normanni* saw its greatest usage, the Carolingian dream of empire and *Romanitas* was still very much alive, and the Roman culture was always oriented towards the south and the Mediterranean. Thus, as a term to distance someone from the Roman culture, the geographical implications of 'Northman' were seemingly ideal.

The adoption of the ethnonym 'Norman' by the 'proto-Norman' people has been discussed in the previous chapter, and the consistent usage of the word *Normanni* in the Frankish sources after the end of recorded Viking raiding is seemingly self-explanatory. What is less comprehensible, however, is the continued connotations of disinterest that the term bore and, in fact bears for the Franks / French. While

---

8   Weinreich, 'Operationalisation', 302–3.
9   Richer I, 1:4, p. 14: '*barbarorum ignominia*'.

modern British, American and Scandinavian scholars apply a variety of terms to the study of the Scandinavian raiders and migrants in the period (for example, distinguishing 'Northmen' and 'Normans'), modern French usage still reflects an ambiguity in the use of the word *normands*, which, while primarily meaning the people of Normandy, can also be applied as a generalised term for the Scandinavians operating in western Europe in the ninth and tenth centuries (where English-language scholars tend to use Viking / viking).[10] This therefore suggests that there was never any real distinction made in Frankish minds between these Northmen and the Normans, and that the adoption of the ethnonym Norman by the evolving *ethnie* in the Rouennais, while of ultimate importance to the Normans, was, for the Franks, an explicit acceptance of their superiority.[11]

The urge to create a distinct boundary between the two groups might also help to explain the lack of effort on the part of the Frankish writers to distinguish between Franks and Scandinavians in the settled areas. Although Flodoard makes some reference to pre-existing inhabitants when he observes that the grant of Rouen included 'some of its subjects', he is the only Frankish writer to do so, and after the settlement there are only *Normanni*.[12] Richer is even less forthcoming, with a simplistic comment about the concession of the province, which leaves unanswered the question of whether or not the province contained Franks. It is the works of both Adhemar of Chabannes and Rodulf Glaber that give the most interesting information.[13] For Adhemar, there is no pre-existing population, as he observes:

> And the Normans retired; finding the land empty, they constituted a home for themselves in Rouen, with their leader Roso (Rollo).[14]

For Glaber, too, the *gens Normannorum* is a purely Scandinavian one:

> When first they [the *Normanni*] sallied out, they stayed long in regions close in the vicinity of the Atlantic Ocean and were content with a modest living until they came together into no mean *gens*.[15]

---

[10] For evidence of this, see any French translation of a Latin source of the period.

[11] The consideration of Frankish 'superiority' here is a difficult one. Certainly, the acceptance of an essentially derogatory title by the 'Normans' was a victory on a cultural, and no doubt ethnic level, but the implications of this superiority are more far-reaching. It is conceivable that such ideas may have provided legitimisation for the Franks' cultural ideas (*Romanitas*, etc.) not just on this local level, but also in a wider context. The 'Northern barbarians' had contravened the *mores* of 'civilised' (i.e. Roman / Carolingian) society for over a century, but this had culminated with their inclusion into the Frankish social structure as, essentially, the lowest of the low. Francia had proved itself against the 'barbarians', the 'scourge of God'; it had endured (which was more than Rome had managed), and thus it may be that the Franks conceived the settlement and inclusion of these former raiders both as a general acknowledgement by the 'barbarians' that western European society was superior to their own, and as some sort of redemption.

[12] *HRE*, IV: 14, p. 509: '*cum Rotomagensi quam pene deleverant urbe, et aliis eidem subjectis*'.

[13] Richer notes that the province was granted to the settlers on the condition that they became Christian and fought loyally for the king, but does not mention any pre-existing population: '. . . *hæc provincia ei conferretur; ita tamen ut, idolatria penitus relicta, christianæ religioni se fideliter manciparet, necnon et regibus Galliarum terra marique fideliter militaret*' (Richer I, 1:4, p. 14).

[14] Adhemar, 139: '*Et Normanni regressi, terram vacuam repperientes, sedem sibi in Rotomago constituunt cum principe suo Roso*'.

[15] Glaber, 1:5:18, p. 32: '*Hi denique primo egressu diutius circa mare occeanum degentes, breuibus contenti stipendiis, quousque in gentem coaluere non modicam*'.

Both of these accounts seem strange when it is considered that the Normans seem at best tentative about any argument for *gens* purity even as late as the 1050s, in the work of William of Jumièges; prior to this, it is not purity that they extol, but diversity. Consequently, the Frankish sources actually appear to pre-empt the evolution of the Norman *origo*, if William of Jumièges' vagaries are truly the forerunners of an ideology of *gens* purity. This, of course, raises difficulties. The fact that we lack internal sources from the period in which both Adhemar and Glaber were writing means that we cannot say for certain whether or not the Normans were drawing on this Frankish concept to explain their origins in the mid-eleventh century. However, though we can accept it as a possibility, we must also examine this tradition to some extent. Although the Normans apparently drew on Frankish terms to provide an ethnonym during their period of ethnogenesis, it is rather less reasonable to suggest a similar acceptance once their identity was more firmly formed. Through Dudo, it can be seen that the Normans were not claiming *gens* purity at the end of the tenth century; through the *Inventio*, we can see that these ideas were still not accepted in the 1050s. The ambiguities in William of Jumièges' account of the Norman settlement (in which he does not clearly state whether the Northmen settled empty or occupied territory) hint at the evolution of similar ideas among the Normans themselves, but imply that they had not attained too much credibility by this point. If both Adhemar and Glaber, one writing in Aquitaine and the other in Burgundy, could record such a tradition, it is possible that William of Jumièges was aware of it, either because this tale was current throughout the Frankish provinces in the 1020s at least (and William was born *c*.1000), or because the information was prevalent in monastic or Cluniac circles.

It is, of course, possible that William was unaware of this particular viewpoint, being, as he was, only an ordinary monk. While it is fairly certain that he knew of Jordanes, the *Historia Francorum Senonensis*, the *Miracula sancti Benedicti* and the *Vita sancti Aichardi* (and thus the historical traditions of Sens and Fleury), we cannot prove that he knew the works of either Adhemar or Glaber.[16] The lack of clarity in his discussion of the settlement may even be evidence against his knowledge of this tradition: it would make sense, if he knew of it, for him to have either supported or, if he disagreed, vehemently denied it as an imposition, rather than following the line he did. However, while a rapid change in the perceived Norman *origo*, from that of ethnic diversity to purity is hard to credit, such a perception from the Frankish viewpoint is not. It has already been noted that neither Flodoard nor Richer, both writing in the tenth century, made much of any diversity among their *Normanni*, and it would be only reasonable to accept the later considerations of Adhemar and Glaber as components of the naming problem. It must be remembered that *Normanni* in no way distinguishes between Scandinavians and inhabitants of Normandy and thus, rather than trying to postulate a difference between the two, Adhemar and Glaber simply consider them to be a homogeneous *gens* of unified descent.

This approach accomplishes two things. Firstly, it provides an acceptable reason for the tradition that Adhemar and Glaber present while removing the need to conquer the Normans and 'turn them back into Franks': the *Normanni* had never counted Franks among their numbers, and thus there was no need to posit defeats or

---

16 *GND* I, xxxvi; Van Houts, 'History', 108.

conquests of the Franks that had to be avenged. Secondly, it explains the Norman *gens* in a way that was comprehensible within the Frankish thought-world: to the Franks, a *gens* should have a pedigree, and if the Normans were not prepared to provide a 'realistic' one, then the Franks would. In this light, if the tradition was known among the Normans, William's behaviour is also more understandable; by the time he was writing, the belief in ethnic diversity was waning, and the Franks were claiming the Normans to be of pure Scandinavian descent. It was therefore simpler, and far more distinctive, not to comment.

With such pretexts set, it is hardly surprising that the Franks had perceptions of the Norman leaders that were markedly different from the Normans' own. While, for the Franks, the Norman identity that they had constructed and believed did not owe anything to leadership descent, the Norman leader was just as representative of Norman identity for them as he was for the Normans themselves. It is, in fact, rare to find any other specific Norman mentioned in the Frankish sources in this period, and thus the leader often serves as a metaphorical representation of the entire *gens Normannorum*. Consequently, those criticisms and (occasional) praises that we find levelled at the Norman leader are intended to reflect on the Normans in general. Furthermore, the way in which Frankish titles (*comes, dux*, etc.) are applied to the Norman leader reflect how powerful and important he was *felt* to be by the Franks, carrying also some measure of Frankish respect for / dislike of the Normans as a provincial group. These titles have additional importance, as they represent the treatment of the Norman 'minority' in the context of the dominant majority's statuses and institutions.[17]

With regard to status, the few relevant Frankish charters provide us with the 'royal' interpretation, as one would expect. In the 918 charter mentioned above, Rollo is not glorified with any title, and there is no reliable reference to William Longsword. However, a charter of 7th February 966 refers to '*Richardus, Nortmannorum marchisus*'; this suggests that the Norman ruler had earned a certain amount of respect in the eyes of the Franks.[18] This implication is to some extent supported by a forged charter dated 963–4, in which Richard I is given as a signatory by the title '*Richardi filii Guillelmi ducis Normanniae*'.[19] Obviously, for the forgery to be successful it would need to be believable, and notably the leader is not only depicted as a *dux* (the highest non-royal title), but also the *dux* of a politically constituted territory (*Normannia*) rather than some amorphous barbarian people. However, Robert Helmerichs has noted that the person to whom the ducal title applies is unclear, and has warned that this must be treated 'at best as evidence for nomenclature in *c.*963, and at worst a later interpolation'.[20] It is certainly extremely difficult to establish when the forger was working – we have only a fourteenth-century copy, included in a cartulary in which the earliest genuine charter dates from *c.*1155 – and thus the importance of the use of this title is uncertain. Later charters are no more helpful to us, unfortunately: the disorganisation caused by the change of dynasties means that we lack early Capetian charters in any numbers.

---

[17] Barth, *Ethnic Groups*, 31.

[18] *Actes de Lothaire et Louis V*, ed. Halphen, no. 26, pp. 53–7; quote p. 56. For discussion of the titles of the Norman leaders, see above, pp. 29–30.

[19] *Actes de Lothaire et Louis V*, ed. Halphen, no. 59, pp. 137–8; quote p. 138; see also *Actes des Ducs*, ed. Fauroux, no. 1, pp. 67–8.

[20] Helmerichs, 'Rollonid Designators', 63.

In the narrative histories, the Frankish writers provide no further information about Rollo. In all these sources he is a relatively misty figure, and it is entirely possible that the upheavals created by the process of settlement and the incipient ethnogenesis of the *gens Normannorum* created an information barrier similar to the English Danelaw.[21] Rollo is, however, generally treated by the Frankish writers as a typical Scandinavian leader, and though he is called '*duce Rollone*' by Richer, the title may here retain its classical significance of a war-leader.[22] Generally, the Franks seem to have found Rollo to be quite unremarkable; he was, of course, as uncultured as the next *Normannus*, but not otherwise special, and certainly no '*præstantissime princeps*' as Dudo would have it.[23] There is, in fact, one interesting anecdote told of Rollo, but this does not appear until a century after his death, in the work of Adhemar of Chabannes. Adhemar records that, before he died, Rollo sacrificed many Christian captives to the pagan gods that he had abandoned, while also distributing a large amount of gold to the Church.[24] This event may well reflect the intense cultural confusion prompted by the settlement, and thus represent a later version of a tale that was actually in circulation at the time of Rollo's death. If the situation in the Rouennais had been confusing to the future Normans, it was surely more so to outsiders, and Adhemar's tale reflects this uncertainty.

With regard to William Longsword, our narratives are much fuller, most likely a consequence of William's closer interaction with Frankish politics and society: we have already witnessed William's avid interest in all things Frankish. A similar situation is true of Richard I, again probably the result of close interaction, and it is in the evolving traditions surrounding the murder of William and succession of Richard that the most import Frankish perceptions can be observed. The vast importance of these two events to both sides does not, unfortunately, transmit itself to the *Historia Francorum Senonensis*, but our other Frankish sources provide quite full accounts. The motivation of Arnulf I of Flanders (918–65) in having William Longsword murdered was almost certainly to avenge the slight done to him when William helped Herluin regain Montreuil-sur-Mer, the coastal fort of which Arnulf had dispossessed him.[25] However, Arnulf already had reasons to dislike the Normans; he had been personally involved in the defeat of Rollo at Eu in 925, and William's involvement in Frankish power politics was hardly likely to be welcome to one of the most powerful Frankish magnates.[26] Though the Vikings had been an accepted part of Frankish political life, as both mercenaries and raiders, since the first half of the ninth century, they were considered outsiders until they swore fealty or accepted Christian baptism, and even then were expected to behave in a certain way.[27]

---

[21] The *Cultural Atlas of the Viking World*, ed. J. Graham-Campbell (New York, 1994), refers to the Danelaw as a 'historical black hole' (p. 134).

[22] Richer I,1:28, p. 62.

[23] Dudo, 153.

[24] Adhemar, 139–40: '*Qui factus christianus, captivos plures ante se decollare fecit in honore quos coluerat deorum. Et item infinitum pondus auri per ecclesias distribuit christianorum in honore veri Dei, in cujus nomine baptismum susceperat*'.

[25] Richer I, 2:12–15, pp. 140–4.

[26] Bates, *Normandy*, 10 mentions Arnulf's involvement at Eu.

[27] See, for example, Nelson, *Charles*, 31, 36, 39, 125, 151, 153–4, 158 and McKitterick, *Frankish*

William's attempt to *be* Frankish, to be involved in politics as a Frankish magnate, was stepping beyond these boundaries.[28]

From the previous chapter, it can be seen that the Norman writers of the period viewed William's murder as an act of treachery. There was no reason here good enough to countenance such an act, and it was a rarity for Franks to murder one another.[29] This makes it all the more strange that Flodoard's account of the murder should have been so emotionless. Flodoard observes that Arnulf had William killed by treachery, true, but his obvious lack of interest in the whole affair is only aggravated by the contemptuous description of Richard as 'born of a Breton concubine'.[30] Though Flodoard has often been accused of 'stressing the royal point of view', one would expect a chronicler and monk to be somewhat more concerned.[31]

Eleanor Searle, however, advanced a possible explanation for Flodoard's acceptance of events, looking back on a tradition in which Carolingians blinded Carolingians, but murdered Norsemen.[32] This view is more compelling in light of the discussion of the term *Normanni* above: we know that Flodoard was writing at Reims within the confines of a long Carolingian tradition, and if he considered the Normans and, more particularly, William to be Scandinavian, then his acceptance of the situation seems almost reasonable. A prejudicial attitude against these 'Northmen' also explains his attitude towards Richard who was, as Searle notes, 'some bastard'.[33] This was dismissal, disinterest and, above all else, superiority at work.

If this was, however, acceptable in the 960s, it was not so in the 990s. Richer, like Flodoard, wrote of a murder by treachery, but his is not a simple tale of political interference. Richer shows that he has little respect for either William or Richard I, describing them as '*piratarum dux*' and '*piratarum principi*', but he is educated and writing under different traditions from those that influenced Flodoard.[34] His education, under Gerbert of Aurillac's 'new studies' programme, provided him with a strong pull towards the literary and away from the traditionalist concentration on the Carolingian kings, made impossible by the accession of the Capetians. This change in attitudes in both education and accepted behaviour led Richer to look elsewhere for a motive for Arnulf – a simple clash of political swords was not enough. Richer instead creates an anecdotal tale in which William, denied entry to an assembly of

Kingdoms, 232, 234, 249, 272. For baptism and fealty, Nelson, *Charles*, 68 & 77; McKitterick, *Frankish Kingdoms*, 228–30.

28 Above, pp. 31–2.
29 Searle, *Predatory Kinship*, 58; Eleanor Searle, 'Frankish Rivalries and Norse Warriors', *ANS* 7 (1985), 212.
30 Flodoard, p. 86: '*nato de concubina Britanna*'.
31 *GND* I, pp. 122–3, n. 2.
32 Searle, 'Frankish Rivalries', 200.
33 Searle, *Predatory Kinship*, 58.
34 Richer I, 2:20, p. 152; I, 2:28, p. 164; II, Notes, p. 308. Richer's use of the term *pirata* to describe the Normans may well be a Latinisation of the 'viking' concept. Certainly the words *viking* and *víkingr* used in written sources refer to piracy, though the derivation of the word is in some doubt. Gwyn Jones suggests various derivations relating to either OE *wic*, Latin *vicus* or ON *víkja*, while Alfred Smyth has proposed more geographical association, abandoning a 'commonly accepted meaning' of 'the men from the fjords' for ' "the men from the Vík" – or those pirates who infested the Skaggerak and Oslofjord' (see Gwyn Jones, *A History of the Vikings*, 2nd edn (Oxford, 1984), p. 76, n. 1 and Alfred P. Smyth, *Scandinavian Kings in the British Isles, 850–880* (Oxford, 1977), 34).

provincial governors, Louis IV and Otto the Great, forces his way in. On entering, however, William discovers that Otto is seated at a slightly higher level than Louis, and calls Louis to his feet ('Get up for a moment, king!'), insisting that he take the higher seat. William then takes the lower for himself, leaving Otto standing.[35] The insult to Otto is obvious, but the situation ridiculous; Richer here constructs a scenario in which Norman inferiority is showcased, and inevitably results in William's 'removal' from Frankish politics. Having been excluded once, William demonstrates his barbarity by bursting in, his political incapacity established by his rudeness and blind anger, during the course of which he deals an unforgivable insult to Otto.[36] His death is the Frankish response to Norman violence and petulance, and indicates quite clearly the Frankish perceptions at the end of the tenth century: if, for Richer, the Franks had evolved as a race to new moral and social heights, the Normans certainly had not.

Richer's approach to Richard I is also different from that of Flodoard. While he is equally dismissive of his birth, as the *'filium de Brittanna concubina'*, in Richer's version of events Louis IV concedes the lands held by William to him, receiving him with distinction and remarking upon the grace of the young man.[37] While this is a far cry from the Norman reports of Richard's kidnapping and imprisonment, it would appear that Richard is more acceptable to Richer, and to the Franks in general, than ever his father had been. This indicates, therefore, that by the end of the tenth century Frankish attitudes towards the Normans were beginning to become more positive. Richer, writing at the end of Richard's long period of rule, could look back on this period and yet say few overtly negative things about Richard himself: although Richard was still leader of the 'pirates', he was less naïve than his father. This comparatively positive assessment of Richard may, in part, be explained by the change in royal dynasty. For Flodoard, the Normans were quite an unsuccessful people, and even William Longsword's attachment to Louis IV, of whom he was the sole supporter between 940 and 942, could not save him from murder.[38] The apparent apostasy in the Norman territories after his death, and the generally weak state of the *gens Normannorum* in the face of the *gens Francorum* at the start of the 960s revealed to Flodoard no improvement.[39] Richer, on the other hand, saw the fruits of a long-term plan based around an 'old custom' of Norman–Capetian alliance, by means of which the Normans, with the accession of the new dynasty, had attained far greater political prominence.[40] As Richer records a tradition that the conspiracy for the death of William Longsword took place between Arnulf of Flanders and Hugh the Great (father of Hugh Capet and the *dux Francorum*), it seems

---

[35] Richer I, 2:30, pp. 166–8; ' *"Surge," inquit "paululum rex!"* ', p. 168.

[36] Significantly, Richer's patron, Gerbert of Aurillac, had been sent to the court of Otto I by Pope John XIII in the early 970s, and taught the young Otto II; this may help to explain the strength of the Frankish response to the insult dealt to Otto by William (*Letters of Gerbert*, 4).

[37] Richer I, 2:34, p. 174; '*Rex adolescens elegentiam advertens, liberaliter excipit, provinciam a patre pridem possessam, ei largiens*'.

[38] Felice Lifshitz, *The Norman Conquest of Pious Neustria: Historic Discourse and Saintly Relics 684–1090* (Toronto, 1995), 176.

[39] For the apostasy: Bates, *Normandy*, 13–14; for the weakness of the Normans until *c.*960, see Searle, 'Fact and Pattern', 131–2.

[40] Donald Matthew, *The Norman Conquest* (London, 1966), 44 makes reference to the custom.

only reasonable that he should attribute this success to Richard, and thus credit him with more respect than Flodoard does.[41] The tone of Richer's prose, however, suggests that he did not encourage such an alliance.

The development of respect for and acceptance of the Norman rulers and, by association, the Norman people can be seen in later redactions of the William Longsword story. Even though the event gets little coverage in Adhemar's work, the distinguishing feature for him is the fact that William was 'deceitfully killed by Arnulf'; there is no mention of a reasonable motive, and the fact of the murder stands therefore as an unequivocal crime.[42] Richard is simply referred to as William's son – no elaboration concerning his birth is present.[43] Shortly thereafter, when Rodulf Glaber was writing his *Historiarum libri quinque*, the story had evolved to a further level. Again, the act of the murder is treacherous – Glaber even refers to an accomplice of Arnulf's by the name of Theobald 'the Deceiver' – but William does not in any way deserve the murder. On the contrary, it is William's trusting, naïve nature that causes his death; and it is God who avenges him, by killing Theobald's grandson Odo in battle.[44] Although Glaber is less forthcoming about Richard I specifically, his attitude towards the Norman leaders is clear when he states that from the alliance of the Normans with the French and Burgundians there 'arose an outstanding line of dukes, first William, then those that took the name Richard after a father or grandfather'.[45] The highest praise of both Adhemar and Glaber is, however, reserved for Richard II, whom Adhemar calls the 'true count of Rouen' and Glaber 'the venerable duke of the Normans'.[46]

Adhemar's statement is the more interesting of the two. The appellation 'true count' may suggest that Richard's predecessors did not hold the countship of Rouen with the same validity, which has implications on two levels. It may be the case that Adhemar considered Richard II to be the first Norman leader to be genuinely Frankish, or at least Frankish enough to hold such an office; there is no evidence to support the potential implication that Richard had a rival for the position. Alternatively, this may be a veiled reference to the fact that Richard II was the first Norman ruler to have inherited his patrimony legitimately, his grandfather and father both having been the sons of concubines. Whichever is the case, it is clear that the Frankish attitudes examined here reflect a gradually increasing respect for the Norman leaders, and acceptance of them within Frankish society. Indeed, it was not only the people that were gradually accepted in this manner, but also their identity. Although in the mid-tenth century Flodoard of Reims wrote of the *Normanni* as if they were beneath his notice, by the mid-eleventh century Rodulf Glaber could write thus of the dukes:

> The whole of the province subject to their might lived as one clan or family united in unbroken faith.[47]

---

[41] Richer I, 2:32, p. 170.

[42] Adhemar, 148: '*Willelmo ab Arnulfo, Flandelensi comite, dolo interempto . . .*'.

[43] *Ibid.*, 148: '. . . *filius ejus Richardus . . .*'.

[44] Glaber, 3:38–9, pp. 162–4.

[45] *Ibid.*, 1:21, p. 36: '*Indeque orti duces excellentissimi, Willelmus uidelicet atque post ipsum quique denominati paterno seu auito iure Richardi*'.

[46] Adhemar, 178: '*vero comite Rotomagi*'; *Vita Willelmi*, vii, p. 270: '*Normannorum dux uenerabilis*'.

[47] Glaber, 1:21, p. 36: '*Nam omnis prouintia quae illorum ditioni subici contingebat ac si unius consanguinitatis domus uel familia inuiolatæ fideli concors degebat*'.

This united family to which Glaber refers is the *gens Normannorum* and, as an external writer, he shows that the perceived internal unity written of first by Dudo, and later by William of Jumièges, had achieved outwards expression. The Normans were, by this point, considered a separate people who were united by bonds of commonality, which the Franks had come to recognise to a gradually increasing extent. The various and chaotic *Normanni* of the tenth century had disappeared, and had been replaced in the Frankish mind by a comprehensible and quantifiable *gens Normannorum*. The defining elements of this *gens* were, naturally, components of the Norman myth / symbol complex, and we can see the slow recognition of the *gens Normannorum* reflected in the increasing *alter-ascription* of what were *ego-recognised* qualities.[48] This is most evident in the areas of military and religious achievement.

Although the concepts of conquerors and great warriors are inherent aspects of modern ideas of the Normans, the tenth-century Franks had no such illusions. In Flodoard's works, the *Normanni* are only ever truly victorious against the Bretons.[49] Against the Franks, even when they are relatively successful, they always lose the field, and although they achieve victories later, this is when fighting *for* Hugh the Great.[50] In Richer, this theme is in some cases even more pronounced. The *Normanni* are regularly and soundly beaten by a succession of Frankish kings, and it is in one such battle that Rollo loses his life.[51] The pagan uprisings following the death of William Longsword provide Richer with even more material, and he relates one instance in which Louis IV, with only 800 men and the protection of God, attacks a massively larger Norman force, killing 9000 and routing the rest.[52] While these figures are obviously inaccurate (one suspects that the 'protection of God' is actually a rogue zero), they leave no doubt that the tenth-century Franks held nothing but contempt for the military prowess of these *Normanni*.

In the eleventh century, we see a markedly different story, in which the Normans are warriors worthy of respect. For Adhemar of Chabannes, the most revealing incident is that between a group of *Normanni* under King Storin, and a force under the Aquitanian William 'Ironcutter'. In the battle recounted by Adhemar the Normans hold their own (this is, it must be remembered, against Adhemar's countrymen), and the encounter was decided by single combat, in which William was victorious.[53] This is not, however, to say that Adhemar thought the Normans were particularly special in a military capacity, and their ignominious slaughter at the hands of the Irish shows that they were no better than anyone else.[54] It is, again, in Glaber that we see the fullest development of this idea, as he attributes the highest capacity to the Normans and their leaders: 'These dukes surpassed all men in their military might, in desire for peace and liberality'.[55] Such praise is clearly excessive, and undoubtedly motivated by the Norman adoption of the Cluniac monastic tradition, from which he himself came,

---

[48] See above, p. 5, for these terms.
[49] See, for example, Flodoard, 1 & 94.
[50] The loss of the field occurs against Hugh the Great: Flodoard, 88.
[51] Richer I, 1:50, pp. 96–8: the chapter is entitled '*Rollonis pyratae interitus suorumque ruina*'.
[52] *Ibid.*, 1:35, pp. 176–8.
[53] Adhemar, 149.
[54] *Ibid.*, 177.
[55] Glaber, 1:21, p. 36: '*Cum igitur predicti duces ultra ceteros uiguerint militiæ armis, tum perinde pre ceteris gratia communis pacis ac uirtute liberalitatis*'.

and by the successes of Norman adventurers in Italy (known of through his mentor, William of Volpiano (Dijon)). Even so, it still suggests that, by the time William of Jumièges was writing, the much-vaunted military prowess of the Normans was no longer so idly dismissed by their Frankish contemporaries.

Glaber's bias here leads us naturally towards the area of religion, in which again we can see an evolving degree of praise among the Franks. Although Flodoard does not generally make explicit reference to the religion of his *Normanni*, when he does it is to remind us that they had been pagan, not Christian in the main. He does discuss the conversion of the *Normanni* of the Seine (i.e. those under Rollo), but he is more detailed about those on the Loire, in whom he presents a painfully slow progress of conversion.[56] Even after the conversion, the *Normanni* performed no overtly Christian acts, and it is as though their conversion had not affected them at all. A similar situation can be seen in Richer, who also makes few references to the Normans' religious attitudes; again, this is perhaps because their conversion seems to change the nature of his accounts little. Thus our tenth-century writers do not appear to consider the religion of these *Normanni* worthy of any particular note, unless it is to comment when paganism resurfaced.

In the eleventh century, again, this changes. Adhemar, although giving a comparatively small amount of space to the post-settlement *Normanni* in his work, observes that Norman religious tendencies were towards Christianity. He notes that William was baptised as a youth, and that, when Richard succeeded, he was 'most Christian'.[57] He then goes on to attribute the foundations of both the monasteries of Mont-St-Michel and Fécamp to Richard – to Adhemar, Richard was clearly a powerfully Christian leader. Glaber is even more full in his praise, and this is probably again the result of his relationship with William of Volpiano. William had been invited to Normandy in 1001 by Richard II, to reform monasteries after the Cluniac tradition.[58] We know that Glaber studied at St-Bénigne at Dijon under William, and this no doubt led to Glaber's sympathies being directed towards the Normans, especially as he was responsible for a *Vita Willelmi*. Nonetheless, even though he is clearly impressed by many aspects of Norman religious life, he is not universally accepting. He refers to the care given to the needy, poor and pilgrims, and also the generous gifts made by the dukes to the churches of 'almost the whole world', recounting the story of how monks made annual visits from Mount Sinai to collect gold and silver, and Richard II sent one hundred pounds of gold to Jerusalem.[59] However, the ducal monastery at Fécamp is referred to as 'an inconsequential little congregation of clerics living in a carnal manner unfettered by the burden of the rule' before its reformation by William; the Normans weren't perfect, after all, but their religious life was clearly healthier, at least in Frankish eyes, than it had been in the tenth century.[60]

Use of the Frankish sources has therefore allowed us to examine Norman identity from an external viewpoint, armed already with the knowledge of the way in which

---

[56] For example, after the concession of Nantes, only five of them convert: Flodoard, 6.

[57] Adhemar, 148: '*christianissimus*'.

[58] *Vita Willelmi*, p. 272, n. 1.

[59] Glaber, 1:21, p. 36.

[60] *Vita Willelmi*, vii, p. 272: '*Erat enic illic more uiuens carnali iugo soluta regulari clericorum leuis conciola*'.

the Normans perceived themselves in the same time periods. It seems that the relationship between the Franks and the Normans, at least during the earlier part of the settlement period, fits quite well with models of ethnic minority situations.[61] The Normans, initially, were judged very much in context of the Franks' own cultural framework, which did not prove to be particularly receptive to the Normans' ideals and behaviour.[62] The response to the derogatory image created by the Franks was, apparently, an acceptance of the label 'Norman', but also an attempt, in certain cases, to cross the social barrier that existed between the two ethnicities (by William Longsword, for example). Yet the attitude present at the end of the tenth century suggested that such attempts were ill-fated, and the majority/minority relationship was therefore maintained.

In the eleventh century, however, there is a noticeable shift in attitude, in line with an increasingly explicit, non-Frankish definition of the *gens Normannorum*. As the Franks came to see the Normans as of purely Scandinavian constitution and therefore more alien, the treatment of even the most 'civilised' Normans as second-class Franks seems to have dwindled and been replaced by something approaching respect. It would appear that the reinforced boundaries created not only a stronger sense of separateness but some form of realisation that the Normans might be understood as a *gens* in their own right, rather than by reference to Frankish norms; this perhaps indicates that the Normans had ceased to be regarded as an ethnic threat. Such acceptance speaks highly of the robustness of Frankish identity in the eleventh century.[63]

It is also clear from this examination that the perceptions that the Franks held of the Normans were very different from those the Normans held of themselves, and yet no less important to this study. It took considerable time for the Franks to become acclimatised to the *gens Normannorum*, which had essentially evolved on their doorstep. If *Normanitas* conditioned the way that the Normans thought, it equally conditioned the way in which they acted, and it was only with time that the salient aspects made themselves clear to the external observer as symbols of the *gens Normannorum*. Clearly, then, it is not enough for a *gens* to be self-conscious. While a people may abide by a code of behaviour / symbolism, unless this is externally recognised and those characteristics that people see in themselves can be equally viewed by others, a group affiliation is not fulfilling its function – a *gens* is not distinctive and positive if no-one notices the distinguishing symbolism. While we can thus accept that the Franks, in such close proximity to the Normans, gained a progressively increasing understanding of *Normanitas*, and could thus recognise and accept this symbolism, we must look elsewhere to see the performance of this newly formed identity in the face of other challenges. Were those representations of the *gens Normannorum* that had finally evoked such strong responses in the Frankish sources capable of maintaining their distinctiveness in new and less disordered contexts?

---

[61] Weinreich, 'Operationalisation', 301–5.
[62] Barth, *Ethnic Groups*, 31.
[63] Weinreich, 'Operationalisation', 302–3 indicates the accepting responses of dominant communities with robust identities when confronted with minorities.

PART II

The Normans in the South

4

Sources to 1154

Unlike the early period in Normandy, the setting of Norman southern Italy and Sicily has provided us with numerous sources on which to base a study of Norman identity. Though there are similarly few sources that provide useful contemporary opinions from the very earliest years (*c*.1018/19 onwards), from *c*.1030 there are only occasional periods when we lack some form of narrative history that can provide an insight into the way in which the Normans were viewed as an *ethnie*. Furthermore, the Normans' retention of at least some connections with Normandy provides us not only with simple internal and external viewpoints, but also sets of ideas that are born of different sets of preconceptions, stimulated not by witnessed actions but rather by reports. With these things in mind, it seems most sensible to divide the sources to be used into three categories. The first two categories focus on the local sources, produced both internally and externally in the area of, or immediately around, southern Italy and Sicily in the period between the arrival of the first Norman mercenaries and the death of King Roger I of Sicily. The third focuses on sources produced far to the north, in France, by writers who had motivations entirely different from those of the local historians, but whose opinion is no less important to this study.

It is both a help and a hindrance that three of the four main local, internal sources are very near contemporaries. The works of Amatus of Montecassino, Geoffrey Malaterra and William of Apulia were all completed in the closing decades of the eleventh century, and it is unfortunate that the internal opinions that they provide in their histories (written for Normans, if not necessarily by them) are not more widely spread. Even so, the corroboration that such closely grouped histories can provide is a fair compensation, and this allows one of the clearest views of Norman self-perception in any period of their history. This is even more important when it is considered that we are not certain of the background of any of these three writers, making their personal motivations all the more difficult to analyse.

Of the three, Amatus of Montecassino was the first to set down his *Historia Normannorum*, which has unfortunately only survived in an Italianate Old-French translation (as *L'ystoire de li Normant*), made some time in the fourteenth century. As a consequence, Amatus is both hard to identify and hard to date. His two editors, Louis Champollion-Figeac (1835) and Vincenzo de Bartholomaeis (1935), both give the dedicatory letter to Desiderius, abbot of Montecassino, as evidence for setting a final date on the piece: Desiderius was consecrated as Pope Victor III on 24 May 1086, so the work must have been completed before this date.[1] Precisely when

---

[1] For dating arguments, see Amatus, lxvii–lxx, and *L'ystoire de li Normant, et la chronique de Robert*

is, however, uncertain. Amatus mentions the death of Richard of Capua in 1078, so he was evidently writing after this event, perhaps commencing, as de Bartholomaeis believes, after July 1080.[2] This gives us an approximate dating of *c*.1078×1086 for the production of the history; even so, a number of historians have suggested the wider span of *c*.1071×1086.[3]

As to Amatus' origins, they are no less vague. '*Amatus episcopus, et Casinensis monachus*' is mentioned in the work of Peter the Deacon: this is supported by Leo of Ostia, who says Amatus was a bishop and monk of Montecassino, and by necrologies giving the date of death for one Amatus, '*episcopus et monachus*' as 1 March, but without a year of death; however, one of these necrologies can be dated before 1101.[4] Champollion-Figeac and Kenneth Wolf have, however, found very different 'Amati' to apply this evidence to. Champollion-Figeac, quoting Marcus' edition of Peter the Deacon's *Biographies*, distinguishes our Amatus from Archbishop Amatus of Bordeaux, before going on to cite Ferdinand Ughelli's *Italia sacra* of 1721, which cites eight Italian bishops called Amatus, only one of whom was a contemporary of Desiderius. Amatus was, he argues, bishop of Nusco, in Campania, and died in 1093; he was made bishop, perhaps, as a reward for the writing of his history by Pope Victor III.[5] Wolf, on the other hand, finds mention of an Amatus who was bishop of Pesto-Capaccio from 1047 to 1058, and suggests Amatus may have retired to Montecassino, and written his history as an old man.[6] It is impossible to tell which hypothesis is correct, though the fact that most bishops of the time died in office detracts somewhat from Wolf's argument.

It is no easier to identify Amatus' near-contemporaries, Geoffrey Malaterra and William of Apulia, though they are somewhat easier to date. Historians have often assumed that Geoffrey came from Normandy, but there is no specific evidence to this effect, though Geoffrey does observe that he comes from a region on the other side of the mountains (presumably the Alps); his surname was apparently an ancestral nickname, and thus provides no further clues.[7] Recent work has instead suggested that he was a co-opted pilgrim.[8] Although we do not know when he commenced writing, it seems clear from the contents of his work that he wrote the last section some time after Urban II issued his bull regarding the First Crusade, but

---

Viscart, par Aimé, moine du Mont-Cassin, ed. Louis Champollion-Figeac (1835, repr. New York, 1965), xxxiii.

2   This argument is based around the fact of Robert Guiscard's excommunication by Pope Gregory VII on 3 March 1078. Although there is no specific mention in the text of the reconciliation of July 1080, de Bartholomaeis considers it likely that Amatus knew of the reconciliation from the way that he enthuses about both Robert and Gregory; as a monk, it would be expected that he would denounce Robert after his excommunication unless this had been retracted (Amatus, lxviii).

3   See R. Allen Brown, *The Normans* (Woodbridge, 1984), 96 and David C. Douglas, *The Norman Achievement, 1050–1100* (London, 1969), 17.

4   *L'ystoire*, ed. Champollion-Figeac, xxxvi; Kenneth Baxter Wolf, *Making History: the Normans and their Historians in Eleventh-Century Italy* (Philadelphia, 1995), 88.

5   *L'ystoire*, ed. Champollion-Figeac, xliv–liii.

6   Wolf, *Making History*, 88.

7   See, for example, John Julius Norwich, *The Normans in Sicily: The Normans in the South 1016–1130/The Kindom in the Sun 1130–1194* (1967, 1970; omnibus: London, 1992), 339; Brown, *Normans*, 96. Malaterra, 3: '*a transmontanis partibus venientem*' & 5.

8   Wolf, *Making History*, 143–4.

before (or soon after) June 1098, as he mentions Bohemond's departure, but not the fall of Antioch.[9] William of Apulia's work can be dated in a similar manner – he refers to the beginning of the First Crusade, but makes no mention of the taking of Jerusalem, providing a date of 1095×1099; this can be supported by his dedication (to Urban II and Roger Borsa), his talk of the completed conquest of Sicily, and his coverage of Byzantium.[10] However, we know even less about William than we do about Geoffrey: we have no record at all of his origins beyond what is implicit in the name 'of Apulia'.

All three of these works focus on the Norman leaders of their day, and it is this that makes them so useful as a group. Amatus, although his work is titled as a general Norman history, primarily follows the careers of Richard of Capua and Robert Guiscard; the weighting here would seem to be towards Richard, as the work ends with his death. Geoffrey's work, sponsored by Count Roger I of Sicily, has more of an interest in Roger's undertakings than those of his brother Robert, while William of Apulia's *Gesta Roberti Wiscardi* is precisely that. These are complemented by the fourth internal source, Alexander of Telese's *Deeds of King Roger* (*Gesta Rogerii*), written *c.*1136 and focusing entirely on King Roger I of Sicily. Alexander was abbot of S. Salvatore, near Telese, who wrote at the request of Matilda, Roger's sister. His work breaks off abruptly in the middle of an account of 1135, and appears to have been presented to the king in this state.[11] However, Alexander provides us with coverage of the fourth of the major figures to whom the Italian and Sicilian Normans looked for their leadership, and thus makes an essential contribution to the study of Norman identity.

Of the many local, external sources we have at our disposal, there are three that seem of primary importance to this study. The earliest of these is Leo of Ostia's *Chronica Monasterii Casinensis*, written some time before 1105. Leo was a personal friend of Abbot Desiderius, and had entered Montecassino *c.*1061; he was created cardinal-bishop of Ostia some forty years later, and is known to have died in 1115.[12] The dating of Leo's work is based upon archive and oral traditions, and it is usually considered to have been written between *c.*1099 and 1105.[13] The import of this work stems not just from the nature of the comments on the Normans as a people, but also from its comparative value. Produced at Montecassino initially without the help of Amatus' work of a few decades earlier, it was later revised to 1075 using the *Historia Normannorum*. However, the later sections never received alterations of this basis, as they referred to events after Amatus had stopped writing, and it is therefore possible to examine the evolution of opinions about the Normans at Montecassino throughout the second half of the eleventh century.

Our two other sources, the *Chronicle* of Falco of Benevento and the *Alexiad* of Anna Comnena are far harder to date. The extant version of Falco's work lacks both a beginning and an end, commencing in mid-sentence during an entry for the year

---

[9] *Ibid.*, 146.
[10] Apulia, 11–12.
[11] G.A. Loud, 'The Genesis and Context of the Chronicle of Falco of Benevento', *ANS* 15 (1993), 177; Norwich, *Normans in Sicily*, 340; Donald Matthew, *The Norman Kingdom of Sicily* (Cambridge, 1992), 39.
[12] Norwich, *Normans in Sicily*, 340; Wolf, *Making History*, 78.
[13] Brown, *Normans*, 96.

1102, and ending similarly in 1140. His coverage of events is rather uneven, with the focus of entries being on Benevento before 1127 and the death of Count William of Apulia; his account is, however, not based primarily on written sources, but rather on his own experiences and eyewitness testimonies.[14] The date at which he was writing is subject to extensive debate. The translation of the words *'execrandae. . . memoriae'*, used of King Roger of Sicily, has led some historians to suggest that Falco was writing after his death in 1154; others have suggested that he may have been writing as early as 1112.[15] G.A. Loud's 1992 paper on this chronicler concludes otherwise, based on Falco's career. Active as a notary in 1107, Falco ceased judicial activity after 1143 and his son was old enough to be a civic notary in 1137: this all suggests that Falco was dead by 1154. The apparent end of the coverage in the *Chronicle* is 1144, and Loud proposes a completion date near to this, though Falco's ambiguous attitude to certain major players suggests an evolving work, written over an extended period. The conclusion is, therefore, that Falco began his work in the 1120s as a civic chronicle, but his interests expanded *c.*1130, and his work ceased in 1144 or shortly afterwards.[16]

Far less can be said of Anna Comnena. We know that she was born on 1st December 1083, the daughter of the then Byzantine emperor, Alexius Comnenus, but it has proven impossible to establish her date of death.[17] Anna seems to have produced the majority of the work while in exile, and her intention was to set down the achievements of her father, of whom she was extremely proud. Her coverage of Byzantine affairs includes, of course, Robert Guiscard's campaigns into Byzantine-held territory, and her sources for these seem to have been her family – she herself was only two years old when Guiscard died, in 1085. She also recounts the circumstances surrounding the First Crusade and the presence of the Normans, among others, in Byzantium and the taking of Antioch; she was an eyewitness to many of these events (although such considerations are, unfortunately, irrelevant to this study). Unfortunately, although she was still writing in 1148, we do not have any other dates to apply to her work; however, her removal from the political sphere and the 'pulse' of Greek society suggests that she may preserve a view of the Normans from the turn of the century.

With regard to the more distant sources, we have information both from internal (Norman / Anglo-Norman) and external (French) perspectives. The external sources at our disposal are the works of Adhemar of Chabannes and Rodulf Glaber, who have been examined previously in the context of the duchy of Normandy itself.[18] Those 'internal' sources that were produced in Normandy have, however, been omitted from the analysis, because they cannot reasonably be said to represent the state of *Normanitas* in Italy. A lack of local information and close contact with the people who are the subject of this area of the study, while not a handicap for an external source, is hardly a recommendation for a supposedly representative, 'internal' source. Additionally, it seems far more sensible to treat those tales of the Normans in Italy

---

14 Loud, 'Genesis', 178 & 182 ; Matthew, *Norman Kingdom*, 19.
15 Loud, 'Genesis', 183; Matthew, *Norman Kingdom*, 19.
16 Loud, 'Genesis', 185, 191–2.
17 *Alexiad*, 12.
18 Above, pp. 16–17.

that were being recorded in Normandy and England in the context of those areas; these were 'internal' tales of the exploits of the *gens Normannorum* far from home, and the qualities and successes represented in them naturally reflected those of the environment of the authors.

The collection of sources that we have at our disposal for the examination of Norman identity in southern Italy and Sicily is therefore reasonably full and wide-ranging. Even so, there are periodic lacunae in the coverage: there is no coherent narrative for the period 1085–1127, for example.[19] Nonetheless, the sources provide a good deal of interesting information about the perceptions held of the Normans, both by themselves and by 'others', as they went through the transition from mercenaries to kings.

[19] Matthew, *Norman Kingdom*, 19.

5

Internal Identity

It is readily apparent that the Norman (-Italian) society in Apulia, Calabria and Sicily underwent many changes during the period from the arrival of the first mercenaries *c.*1016 through to the death of King Roger of Sicily in 1154. For our purposes, the most interesting and astonishing aspect of these changes, however, is the way in which they mirrored the earlier and more gradual transformations to the north, in the duchy of Normandy. When the Normans arrived in Italy they were mercenaries and raiders, as their Viking ancestors had been before them. After a time they were granted land on which to settle, and from this base carved a home for themselves, the future duchy of Apulia and Calabria. At their peak, they conquered a great deal of land before becoming identified with an island kingdom, that of Sicily. The southern Italian Normans were repeating the exploits of their northern brethren, only over a shorter period of time.

The identity of those Normans who established themselves in southern Italy and Sicily during the eleventh and twelfth centuries is the most complicated of all Norman identity constructs. Aside from this rapid development, there is no simple struggle here, as elsewhere, between an existing majority and a newly arrived minority; rather, the Normans in the Italian area interact constantly with numerous groupings, each possessing their own identity (i.e. ethnic, linguistic, regional or civic) and their own opinions of who and what the Normans were. Consequently, models of minority interactions will be rather less helpful here. The variety of contacts provides a complicated backdrop to the evolution of Norman identity in this area, an evolution confused even further by viewpoints that were based not on contact, as those of the Greeks were, for example, but on reports at distance, or on an archetype derived from the *Normanitas* of their northern relations. We are left, therefore, with an identity constructed by the Normans themselves, along with a whole host of external viewpoints. It is the study of the 'internal' perspective that concerns us here.

As it is not possible to view the Normans in southern Italy and Sicily in the same way as those in Normandy, a careful account must be taken of the developments in their identity in this area. While the circumstances of these Normans changed greatly and, historically speaking, rapidly between *c.*1016 and 1154, it is still possible to divide their exploits and circumstances into four main periods. The period from the initial Norman arrival to the recognition, by the Normans, of William Iron-Arm as Duke of Apulia and Calabria in 1042/3 was a time in which the Normans were establishing themselves in the area, gradually obtaining a 'stake' in southern Italy.[1] In the

---

[1] There is some disagreement among historians as to William's recognition as duke. Lord Norwich

following years, the Normans changed yet further, from settlers to conquerors, ever expanding their territory. During this second period, many important events occurred – the arrival of Robert Guiscard in the area in 1047, and the great victory at Civitate are but two of these. After Guiscard's death in 1085, however, the Normans of Apulia and Calabria had something of a change of fortunes; they suffered reverses in military campaigns, and had their numbers decreased by the call to crusade of 1096. However, in Sicily their situation consistently improved, until it reached new heights with the coronation, in 1130, of Roger I as the first Norman king of Sicily. From 1130 until Roger's death in 1154, the Normans saw a fourth transformation, as the rulers of an important medieval kingdom.

The First Phase – Arrival and Settlement

According to Amatus of Montecassino, the first Normans to arrive in Italy were a group of 40 pilgrims who, having landed in Salerno and gained audience with Guaimar, '*serenissime principe*', asked to be given weapons and horses in order to fight the Saracens '*por lo amor de Dieu*'.[2] William of Apulia recounts a slightly different story in his *Gesta Roberti Wiscardi*. In his *origo*, once again Norman pilgrims play the pivotal role, this time visiting the sanctuary of St Michael on Mount Gargano, where they encountered a Greek by the name of Melus who desired their aid. The Normans, for their part, promised him help when they had returned to their duchy to recruit more men.[3]

While these 'origin' stories are not exactly the same, they contain a number of important and interesting similarities. In the first instance, they talk of these people as 'Normans', and not as 'Franks' or 'Frenchmen', who gave aid to those in need. Although none of these men elected to stay in Italy, all of them talked of sending forces back from Normandy when they had returned home; this response is reflected in the opening pages of Geoffrey Malaterra's *Gesta Rogerii* with reference to the brothers de Hauteville. Finally, in each case the Normans were on pilgrimages, and had encountered these situations of need on these religious journeys: the motif of divine inspiration, while implicit in the writings, is obvious. There are stark similarities here, also, with the early history of the duchy as Dudo of St-Quentin recorded it. The Normans here, as there, were new to this environment and proceeded initially not by conquest but by the provision of aid to their neighbours: Rollo helps the English, and these Normans help the Lombards / Greeks.[4] The motif of the divinely inspired journey is also consistent: Rollo's journey stems from a dream of a 'promised land', these are, as William of Apulia says, from a religious vow (*votum*).[5]

suggests that, having been recognised as count of Apulia by Guaimar of Salerno in 1042, he was acclaimed as duke by the assembled Normans at the end of that year (Norwich, *Normans in Sicily*, 66). Kenneth Wolf has, however, indicated that Guaimar assumed the title of 'duke of Apulia and Calabria' in February 1043 (Wolf, *Making History*, p. 13, n. 56, citing Ernesto Pontieri, *I Normanni nell'Italia meridionale*, 2nd edn (1964), 113 and F. Chalandon, *Histoire de la domination normande en Italie et en Sicile* (1907), I, 105).

[2] Amatus, 22–3.
[3] Apulia, 98–100.
[4] Dudo, 147–8; Dudo (tr.), 30–2.
[5] Apulia, 98.

Unfortunately, however, these tales tell us nothing at all about the identity of the first Normans to arrive in southern Italy. They were written in a different period in the history of the Normans, much later in their development, and serve not to enlighten us but rather to confuse us in any study of the Normans' mercenary identity. The intentions that Amatus reports of these Normans – namely, to fight against the Muslims for religious reasons – probably date more from Amatus' own time than from 1016 and do not, therefore, reflect the realities of the situation: the Normans seemingly intended to fight the Greeks, as William of Apulia tells us, and made war on the Sicilian Muslims only from 1035 onwards.[6] Additionally, the concept of pilgrimage must be treated with care here: undertaking a pilgrimage meant 'suspending one's martial profession, since the pilgrim stopped being a warrior for the duration of his travels', which may help to explain the Norman need to return home and recruit men; the Normans of Amatus' *Historia Normannorum* seem more in keeping with popular ideas of crusaders than with those of pilgrims.[7] In order to truly examine the identity of the early Norman mercenaries, it is necessary to examine the writings of their contemporaries.

We have, unfortunately, no usable Norman sources from the period *c.*1016–1042/3 at all. Back in the duchy, Dudo's work ends a few years too soon; William of Jumièges, writing rather too late anyway, makes no reference to these mercenary Normans in his history. In Italy, the earliest 'Norman' writer, Amatus of Montecassino, did not begin writing until the 1070s, and this is well within the second period. This obviously creates fundamental problems for any study of Norman identity at this time. We cannot say with certainty that *any* of the origin stories, as told by these later writers, resemble the actual events of the Norman arrival; the same is true of any information gleaned from these sources. However, there are still some areas that may (and, indeed, should) be explored, based on what little information we do have.

That these newcomers were using the name 'Norman' to describe themselves seems undeniable. All three of the eleventh-century southern Italian historians adhered to this name, and each gave a version of the etymology from which it derived. Amatus of Montecassino, in his *Historia Normannorum*, tells of '*li Normant*', who came from France but had originally lived on a isle by the name of '*Nora*'; therefore, they were called *Normant*, '*home de Nore*'.[8] William of Apulia derives the name from a similar root, a Germanic version of '*homines boreales*', while Geoffrey Malaterra comments that '*quia ipsi ab aquilone venerant, Normanni dicti*'; such etymologically correct interpretations were also geographically helpful in Italy.[9] The fact was that this name endured, not only to be mentioned by all three historians here but also to be associated, by Alexander of Telese, with those who 'had attacked Apulia'.[10] When one compares this consistency of naming with the almost indifferent attitude the external chroniclers seem to have taken to the 'invaders', it is quite

6   Carl Erdmann, *The Origin of the Idea of Crusade*, tr. Marshall W. Baldwin and Walter Goffart (Princeton, NJ, 1977), 109–10.
7   *Ibid.*, 305.
8   Amatus, 9–10: '. . . *laquel gent premerement habiterent en une ysulle qui se clamoit "Nora"; et pour ce furent clamez "Normant", autresi comme "home de Nore"* '.
9   Apulia, 98; Malaterra, 8.
10 Telese, 58.

evident that this ethnonym was provided by the Normans themselves and not, as in Francia, by external perceptions.[11]

With this in mind, it must be remembered that the name Norman was not a simple identifier of a place of origin, as in such constructs as '*x* of Normandy'. As has already been shown (Chapter 2 above), *Normanitas* was a living concept, which had evolved to a certain point by *c.*1016, the time at which these first inroads into Italy were being made. To call oneself a Norman was to make oneself heir to the culture surrounding the name and, further, to brand oneself as a product of this culture, as one who upheld that *ethnie*'s *mores* and customs. Those early arrivals in Italy brought with them from their homes in the duchy a set of ideas and ideals, a myth / symbol complex encapsulated by the name Norman. Though this ethnonym and its associations may have meant rather less to the people of southern Italy and Sicily than they did to the people of Francia, their meaning to the Normans themselves was consistent, and so this 'cultural baggage' was retained.

Further, as has previously been seen, the ethnonym 'Norman' was not simply an identifier, but also a unifier; it had come to represent (at least for the Normans) a defined *gens*. The history of this early period, however, presents a picture of small Norman mercenary groups operating independently of one another, and often fighting for different people. These small groups, according to tradition, also included a number of malcontents. Amatus tells of a disagreement between one Gisilbert (or Gilbert) Buatere and a certain William, both recorded by him as '*princes*'. The resultant contest of honour left William dead and the then count, Robert (1027–35), tremendously angry: Gisilbert, and his four brothers, 'Raynolfe' (Rainulf), 'Ascligime' / 'Aséligime' (Ascletin), 'Osmude' (Osmund) and 'Lofulde' (?), fled to Italy to escape Robert's ire.[12] In these circumstances, it is difficult to see the 'Norman' banner as a unifier of any sort; however, there is evidence to suggest that it remained, or at least soon became, one. In 1030, the Normans began settling in the area of Aversa, which had been granted to Rainulf, who became count shortly thereafter.[13] Although we have no contemporary Norman sources on which to rely, it would seem that the presence of a titled leader provided the Normans with a renewed sense of unity: Lord Norwich concluded that, under Rainulf, 'in any battle in which the Normans fought on both sides' it became 'the regular practice for those on the winning side to seek clemency for their less fortunate compatriots'.[14] This suggests that these mercenaries, while operating in smaller groups, still considered themselves members of a larger Norman *gens*.

It is, of course, tempting to perceive a complete lack of unity among these Norman groups. Certainly, if this period in the history of the Normans in Italy is compared with the relevant phase in the north, we would be looking for commonality among a number of amorphous viking groups, at least until the alleged land- and title-grant of 911, which resembles the Aversa grant of 1030. Is this such a

---

[11] For external chroniclers, see below, Chapter 6.

[12] Amatus, 25; *L'ystoire*, ed. Champollion-Figeac, 17 (for the alternative name form 'Aséligime'). Amatus, pp. 25–6, n. 1 has more information on the identification of these names; 'Lofulde' is perhaps 'Rodulf' / 'Rudolf'.

[13] Matthew, *Norman Kingdom*, 144; Amatus, 54.

[14] Norwich, *Normans in Sicily*, 34.

far-fetched idea, though? The Vikings had clearly been able to co-operate with one another when the need arose, for invasions such as that performed by the *micel here* in England and elsewhere, and it is evident that the Vikings who settled in Normandy were not from a single area or bloodline. It is reasonable to assume that these Normans would have been united by their profession as mercenaries if nothing else, and their origin in a very specific area of northern France would no doubt promote further unity, as would their language and the external recognition, discussed below, of these men as 'outsiders' to the Italian area. This is not to say that relations among the Normans would have always been harmonious, however – William of Apulia gives an example of troubles within the ranks – but their difference from those around them would have provided a certain sense of unity.[15]

After the grant of 1030, the Normans were beginning to settle in the region, and the unity provided here is doubtless of vital importance. At a stroke, the Normans were provided both with a territorial centre (Aversa) and a figurehead (Count Rainulf); both of these things were central to ideas of Norman unity. The importance of such political elements in ethnic consciousness has already been mentioned, and here we see the territorial constitution of the *gens* on Italian territory, through the process of political leadership.[16] Aversa served as a 'second Rouen', and from here the *gens Normannorum* could expand their operations throughout the peninsula. However, if such unity existed, it appears not to have endured for long: the arrival, in *c.*1038, of the three brothers d'Hauteville, William, Drogo and Humphrey, was seemingly the beginning of its end.[17] In 1042 or 1043, William was given the title 'count of Apulia', under Guaimar of Salerno; one would expect a divide to have been inevitable, as William's power base was not, like Rainulf's, in Aversa, but instead in the more recently captured Melfi.

The Second Phase: Conquest

The period between *c.*1042/3 and the death of Robert Guiscard in 1085 is, for most of its length, no less opaque in the Norman sources than that from *c.*1016. The only internal writer in this period in Italy was Amatus of Montecassino (who only wrote towards its end), and we are thus left, once again, with a largely uncharted period in which the Norman identity was evolving. Following this, we gain our first real insight into the product of this evolution, through Amatus; from that point onwards, we are better served by our sources.

There is little to reveal the development of Norman identity in the period before Amatus wrote. However, the few things of which we can be certain do appear to highlight particular areas within the variety of *Normanitas* alive in Apulia, Calabria and, later, in Sicily. It is overwhelmingly clear that military successes retained their great importance to the Normans, and were both internally and externally defining. The role of victory as an aspect of Norman leadership in northern France has

---

[15] William records an incident where the Normans transferred their loyalties from their twelve chiefs to Adenolf of Benevento (Apulia, 116).

[16] Above, pp. 6–7, and Goetz, et al., *Regna and Gentes*, 623.

[17] Orderic, vol. II, bk III, p. 58, n. 3.

previously been discussed, and the situation in Italy was no different. The effectiveness of the Norman cavalry against the predominant military tactics in use in the area is apparent, and to this was added a discerning tactical element; prior to the defeat of Roger at Messina, the Norman military record had been extremely good. The Normans did not involve themselves in battles which they didn't believe they could win, especially as they had a heavy reliance, at least initially, on immigrants from the duchy for their major strength.[18]

It is at the time of perhaps the greatest military success of the period that Norman unity again comes to light. The Battle of Civitate of 1053 was the most important demonstration of Norman military prowess that had yet occurred in Italy, and a great embarrassment to the reforming pope, Leo IX. Concerned for the well-being of the Church in the face of the Norman threat to Rome, Leo forged an alliance with Constantinople to drive the Normans from Italy, and summoned an army. In the aftermath of the Norman victory, the Greek army withdrew and Leo was humiliated and became a virtual prisoner of the Normans, finally giving up papal recognition of the Norman acquisitions in Italy. For the Normans, also, Civitate marked another milestone, outside the resultant alliance with the papacy, commenced at Melfi in 1059. There is universal agreement in our sources not only that the Normans succeeded in this great undertaking but, more significantly, that they fought together as a single and unified people. This is, perhaps, unsurprising, given that the aims of Leo seem to have focused on the Normans as an ethnic group. Thus, while the Normans of Aversa and Melfi might have been expected to hold separate identities, these regional 'particularisms' were not the only identities among the Normans in southern Italy, merely important ones. The conflict was instigated on an ethnic level; it was as a *gens* that the Normans were threatened, and as a *gens* that they responded. This threat was important enough to necessitate the suspension of differences between the various Norman camps, a change in dominant identity, in order that the *gens* might prosper.[19] The Normans' continued consciousness of their basic unity is here made clear.

The *Historia Normannorum* of Amatus of Montecassino provides an interesting continuation of the idea of Norman unity, though the use of this source to investigate Norman identity causes some difficulties. In the first instance, it is necessary to treat Amatus with a certain amount of caution. The text we have received is an Italianate Old-French translation, dating from the fourteenth century, meaning that we do not have the original Latin that Amatus wrote. This concern is compounded by the consideration that the translation is more of an adaptation than a straight translation, and thus certain sections may represent views that were not those of Amatus. Indeed, evidence suggests that at least one ethnically loaded comment is absent from Leo of Ostia's second redaction of the *Chronicle of Montecassino*, which preserves selections from the original Latin.[20] However, Kenneth Wolf has observed that

---

18 Norwich, *Normans in Sicily*, 137.
19 For changing identity priorities and conflict, see for example Weinreich, 'Operationalisation', 300 & 309; Heather, *Goths*, 6; Amory, *People and Identity*, 13.
20 Albu, *Normans in their Histories*, 109. The missing comment concerns the worthiness of Normans relative to Greeks (Amatus, 67). See below, pp. 93–6, for some comparison of Amatus' *Historia* with the works of Abbot Desiderius and Leo of Ostia.

comparison between the *Chronicle* and the French version of Amatus' history suggests that the French is not hopelessly corrupt.[21] Furthermore, the attitude presented throughout Amatus' history seems reasonably consistent; even it was a later addition, the missing ethnic comment is not out of character with the rest of the history, and thus the text would seem to be admissible as a presentation of eleventh-century attitudes. That said, it is clearly necessary to exercise a certain caution, lest the 'eleventh-century' perceptions gleaned from Amatus prove to be those of a rather different time.

Amatus was, without a doubt, a pro-Norman writer. His discussion of the Normans is filled with positive adjectives: the Normans are *'vaillant'* and *'fortissime'*, their leaders 'adorned with knightly virtues'.[22] However, his classification as an 'internal' writer requires a good deal of justification. Like Dudo of St-Quentin, Amatus was a non-Norman writing a history of the Normans that focused on the major figures in the Norman society of his area – in this instance, Richard of Aversa / Capua and Robert Guiscard. Unlike Dudo, though, Amatus' work was not commissioned by the Normans themselves, and it is therefore more difficult to argue that Amatus was writing what these Normans wanted to read, and that he can thus be considered to be providing information about Norman identity. Amatus wrote at the instigation of Desiderius, the abbot of Montecassino between 1058 and 1086 (when he became Pope Victor III); as a monk of this same monastery, it is likely, though not certain, that Amatus was of local, 'Lombard' extraction. As a consequence, he was a complete outsider to the Normans and, seemingly, not writing specifically to please them. Yet his work is, as has been noted, very much pro-Norman and positive about them and their deeds. Given in particular our concerns about the lateness of the translation at our command, we must question Amatus' motivation here.

The explanation for the nature of Amatus' work seems most likely to reside in Montecassino's good relations with the Normans (both of Aversa / Capua and Melfi) under Richard of Aversa and Robert Guiscard. Wolf has noted that, for Amatus, both Richard and Robert played important roles in the religious structure of southern Italy, and Amatus perceived Richard as the protector of Montecassino, and Robert as a protector of the Church as a whole.[23] Although the early Norman castellans of the citadel at Montecassino had been depicted by the same Abbot Desiderius as aggressors in his *Dialogues*, their support of Montecassino had, it appears, been largely steadfast during the countships / dukedoms of Richard and Robert, and Amatus' work serves to an extent to commemorate this relationship of trust; as he himself observes, *'pour perpetuel memoire'*.[24] The work highlights these two leaders specifically, ending very shortly after a record of the death of Richard on 5 April 1078, and recounts their deeds in support of the monastery; and yet, there is clearly something more here. Amatus' depiction of events unrelated to the monastery, those conquests and battles for which both Robert and Richard were so famous, are vivid and positive.

---

[21] Wolf, *Making History*, 89.

[22] Amatus, 22 & 90, 130, 53: *'aorné de toutes vertus qui covenant à chevalier'*.

[23] Wolf, *Making History*, 90. Amatus was, of course, writing after the Battle of Civitate and the reform papacy's acceptance and investment of the Normans leaders as the defenders of the reformers against German and Tusculan pressures.

[24] *Ibid.*, 73; Amatus, 4.

Equally, controversial events are glossed over, as is the case with Robert's excommunication of 3 March 1078, concerning which Amatus simply observes, without comment, that '*lo Pape, pour ceste chose* [besieging Benevento] *et pour autre, assembla lo consistoire, et excommunica lo Duc et tout ceuz qui lo sequtoient*'.[25]

From the nature of his coverage, then, it would be reasonable to suggest that Amatus did have a real and positive interest in the deeds of the Normans, which was not simply limited to their operations that immediately concerned the monastery at which he was based. His work *is* a *Historia Normannorum*, and written in a format that Normans could appreciate; it is compelling evidence of the enduring interest it created that our manuscript is in Old French (rather than the original Latin). Of course, one might be cynical enough to suggest that, as Guiscard was probably still alive when Amatus completed his work, Amatus wrote in fear of retribution, but this is a doubtful, if amusing, consideration. While Amatus wrote outside the environment of the 'Norman camp', he appears to have produced a history that was acceptable within it. Although the veracity of such a piece may be held firmly in doubt, the fact that the history seems to have been accepted suggests strongly that it was valued by the Normans; if not the actual truth, then it was a fiction about themselves that the Normans were happy to believe, and therefore identify with. It was, in essence, a presentation of the historical myth of the southern Italian Normans that fitted with their internal perceptions. It is, therefore, possible to accept Amatus' work as providing a helpful insight into southern Italian Norman identity.

The perceptions provided by Amatus of Norman ideas of unity are once again of paramount importance, not only because they impact on our considerations of *Normanitas* in this area, but also because they seem to refute certain historical assumptions made about the southern Italian Normans. In the first instance, the *Historia Normannorum* provides yet more evidence that there was no fundamental divide between the Normans of Aversa / Capua and Melfi. Lord Norwich may have been correct in thinking that the two areas retained separate identities under Richard and Robert Guiscard, but Amatus' work reminds us that the sense of Norman ethnic unity, if not the dominant identity, was still present.[26] Amatus grants equal compliments to both Richard of Aversa, later prince of Capua, and to Robert Guiscard. Richard is, for example, recorded as having been 'loved and honoured by everyone', 'most valiant and skilful'; Robert was 'the noble and powerful duke', 'glorious in all his acts'.[27] Both are heroes, who are filled with the values of *Normanitas*, and as such they are members of a *gens* distinguishable from the others around it by the qualities which these men exemplify. They function not only as focal points for the identity of the Norman *gens*, therefore, but as a physical display of the extensive cultural symbolism manifested by Norman ethnicity; they represent the pinnacle of *Normanitas*. These qualities thus unify not just these two men, but the people under them, through the Norman name and ethnic construct.

Of equal importance is the sense of a wider unity, with Normans elsewhere. R.H.C. Davis suggested, in 1976, that any perception of a wider Norman identity

---

[25] Amatus, 372.
[26] Norwich, *Normans in Sicily*, 108.
[27] Amatus, 110: '*de tout lo monde estoit amé et honoré*'; 201: '*molt vaillant et esprouvé*'; 249: '*le noble et puissant duc*'; 284: '*glorioz en touz ses faiz*'.

was the 'idiosyncratic view' of 'one eloquent historian' (Orderic Vitalis). Amatus'
work, and indeed that of the historians who followed him, refutes this.[28] In the third
chapter of his first book, Amatus gives an epic account of the Norman conquest of
England, in which Duke William crossed the channel with 100,000 knights, 10,000
crossbowmen and more besides, to fight that '*maledit home*' Harold; two years later,
Amatus reports, William also vanquished the King of the Danes, who came with 'a
great and innumerable multitude of people'.[29] Indeed, it was not only the conquest
of England that was held up as an example of the exploits of '*ceste fortissime gent*', but
also the deeds of Robert Crispin in Spain.[30] All these occurrences were part of the
expansion of the *gens Normannorum*, and therefore the origins of the people about
whom he now wrote his history. While Normandy was a land 'full of trees and
various fruits', there was simply not enough to support all the Norman people;
consequently, they burst forth and 'scattered themselves here and there, into various
groups and countries'.[31] And all these groups, in their various countries, were united
in purpose as well as in origin: 'they wanted to have all *gentes* under their subjection
and lordship'.[32]

It is therefore clear that the Normans retained an awareness not only of the deeds
of their countrymen elsewhere, but also of their kinship of purpose and origins with
these countrymen. Certainly, by the 1070s and 1080s, when Amatus was writing,
the Normans had remained true to these dictates, and had brought vast areas of new
land under Norman control. This in itself is evidence of the continuation of those
concepts of *Normanitas* imported from Normandy in the early eleventh century. The
importance of military success and prowess had been retained within *Normanitas*; it
would, in fact, be surprising if a *gens* that saw itself destined to conquer did not value
such things highly. As an aspect of Norman identity, the Normans' military glory
shines from the pages of Amatus' *Historia*, but this is not the only aspect of Norman
identity present, though it appears to have been a centrepiece from which many
concepts stemmed. It seems very much the case, in fact, that it is through the
language of conquest that Amatus makes us aware of those things that were important to the Normans' ideas of themselves, their own internal perceptions, and thus
held a fitting place in this 'History of the Normans'.

From this perspective, those things that characterised the body of the Norman
people were all military in nature. They were 'the valiant Normans, strong, and bold
as lions', and their *Historia* is filled with tales of their victories against all others.[33]
Even in times of great adversity, when vastly outnumbered, they fought bravely and
well: 'For every Norman [casualty], more enemies were dead'; the Normans 'always
stood firm'.[34] It is perhaps for this reason that the disregard of other *gentes* is also so
clear in Amatus, no doubt reflecting Norman arrogance against those whom they
seemed to best so easily. Under Melus, they fought against the Greeks, 'and saw that
they were as women', and there is a definite dismissiveness to Amatus' statement

28 Davis, *Normans and their Myth*, 15.
29 Amatus, 11–12: '*grant multitude de gent sans nombre*'.
30 *Ibid.*, 13–16; quote p. 11.
31 *Ibid.*, 9–10: '*s'espartirent sà et là, c'est en diversez parties et contrées*'.
32 *Ibid.*, 11: '*voilloient avoir toute gent en lor subjettion et en lor seignorie*'.
33 *Ibid.*, 90: '*li vaillant Normant, fort, hardi come lyon*'.
34 *Ibid.*, 28–30: '*pour un de li Normant furent mort molt de anemis*'; '*estoient touzjours ferme*'.

that, when the Greeks set the 'strongest men that they could find' against the Normans, still 'the Greeks lost'; in fact, the Greeks only ever defeat the Normans with the advantage of one hundred times as many men.[35] Amatus' belief in this is evident and he observes that, when William de Hauteville arrives from Normandy with Drogo, Humphrey and a mere 300 men, 'to tell the truth, the hardiness and prowess of these few Normans was more valued than the Greek multitude'.[36] Of course, the Normans' other enemies were little better – the Lombard inhabitants of 'Ascle' were '*homes plus febles*', and even the emperor had great respect for 'the boldness and strength of this *gens* from Normandy'.[37]

Of course, these warriors had leaders, and as the men who served them were instilled with valour and strength second to none, so these leaders were the very personification of such qualities, the physical manifestations of the ideas of *Normanitas*. Rainulf of Aversa was 'a man adorned with all the virtues which are agreeable to a knight', William de Hauteville 'a man most valiant in arms, adorned with all the good customs, and handsome, and kind, and young', of 'noble lineage'; likewise, 'Asclitine' was 'worthy for his prowess and beauty' and Drogo was a 'wise and remarkable knight'.[38] We have already seen similar examples concerning Richard of Aversa / Capua and Robert Guiscard.

It is clear from these brief descriptions that the Normans expected a great deal from their leaders. As in the early period in the duchy, they were expected to be great warriors, unparalleled in military prowess, but here in Italy we can also see new facets emerging in the Norman concept of leadership. Firstly, the Norman perception seems to have begun to be infiltrated by the burgeoning ideas of chivalry that were to become so prevalent in the culture of the twelfth century, and it is no doubt the influence of such ideals that sets Norman heroes in this mould.[39] For how better to glorify an individual above others than to believe that person only comparable with figures from epic tales? This combines with the second issue, that of youth and beauty – an old soldier may have been skilled but he often lacked the fire and drive that was the mark of youth, and the sheer physical power that is here recognised as 'beauty'. And for those who were not so young, they then had virtue and wisdom to replace this fire.

All this conspired to elevate these men to legendary status. The role of leadership was, once again, proving to be an enduring aspect of Norman ethnicity. In fact, the more military atmosphere of the southern Italian arena made the prowess of a leader all the more important, and the exaltation of youth and strength no doubt relates in some way to this increased level of danger: the small numbers of Normans in the area, even with continued immigration, suggests little time for the older members of their

---

[35] *Ibid.*, 27: '*et virent qu'il estoient comme fames*'; 28: 'li plus fort home qu'il put trover', 'Mès li Grez perdirent'; 81.

[36] *Ibid.*, 67: '*à dire la verité, plus valut la hardiece et la prouesce de ces petit de Normans que la moltitude de li Grex*'. See above (p. 65) for the absence of this phrase from Leo of Ostia's *Chronicle*.

[37] *Ibid.*, 79 & 83: '*la hardiesce et force de ceste gent de Normendie*'.

[38] *Ibid.*, 54: '*home aorné de toutes vertus qui covenent à chevalier*'; 93: '*home vaillantissime en armes et aorné de toutes bones costumes, et beauz, et gentil, et jovene*'; 94: '*noble parentece*'; 98: '*dignes pour sa proësce et pour sa biauté*'; 101: '*sage chevalier, singuler*'.

[39] Though see Maurice Keen, *Chivalry* (London, 1984), 1ff. for the problems of defining the temporal bounds of an 'age of chivalry'.

society, or the militarily useless. Equally, they were uninterested in leaders from other groupings or families: Amatus records that the people of Aversa, having endured the rule of 'one who called himself Raoul', 'did not want another count of another *gens* or lineage'.[40]

Interestingly, and as will be evidenced later, the legendary trappings of these heroes continued to grow in subsequent histories. One piece of supporting evidence for this is the epithet 'Iron-Arm', which has come down to us concerning William de Hauteville. At no point does Amatus show any knowledge of, or make any reference to, this cognomen, or its supposed origin in William's slaying of the Emir of Syracuse. Equally, by the time that Amatus was writing, the Hauteville family, while powerful, did not have total control of the peninsula, and Richard of Capua (Aversa) had remained strong until his death. In every generation, therefore, the Normans required two heroes, one for each of the two groupings, in order to give all their victories equal validity under *Normanitas*.

There is also in Amatus an element that perhaps goes some way towards explaining many of the changes within Norman identity, both in terms of this new concept of 'wider unity', and also the seemingly increased importance of military skills and prowess to the virtual exclusion of all else. This explanation rests once again in the military sphere, in the clear Norman awareness that there really were not very many of them. It must remembered that, while the number of Norman immigrants into England was small by comparison to the existing population, in Italy it was smaller still.[41] Those early battles depleted the Norman forces to a mere 500 men, and though reinforcements soon arrived from the duchy, the Normans kept fighting and men kept dying.[42] It is therefore no surprise that the dowry of 'Adverarde' (the young aunt of Gerard, the Norman lord of Buonalbergo), of some 200 knights, is seen as worthy of note.[43]

There is, in fact, no sense in Italy, as there was in France, that the inhabitants of the areas under Norman control became Norman by default. As one might perhaps expect, the ongoing conflict and military pressure on the Normans as an ethnic group gave ever more definition to their identity boundaries. In addition, the Norman *gens* in Italy was ever a small one, enough to be remarked upon by the Greeks, who 'despised the Normans, because they were few in number'. Consequently, the Normans were extremely demanding about the prowess of these few, and the escalating need for skilled warriors added yet more strength to the ethnic boundaries, precluding the entrance into the *gens* of any members of the 'other', for whom Norman disrespect grew.[44]

However, even though the Normans nurtured their vitally important military skills, as an integral part of their ethnic expression, they continued to win victories, which was clear evidence that God was on their side. Both in the eyes of the people, whom He supported through their constant wars against enemies of His Church, and their leaders, God was essential to their success. Amatus' emphasis of this aspect

40 Amatus, 98–9: '*qui se clamoit Raül*'; 103: '*non voloient autre conte de autre gent ou lignage*'.
41 See Matthew, *Norman Sicily*, 144.
42 Amatus, 31.
43 *Ibid.*, 126.
44 *Ibid.*, 81: '*desprizerent li Normant, por ce qu'il estoient petit de gent*'.

leads Wolf to suggest that he placed the Norman involvement in Italy within the framework of an extended campaign against the Saracens, but there was obviously much more to this aspect of Norman identity.[45] Even in the same breath as he recounts the rather dubious repudiation of Alverada by Robert Guiscard, Amatus observes that 'the hand of God helped him in all things'.[46] In a speech attributed to Guiscard, concerning Sicily, he expresses his wish 'to deliver the Christians and the Catholics, who are constrained to the servitude of the Saracens', and this was supported by God, who allowed Guiscard to vanquish Palermo in just five months.[47]

Over and above all this religious support of the Norman *gens*, though, is a concept that exists throughout Norman identity, both back in the duchy and in Italy, and is here evidenced in Amatus – the idea that the Normans are a 'chosen' people, and that the lands they conquered were divinely ordained as theirs. As Rollo experienced a vision of the bounties of Normandy, so (according to Amatus) John, bishop of Salerno has a similar experience here, when St Matthew the Apostle appears before him with these words: '*Ceste terre de Dieu est donnée à li Normant*'.[48] Thus it can be seen that the Normans perceived themselves not only as a *gens* purposed to conquer, but one with divine support in so doing.

The Third Phase: Consolidation

From 1085 onwards, however, it is difficult to see how such an identity could remain viable, given that the Normans of southern Italy were conquering little of anything between this date and the coronation of Count Roger II as King Roger of Sicily in 1130. With even the conquest of Sicily completed in 1091, and the (unfortunate) failure of Guiscard's plans for the Byzantine empire, it must have seemed as if the work of conquest had been completed in the southern Italian (and Sicilian) area. This appears to have resulted in two things. Firstly, when the call to crusade came in 1096, it was readily acknowledged by many of the younger Normans inhabiting Apulia, Calabria and Sicily, perhaps motivated by a continued perception of themselves as members of a conquering *gens* and by the previous conquests of Muslims in Sicily. Secondly, the Norman histories of this period in the Italian area are notably lacking, and the focus is very much on the years before Guiscard died. The two historians writing in the area, William of Apulia and Geoffrey Malaterra, both wrote in the 1090s, and we are left, unfortunately, without an internal source for the early part of the twelfth century.

The two main histories we have are of the traditional Norman *gesta*-type: each focuses on the Hauteville dynasty and, more particularly, on one of the two great members: Robert Guiscard and his brother Roger. William of Apulia produced a great epic poem exalting Guiscard and his family, and Guiscard's life, from his arrival in Italy to his death in 1085, is his primary area of interest. Geoffrey, too, attempted a

---

[45] Wolf, *Making History*, 93.
[46] Amatus, 194: '*la main de Dieu en toutes chozes estoit en son aide*'.
[47] *Ibid.*, 234: '*Je voudroie delivrer li Christien et li Chatolici, liquel sont constreint à la servitude de li Sarrazin*'; 284.
[48] *Ibid.*, 151.

poem, but reverted to prose after only a few lines; he also has a marked interest in the Hauteville dynasty, but the hero of his piece is Roger, count of Sicily.

This provides what would ordinarily be an ideal basis for the study of the changes in an identity. Not only were both these histories written only a few short years after Amatus' *Historia Normannorum*, but both were written within a few years of one another. Furthermore, while Amatus, though pro-Norman, was definitely an outsider to the Norman *gens*, it is entirely possible that both William and Geoffrey may have been Norman (although it is really impossible to tell; we can accurately identify neither man). With these things in mind, the similarities and differences between these two sources, and between them and Amatus, communicate a great deal about the state of Norman identity in southern Italy and Sicily at the end of the eleventh century.

It is ultimately revealing, then, that the works of Geoffrey and William are very different in their basic nature. While both are telling similar stories, writing as they are of many of the same events, from the commencement of both works there is a sense of a divergence between them. The possible explanations for this are numerous; one that can immediately be arrived at is that the two were writing in somewhat different environments. As his name suggests, it is likely that William was writing in Apulia (although the epithet may simply derive from the subject of his work or his origin); Geoffrey, Wolf suggests, was writing from the vantage point of Sicily and, were this the case, it would help to account for differences of perception.[49] Equally, differences in the styles of language used, and in descriptive terminology, could perhaps be accounted for by William's epic style as compared with Geoffrey's more mundane prose.

Yet neither of these explanations seems sufficient. There seem, in fact, to be two possible solutions of primary importance, either or both of which are reasonable conclusions from the evidence cited below. The first of these concerns William's origins, and the suggestion that he may not be Norman at all, and is not therefore giving an internal view of Norman identity. The second, and rather more compelling of the two, is the consideration, raised above, that the identity structures described by Amatus were, even this soon afterwards, losing their validity.

This difference is immediately evident in the approaches taken to ideas of Norman unity, not just in the Italian area, but in the wider sense. As we have seen, both Geoffrey and William provide an etymology for the ethnonym 'Norman', and both derive this from the fact that they came from the north. Yet to this William adds a qualification, commenting that 'man is for them what for us is called *homo*'.[50] To Wolf, this is a simple linguistic comment that separates 'Norman' from the Latin language, yet the very structure of the sentence suggests that William is not a member of the people to whom he is referring, precisely *because* he makes this linguistic distinction – there is thus the possibility that William was an Italian, or perhaps a French speaker who was not acquainted with the Germanic languages.[51]

These differences extend further into both works. Throughout his *Gesta Rogerii*, Geoffrey diligently refers to the Normans as *Normanni*, the common Latinate form.

49 Wolf, *Making History*, 143.
50 Apulia, 98: '*man est apud hos, homo quod perhibetur apud nos*'.
51 Wolf, *Making History*, p. 126, n. 35.

William, however, diverges from this. Perhaps owing to his 'epic style', he uses the term '*Galli*' to describe the Normans; less easily explainable is his use of '*Franci*'.[52] In the previous chapters, we have seen that the Normans in Normandy spent some 150 years forcing (and, indeed, being forced into) a distinction between *Normanni* and *Franci*, yet here William uses the terms interchangeably. But was this a deliberate statement, or did it reflect something else?

Initially, it is difficult to say. William is, of course, not the only writer in this period to use *Franci* as a descriptive term that included Normans. Among the historians of the First Crusade, who wrote in the early twelfth century, the use of the term *Franci* to describe the whole Christian army was fairly commonplace. *Franci* has this sense in the histories of writers such as Fulcher of Chartres and Raymond of Aguilers, and it was clearly not a difficulty for them to accept these men as being Normans as well as Franks – Fulcher, for example, refers to Bohemond as 'an Apulian, of Norman race'.[53] It is revealing that this is true of the anonymous author of the *Gesta Francorum*, who appears to have been a vassal of Bohemond's, probably from Apulia.[54] This author shows his acceptance of this terminology when he has Karbuqa (commander of the Persian army) ask whether Bohemond and Tancred are 'the gods of the Franks'.[55]

This use of the ethnonym *Franci* suggests that a further aspect of Norman identity was being revealed, one that could be recognised both by Normans and non-Normans alike. Indeed, this use of *Franci* as an umbrella term for the crusaders did not just make Normans Franks, it made Franks of all the others too, be they Provençals, Gascons, Flemings or whoever. The role of *Franci* here was evidently a unifying term that was apparently not being employed as an *ethnic* term, but was being used in a way that distinguished the crusaders from those they encountered on crusade. The term might refer, therefore, either to the origin of the crusaders in France, or to the common language they spoke. Given the difficulty of perceiving Bohemond's Apulian forces as 'from France', it might reasonably be supposed that this was a linguistic classification.[56]

Yet the use of *Franci* by William of Apulia seems to express more than a consciousness that Normans spoke French; it appears to be just one element of a rejection of certain Norman 'traditions'. A further example is his apparent disregard for the traditions of unity with the Norman homeland. Geoffrey Malaterra, in his first two chapters, describes the origins of Normandy, mentioning that it had not always been so called until '*Rodlo, dux fortissimus*' was given the land by the king of

[52] Apulia, 100 & 118 for examples.

[53] *The Chronicle of Fulcher of Chartres*, tr. Martha E. McGinty, in Edward Peters (ed.), *The First Crusade*, 2nd edn (Philadelphia, 1998), 57. For examples of a general use of the ethnonym 'Franks', see 48, 64, 75, 77, 79, 87, and Raymond d'Aguilers, *Historia Francorum qui ceperunt Iherusalem*, in Peters, *First Crusade*, 183. *The Chronicle* was completed around 1127–8 (Peters, *First Crusade*, 47), the *Historia Francorum* some time before 1105 (*ibid.*, 156).

[54] *The Deeds of the Franks and the other Pilgrims to Jerusalem*, ed. & tr. Rosalind Hill (Oxford, 1962), xi. For examples of the general use of Franks, see 16, 17, 21, 22, 24, 33, 34 and, of course, the title of the work. The *Deeds of the Franks (Gesta Francorum)* was completed no later than 1101 (*Deeds of the Franks*, ix).

[55] *Ibid.*, 55. Notably, the author of the *Gesta Francorum* refers to Robert Curthose as 'Robert the Norman' (*Deeds of the Franks, passim* and Albu, *Normans in their Histories*, 153–4).

[56] The use of *Franci* as a linguistic classification in England is discussed below (pp. 131–3).

the Franks.[57] Such an awareness of the origins of the Norman *gens* is fairly typical in Norman history – Amatus puts forward something to this effect, also – but William, unusually, omits such a story, contenting himself instead with odd references to an undefined '*patria*'.[58] It is evident that William has far less interest than Geoffrey in continuing the tradition of wider unity that appears in the pages of Amatus; as Geoffrey strengthens it, so William fails to acknowledge its existence. Yet, on a more local level, William happily acknowledges the unity of the Normans within Italy, and does this to a far greater extent than Geoffrey. Reading the *Gesta Rogerii*, one might be forgiven for thinking that nothing of moment had been achieved by the Normans in Italy prior to the arrival (*c.*1038) of William de Hauteville and his brothers, who had left for Apulia when they realised that there was not enough of a patrimony to support all of the sons of Tancred.[59] William of Apulia, on the other hand, tells of how the earliest Norman settlers in the area elected a chief, named Rannulf (Rainulf), 'whose commands it was impossible to oppose', and worked together to set up a settlement site 'without the help of any of the area's inhabitants'.[60] Again later, William records that the Normans 'all united and chose twelve nobles as *duces*'.[61]

So, where does this leave us? It is already quite clear that the identities being portrayed by Geoffrey and William, while focused on the same core events, are different. At first glance, it is tempting to assume that Geoffrey is the more likely of the two to be 'correct', as his work most closely resembles the tradition of which it is a part. However, even he is diverging from the concepts of unity that appear to be so important in Amatus: Geoffrey has little interest, it seems, in driving home the idea of unity between Normans locally, though he does not, it is true, undermine this idea, either. For William, it would now be unreasonable to attribute the divergences to an 'epic tradition' of some sort; while his usage of names shows a classical bent, the lack of acknowledgement of the pre-Italian Norman past is rather against the purpose of the epic. While it might be proposed that everyone in the area knew of the Normans' background, one would still expect to see some mention of the environment in which the hero of the piece grew up. This leads us, then, towards the conclusion that William was perhaps not a Norman, and therefore may have omitted the background of Normandy because he was ignorant of it, possibly because he was more distant from his sources than Geoffrey or Amatus.

This consideration is, however, equally difficult to uphold. William's *Gesta Roberti* was, like Amatus' *Historia*, considered acceptable by the Normans – our two surviving medieval manuscripts exist in Normandy, not Italy – and must therefore contain a presentation of their past and *gens* that the Normans were willing to believe. Additionally, both William and Geoffrey continue the theme of distaste for the non-Normans in the area of southern Italy. Geoffrey describes the Lombards as 'a

---

57 Malaterra, 7–8.
58 Apulia, 100 for example: '*Illi donandum patriae munimine gentis . . .*'.
59 Malaterra, 9.
60 Apulia, 106: '*Cuius mandatis fas contradicere non sit*'; '*quem nullo dante iuvamen / Cultorum patriae*'. Mathieu observes, in p. 107, n. 2, that it is possible to read '*patriae*' with an initial capital, which would then refer to the region around the lake of Patria. It is, of course, equally possible to interpret *patriae* as referring to the Normans, giving a translation 'of any of the inhabitants of their homeland'. This would of course add to the sense of dislocation from Normandy.
61 *Ibid.*, 110: '*Omnes conveniunt, et bis sex nobiliores . . . / Elegere duces*'.

very spiteful *gens*, the Greeks as 'a most treacherous sort'; for William, the Greeks were, once again, as women, and the Lombards provide an appearance of total incompetence throughout his work, mostly in military matters – they are afraid of the womanly Greeks, and are ignorant concerning proper orders of battle.[62] By comparison, the Normans are 'a most astute *gens*', 'distinguished by the ferocity of their cavalry', and 'all trembled before them'.[63] As with Amatus, it is quite clear that the Normans still thought far more highly of themselves than they did of other *gentes*, and that this was to a large extent referenced to their perceptions of their own great military capacity. William of Apulia's work entirely supports this, with rather more subtlety than Geoffrey Malaterra, and both works are clearly in agreement over the continued importance to the Normans of their military prowess.

This correspondence of Geoffrey and William can also be seen in their depictions of Norman leadership. It is readily apparent that the Normans still considered their heroes to be of vital importance as a manifestation of all those concepts they held dear. In some cases, the tales told by William and Geoffrey are perhaps more heroic than those of previous historians, and certainly more so than those of Amatus. William de Hauteville, for example, becomes 'their best hope, experienced in arms', 'energetic in battle', whose 'famous name terrified the Greeks'.[64] In both histories, he now has the epithet 'Iron-Arm' appended to his name, because of his prodigious strength and bravery; this, as has been noted, is not present in Amatus.[65] An increase in 'respect' in fact applies to other members of the Hauteville dynasty: Drogo was 'lauded by everyone'; Humphrey was 'a most prudent man', and 'all Apulia wept and mourned the death of a father' when he died.[66]

As the real heroes of both pieces, though, the greatest praise is reserved for Robert and Roger. Robert was an 'astute and brave duke', 'a man of great wisdom, genius, largesse and bravery'; Roger was 'younger than him, but no less valiant', a 'most handsome youth, tall, graceful of form, very eloquent in speech, discerning, prudent in the ordering of his affairs, in all things jovial and affable, with great strength and ferocious in battle'.[67] As for Robert's epithet, 'Guiscard', according to Amatus this was first given to him by Gerard of Buonalbergo; William first mentions it before his account of the Battle of Civitate, where he observes that 'he was nick-named Guiscard, because Cicero was not so cunning, nor Ulysses so crafty'; finally, Geoffrey claims that he had been called that from birth.[68]

[62] Malaterra, 10: '*Longobardum vero gens invidissima*'; 40: '*semper genus perfidissimum*'; Apulia, 110, 224 & 142.

[63] Malaterra, 8: '*Gens astutissima*'; 18: '*omnes ante eum tremebant*'; Apulia, 98: '*Gens Normannorum feritate insignis equestri*'.

[64] Malaterra, 11: '*in armis strenuus*'; Apulia, 126: '*horum / Maxima spes, aderat Guillermus ad arma paratus*'; '*Terrebat Danaos Guilermi nobile nomen*'.

[65] Apulia, 126: '*Is quia fortis erat, est ferrea dictus habere / Brachia, nam validas vires animumque gerebat*'. Geoffrey simply says '*Willelmus, Tancredi filius, qui Ferrea-brachia nuncupabantur*' (Malaterra, 11).

[66] Malaterra, 14: '*per cuncta laudabilis*'; '*virum prudentissimum*'; Apulia, 152: '*Lacrimans Apulia tota / Flet patris interitum*'.

[67] Apulia, 202: '*dux astutus et audax*'; 174: '*Erat hoc aetate Rogerus / Non virtute minor*'; Malaterra, 9: '*vir magni consilii, ingenii, largitatis et audaciae*'; 18–19: '*Erat enim juvenis pulcherrimus, procerae staturae, eleganti corpore, lingua facundissimus, consilio callidus, in ordinatione agendarum rerum providus, omnibus jocundus et affabilis, viribus fortis, militia ferox.*'

[68] Amatus, 125: '*cestui Gyrart lo clama premierement "Viscart"*'; Apulia, 138: '*Cognomen Guiscard erat, quia calliditatis / Non Cicero tantae fuit aut versutus Ulixes*'; Malaterra, 9: '*dictus a nativitate Guiscardus*'.

However, it is obvious from the above that, with the exception of William 'Iron-Arm', none of these men are being presented as entirely military heroes. All are given claims to skills such as wisdom, prudence and the like that do not fit in with the old Norman image of a leader being effective simply by dint of a strong right arm and victory in battle. Apparently, by the end of the eleventh century, the cultural symbols of the *gens Normannorum* were changing, perhaps in light of the fact that war was no longer their primary occupation. As leaders played such a prominent role in the conception of *Normanitas*, exemplifying the expressed cultural symbols of the *gens Normannorum*, it is in the descriptions of leaders that changes in the Norman myth / symbol complex are most readily discerned. Therefore, such a change of attitude towards leadership can be expected to reflect a similar change in the basic premises of the Normans' identity. This should not be taken to mean that these people were no longer Normans, of course, as these cultural symbols were the product, not the cause, of identity.[69]

Another cultural change is evident in both the works of William and Geoffrey, in the area of fortune. Both seem to attach a large amount of importance to the luck of the Norman leaders, Geoffrey perhaps more so than William. Geoffrey has Guiscard observe, when first coming to Scribla that 'if fortune is prosperous, we shall prevail easily'; elsewhere, he refers to the fickle nature of fortune, and its capacity for deception.[70] William expresses similar ideas, noting that 'the chariot of fortune had turned and begun to elevate the sons of Tancred'.[71] These ideas of fortune do not, as one might expect, replace the support of the divine in Norman actions, they instead merely add to it. To Geoffrey, the Normans were an instrument of God, akin to plague and famine – these were three explosions of danger that hardly anyone was able to survive intact.[72] Even in William's *Gesta Rogerii*, we see the Normans doing God's work: before Palermo, Guiscard exhorts his men with the words 'this town is hostile to God!'.[73] Yet the sense of divine inspiration of the actions of the Normans is decidedly less here than in Geoffrey.

Thus, the works of Geoffrey and William do correspond in a sizeable number of areas, and provide us with an interesting insight into Norman identity at the end of the eleventh century. Yet we are still left with a distinct problem, in that their works are significantly different in certain areas, and while suspicion may fall upon William as a potential non-Norman, owing to his seeming lack of concern with the ethnonym of the *gens* about which he is writing, this is by no means a certain explanation. His lack of knowledge of the earlier deeds of the Normans suggests that he was not

[69] Barth noted that the history of an ethnic group is distinct from the history of a culture, and that ethnic groups have continued organisational existences despite cultural modifications (Barth, *Ethnic Groups*, 38).

[70] Malaterra, 17: '*fortuna prosperante, facile prevalebimus*'; 61: '*Sicque rotabilis fortuna, homines primo prosperis successibus alludendo, illectos spe priorum eventuum deceptos risit*'.

[71] Apulia, 134: '*Curru fortuna rotato / Tancredi natos sublimes reddere coepit*'.

[72] Malaterra, 21: '*Nam una ex parte gladius a Normannis, vix alicui parcens, desaeviebat; ex alia vero fames, viribus exhaustis, perlanguida aestuabat; tertia vero pugna mortalitatis, horribiliter defluens, vix aliquem intactum permittens evadere . . .*'. Wolf's suggestion (*Making History*, 163) that Geoffrey is here critical, and blaming the Normans for causing disruption, seems entirely out of keeping with the character of the rest of Geoffrey's history. It is far more believable that Geoffrey was excusing the Normans' behaviour by means of divine influence.

[73] Apulia, 178: '*Urbs inimica Deo.*'

French; his comments on the Lombards suggest that he was not Lombard Italian. His use of language might therefore represent his perceived membership of a group of Latinate intellectuals or churchmen, the 'us' in his comment on the Norman ethnonym. He clearly did not feel himself to be a part of the *gens Normannorum*, but then neither did Dudo of St-Quentin; little else can be concluded regarding his origins.

A more viable solution to this problem, however, appears to lie within one paragraph of William's *Gesta Roberti*, in which he states that the Normans 'instructed all those whom they saw come [to them] in their customs and language, in order to create a single *gens*'.[74] We have already seen, though, that the Normans perceived themselves to be members of a unified *gens* in a larger sense, even despite occasional regional differences in Italy, so this is clearly a statement of something new, unparalleled in the works of either Amatus or Geoffrey. In fact, the only similar idea can be found in Dudo of St-Quentin, when discussing the initial settlement of Normandy; it is the perception of an assimilation of one group of people into another, somewhat at odds with Amatus' considerations of the small size of the Norman '*gent*'. When these discrepancies are considered together, a explanation can be seen for William's apparent divergences from the preceding identity structures, and Geoffrey's far more rigid adherence.

It would seem that the second of those 'compelling solutions', that the Norman identity had to some extent lost validity, is supported by the attitudes of these late eleventh-century writers. The consideration that they were writing in different parts of the Norman holdings in the area also helps to explain their approaches to *Normanitas*. For Geoffrey, while conquest has (at least temporarily ended), the *gens Normannorum* is in constant struggle to retain its identity in the polyethnic Sicilian environment. Davis noted that, while the Sicilians were initially divided into three groupings, the *Grifones* (Arabs and perhaps some Greeks), the *Longobardi* (Lombards, Latin-speaking natives) and *ultramontei / transalpini* (recent arrivals from northern Europe, of whom Geoffrey was a member), this distinction collapsed over time into one between those born and bred in the kingdom, and those from outside. It is this very collapse that Geoffrey is fighting in his work, reminding the Normans of their valiant ancestry, their heroic past, and their divine support in battle. He is writing about an identity that is fighting for survival. Not so for William, who writes for an audience very much more secure in who they are, to the extent that he has latitude to experiment with the concepts of *Normanitas*. In the more settled climate of southern Italy, where rebellions were far more frequent than conquests, the Normans required a newer identity that focused less upon the fact that Italy was conquered territory and more that it was the 'new' Norman homeland. Many advocates of the older ideas had gone east, in search of those glorious conquests for God in the Holy Land; those who had stayed were the instigators of change.

Further contributions to this situation stem from the fact that Geoffrey was writing for a member of the 'old school' of *Normanitas*, for Roger, born and raised as a Norman knight in Normandy. Thus, Geoffrey writes with a substantial degree of conservatism, from the perspective of an identity that is under threat and vulnerable.

---

[74] *Ibid.*, 108: '*Moribus et lingua, quoscumque venire videbant, / Informant propria, gens efficatur ut una.*'

The identity in question is challenged by the changing circumstances evident in Sicily, but Geoffrey's work implies a lack of flexibility and an unwillingness to change, making the threat more potent.[75] William, on the other hand, wrote for Roger Borsa, for a new generation of rulers, who had not been raised in a purely Norman, military fashion, but rather in this newer environment. Many of this generation had never seen Normandy, never gloried in those trees and fruits whose virtues Geoffrey extols; rather, although there was a perceived debt to that Norman past, it was becoming as much of a constraint as the Viking past had been to William of Jumièges.

Clearly, this new generation were willing to accept the changes that circumstances in Italy brought, and respond in a flexible and open manner; the consequence of this approach was a redefinition of identity. This was, in part, a response to the external pressures detailed in the next chapter: if the 'other' were happy to recognise the Normans equally clearly as Franks, Gauls and Celts, there was no obvious reason why William should not now do the same. While Wolf has observed that there is no evidence for the reproduction of William's manuscript in the years after its completion, and that it had consequently little impact on the way Norman history was written, it must be considered that William reflected rather than instigated this flux in the identity of the southern Italian Normans. The alteration and fluidity of strong identity constructs are natural results of changes in circumstances, and William's history is merely one product of such a change. The difference between William and Geoffrey is that, while the identity of which William wrote had the flexibility to reshape itself (as a construct of a new generation of Norman Italians), Geoffrey's subject matter reflected an older and surer identity, but equally one that was less capable of change, and thus weaker. The result of this difference is evidenced below.

The Final Phase: Coronation and Kingship

It is unfortunate that an identity entering such a crisis period did not produce another history for more than thirty years. While this is understandable, it does prevent us from seeing the evolution of this identity into its next stage, after the coronation of Count Roger II as King Roger I of Sicily. Between 1130 and 1154, however, we do have one history written internally, that of Alexander, the abbot of Telese and author of the 'Deeds of King Roger'. The work was written *c*.1136, and dedicated to its subject, King Roger, with the intention of producing 'something which wisely records the story of [Roger's] most famous victory', namely his coronation as king.[76] It is clear that Alexander's work shows the fruit of those changes that can be seen emerging in the works of William of Apulia and Geoffrey Malaterra, and these changes have misled many historians into believing that the Normans as a *gens* had disappeared from Italy and Sicily by the time that this history was being written.

Such a reaction is entirely reasonable on the surface. To an even greater extent than William of Apulia, Alexander seems unconscious of the past. He does not begin his work with an *origo* of any sort, whether one based upon the Normans' northern

---

[75] For identity challenge and vulnerability, see Weinreich, 'Operationalisation', 300.
[76] Telese, 1.

homeland or on their arrival and integration with the people of Italy. Instead, Alexander looks back at Roger's own family history, but only a short distance, to 'the mighty Duke Robert Guiscard' and Roger 'brother of the above-mentioned Guiscard'.[77] Even this is only a device through which Alexander reminds his readers of King Roger's heroic lineage, for Roger was 'a scion of the Guiscard's lineage through whom the ducal power might quickly be revived'.[78] And though Roger was related to these great figures of Italian and Sicilian history, there is one aspect of unity that Alexander never attributes to him: King Roger, while many things, is never called a Norman.

In fact, Alexander only mentions the name Norman once in his entire work and, when he does so, the reference is very much incidental: 'there was in that same Terra di Lavoro a city called Aversa which had been founded by the Normans at the time when they had attacked Apulia'.[79] There is no delight in great Norman deeds here, merely a vague mention of something that had obviously happened a long time ago for Alexander. This description of Aversa is not dissimilar to that of Naples, 'which Aeneas was said to have founded when he landed there on his voyage', and thus the Norman reference is more a part of casual historical information about the city than any comment on the people in their own right.[80] Alexander's use of vocabulary is equally interesting: the observation that the Normans *attacked* Apulia is suggestive of a negative occurrence and the implication is in no way that this was part of a successful conquest.

Other vague references to Normandy appear in the work, with mention of Robert of Grandmesnil (who returns to the land of his kinsmen 'across the Alps') and the price of bread (being referenced to the value of a 'coin of Rouen' and a 'penny of Rouen'), but there are no other indications that there is any tie between the Sicilian kingdom and the duchy of Normandy.[81] With these considerations in mind, it becomes increasingly clear that Alexander's work does not portray the identity of a *gens Normannorum*. We know that Roger was of Norman descent, but if Alexander considers this so unimportant as to be unworthy of mention, it seems likely that the same response would have been elicited from his patrons, Mathilda (the estranged wife of Rainulf of Alife) and Roger himself. There is, in fact, only one reputed instance in which King Roger showed kinship with the Normans, when he apparently referred to some men who had despoiled a monastery as '*nostri Normanni*'.[82]

Such a comment suggests that, not only was Roger not a member of this group, but that he did not think of himself as Norman – if he did so, there would be no need to distinguish the ethnicity of these men. The statement would suggest that Roger considered these Normans to be *his* men, the ethnic distinction that they were not of the dominant – i.e. Roger's – ethnicity. It seems, from Roger's general approach to

---

[77] *Ibid.*, 7–8.   [79] *Ibid.*, 58.

[78] *Ibid.*, 8.   [80] *Ibid.*, 68.

[81] *Ibid.*, 17; 62 & 79. The coin references are doubtless to *rothomagenses* / *roumois* / *romesini*, silver deniers minted at Rouen and imported by the Normans; these remained in circulation until their abolition by Roger II in his coin reform of 1140 (see Philip Grierson and Lucia Travaini, *Medieval European Coinage – 14: Italy (III) (South Italy, Sicily, Sardinia)* (Cambridge, 1998), 3, 114, 118, 401; Philip Grierson, 'The Coinages of Norman Apulia and Sicily in their International Setting', *ANS* 15 (1993), 117 & 126).

[82] Matthew, *Norman Kingdom*, 170. Matthew does not specify his source beyond 'one document'.

his kingship, that this is not an expression of affiliation to another *gens*, but rather an attempt to set his own ethnicity aside in recognition of the polyethnic character of his kingdom. This appraisal would therefore suggest that, by the time that Alexander was writing, the importance of *Normanitas* and the *gens Normannorum* was a thing of the past.[83]

Further indications of this can be seen in the way that Alexander writes of Roger as a leader. In his youth, Roger appears to evidence Norman aspects: when he fought with his brother and other youths, 'the younger, Roger, was the conqueror' and, when he became a young man, Roger was 'made a knight'.[84] Yet soon after this, he shows attributes that had not previously been present in the Norman leaders. He remains patient and calm in the face of adversity, and, perhaps more importantly, is seen to lose in battle.[85] Additionally, he shows no kinship with the Norman centres of previous years, such as Aversa and Melfi; instead, Roger's interest is in Palermo, 'the chief city of Sicily, which once, in ancient times, was believed to have had kings [who ruled] over this province'.[86] The strong religious element remains, but whereas before there had persisted the idea of a chosen people settling in a divinely chosen land, now there was only King Roger, who had 'triumphed by divine disposition and received the royal crown by divine influence'.[87]

Obviously, the apparent disappearance of the tenets of *Normanitas*, which had proved so strong a unifier to the *gens Normannorum* in previous years, must be accounted for. To some extent, the upbringing of Roger himself is important. His mother and regent, Adelaide, was a Lombard by birth, and seems to have had little love for the Normans and their ideals. Consequently, Roger was not raised to be the knight that his father had been, but rather to be the statesman that his father eventually became. As well as accounting for many of the characteristics that Alexander writes of, this change is reflected in the development of the titles and signatures used by both Rogers and their immediate relations. With the lack of a prevailing vernacular in Sicily, the titles of its rulers were translated not only into Greek, but also into Arabic, initially resulting in such direct transferences as '*Abārt al-dūqa*', 'Robert the duke'. However, from the later part of the rule of Roger I, and through the early period of his son's control, these titles became more formalised translations of their proper feudal titles; thus Roger I became '*sultān Siqilliyya*', 'lord of Sicily', and Adelaide and Roger '*mawlātu-nā al-sayyida wa-mawlā-nā al-qūmmus Rujjār*', 'our lady regent and our lord Count Roger'.[88] Such a variety of titulature shows the statesmanlike approach taken by Roger I in his dealings with the polyethnic environment of Sicily. Roger II's extension of this 'internal diplomacy' was evident before his coronation as, unlike his father, he issued most of his official documents in Greek, rather than Latin.[89]

---

[83] It is interesting that, in some sense, this bears out Davis' hypothesis concerning Orderic Vitalis. When Orderic was writing, around this time, he could easily be said to be creating a false sense of unity with the southern Italian Normans. However, this sense of unity, if no longer extant, had certainly existed in the eleventh century, and it is really only the eleventh-century exploits that Orderic lays claim to.

[84] Telese, 8–9

[85] *Ibid.*, 10 & 12, 37.

[86] *Ibid.*, 23.

[87] *Ibid.*, 84.

[88] Jeremy Johns, 'The Norman Kings and the Fatimid Caliphate', *ANS* 15 (1993), 135.

[89] Matthew, *Norman Kingdom*, 93.

What cannot be explained by Roger II's upbringing are the alterations in this field after his coronation, when he evidenced a move even further away from Latin tradition. His Arabic title transformed into something that was not a simple translation of a Latin title, but an independent Islamic tradition with no traceable ancestor in Sicily: he became 'the royal, sublime, Rogerial, supreme majesty, may God make his days eternal and give strength to his banners'.[90] It is in fact apparent that this tradition bears most resemblance to that of the Fāṭimid Caliphate in Egypt; this suggestion is further supported by the architecture of, and inscriptions in, Roger's palaces, which owe a clear debt to the Ifrīqiyyan palaces of the Fāṭimids.[91] With regard to signatures, Roger occasionally used the Arabic 'al-ḥamdu li-'llāh ḥaqq ḥamida-hu', 'Praise be to God, and thanks for his blessings'; more significantly, he took to signing all Latin documents in Greek.[92] Such written symbolism was further enhanced through the use of Byzantine and Islamic visual imagery in portraits of Roger, enhancing the perceived debt of his monarchy to these two powers.

It is clear that Roger's upbringing in no way explains these significant changes in the portrayal of what we must now call Sicilian leadership. Jeremy Johns' observation that 'he appropriated whatever symbol enhanced his own monarchy' is equally insufficient, because it greatly underrates Roger's ambition in this area. We have observed already Roger's disconnection from the Norman past in all ways other than his immediate bloodline, perhaps the single aspect that marked his kingship with a Latin element. Given the Greek and Arabic elements that he introduced into the concept of monarchy in his new kingdom of Sicily, his kingship then comes to represent, to a greater or lesser extent, the three cultures over which he was ruling in Sicily: Latin, Greek and Muslim. A more distinctive move towards racial unity is hardly imaginable, for Roger was utilising a collection of symbols containing elements that all his subjects could recognise as the marks of a monarch in their own tradition; he was creating a new myth / symbol complex for the leadership of Sicily, which marked him not as a Norman conqueror but as a representative of all those cultures under him.

However, the reasons behind this failure to institute a purely western European kingship model have yet to be understood. The explanation can perhaps be detected in the histories of William of Apulia and Geoffrey Malaterra, and undoubtedly in the years between the production of those histories and the coronation of Roger in 1130; most importantly, though, it can be found in some modern identity models that apply to superordinate communities. Given the uncommon nature of conquests in modern times, the primary application of such models is to migrations, but they explain this conquest equally well, especially when it is remembered that the Norman identity, at the end of the eleventh century, was 'vulnerable'. In this sense, 'vulnerable' refers to the identity of those who find that 'their aspirations have been overtaken by social change and become meaningless given contemporary norms', a fair description of the Normans in southern Italy and Sicily, who had nothing of their area left to conquer.[93] When introduced into the Sicilian environment, which involved interaction with

[90] Johns, 'Norman Kings', 135–6.
[91] *Ibid.*, 136, 139–40, 149, 153, 158.
[92] *Ibid.*, 137; Matthew, *Norman Kingdom*, 93.
[93] For this model, and related quotes, see Weinreich, 'Operationalisation', 302–3.

what were essentially entire translocated communities, the Norman identity that had served them so well was threatened by the alternative lifestyles of the Greeks, Muslims and Lombards. On the Italian mainland, though, the situation was somewhat different, and the evidence here suggests that they did not feel threatened, undoubtedly because they had maintained their identity in this environment after its conquest, and yet had been able (owing to the leadership of, for example, Robert Guiscard) to continue to succeed in new military ventures.

The results of this threat, or lack thereof, are to be found in William and Geoffrey's works. The model suggests that, when an identity is 'vulnerable', its members 'may come to rely increasingly on their core ethnic identity', and 'they will tend to ascribe derogatory "racial" identities' to the threatening groups. Equally, a robust identity would not need to resort to such 'defensive' centrality. As has been noted above, Geoffrey is writing for a Norman identity that is under threat, reiterating the concepts of military prowess that had been the benchmark of *Normanitas* for so many years, and tying these back to the earliest origins of the duchy of Normandy. William, conversely, is experimenting with *Normanitas*, writing of a younger identity that links the Normans and their subjects in Italy more fully, not as a pure *gens* with a lengthy descent, but as an open group happily adopting new members. It is Geoffrey who portrays the Lombards, Greeks and Muslims in the most derogatory way, in contrast to William's subtle superiority, and thus it is Geoffrey who is writing in response to a perceived threat, while William writes in a far less concerned manner.

The net result of this change can be seen quite clearly in Roger's kingship. In Sicily, the Norman identity had become 'vulnerable'; it was essentially incapable of change, and in the intervening years had been 'broken' by the fundamental social changes occurring around it. This was doubtless exacerbated by the process of the constitution of Sicily as a kingdom, which can be expected to have involved at least a notional synthesis of various population groupings.[94] On the mainland, it is clear from William's work that the survival of a Norman identity was more likely, although the lack of a purely mainland internal source makes this difficult to discern. However, the material that we have at our disposal, including Alexander's history and onomastic studies, allows us to make some form of investigation into the 'remnants' of Norman society in this area, with a view to discovering what exactly had happened to the southern Italian *gens Normannorum*.

Studies of names attested in charters and elsewhere have identified some 375 French names from the eleventh and twelfth centuries.[95] While some two-thirds of these are ostensibly 'Norman', there is often no compelling evidence to support them being the names of people of Norman descent; it is quite reasonable to suggest that, as after the Viking settlements further north, people began to adopt Norman names who were not Norman themselves.[96] Joanna Drell has argued that epithets such as 'the Norman' or 'the Lombard' were adopted by people who wished to make explicit their own consciousness of ethnic divisions, but this appears to stem from the false

---

[94] Goetz, et al., *Regna and Gentes*, 610.
[95] Matthew, *Norman Kingdom*, 140.
[96] G.A. Loud, 'How "Norman" was the Norman Conquest of Southern Italy?', *Nottingham Medieval Studies* 25 (1981), 22.

premise that people chose their own epithets.[97] We have already seen, in the example of 'Guiscard' above, that such nick-names were given by others; it is highly likely that to provide one's own nick-name would be to invite ridicule, not recognition. While such names may well have referred to the lineage of the individual concerned, this is not a hard and fast rule, and they may well have also been applied to describe particular combinations of hair and eye coloration, or aspects of personality. Even where they did have connotations of descent, these could easily have been familial recognition of individuals born of mixed marriages who favoured one or the other parent in appearance. As Drell herself notes, 'the issue of names for Southern Italy – especially during the Norman period – is complex and perhaps ultimately an exercise in frustration'.[98]

The *Deeds of King Roger* of Alexander, however, is somewhat more revealing of the continuation of *Normanitas* outside the person of Roger himself. While Roger does not really evidence those Norman characteristics referred to by earlier authors, there are those who do, and a fact of primary interest is that these are not Roger's allies but his enemies. The most prominent of these figures is Count Rainulf of Alife, who is the centrepiece of the opposition to Roger's rule. When reading Alexander's descriptions of Rainulf's activities, one cannot help but be reminded of the various accounts of Robert Guiscard, as Rainulf strives vainly to fend off the vastly superior military strength and finances of the new king. The description of the Battle of Nocera, in which Rainulf rallies his own men by charging single-handedly at the royal lines and instigating a rout among Roger's forces, is in many ways similar to those stories told by Amatus, William and Geoffrey of Guiscard's performance at Civitate – while Rainulf gets through fewer horses, he is clearly a paragon of military prowess and leadership.[99] Even when finally forced to submit before Roger, Rainulf only does so on his own terms, and when the opportunity arises he is once more in revolt.[100] It is not until all his land has been confiscated that he finally gives up the fight, and even then he does so by accepting voluntary exile in Naples rather than submitting to Roger's overlordship.

Perhaps the most intriguing aspect of Rainulf's character, within the *Deeds of King Roger*, is that he is never explicitly criticised by Alexander, even though he is the king's enemy. Though Roger at one point laments Rainulf's disregard for oath and kinship, this oblique reference is hardly damning.[101] The same is true of Alexander's attitude to Rainulf's son Robert, 'made a knight in his earliest adolescence, at a time when despite his youth he was already beginning to attract praise for his great courage and daring', and to Roger de Flenco, a commander under Rainulf described as 'a valiant knight' in the same sentence that he is called 'a great enemy of the king'.[102] Elsewhere, Richard, Rainulf's brother, expresses what could only be called a typically Norman temperament: when a messenger arrived from King Roger demanding his subjection, Richard 'was filled with fury and madly resolved on war. He hurled the messenger to the ground, cut off his nose, and then ordered him to be blinded'.[103] Yet even this explosive act is not overtly criticised by Alexander.

97 Joanna Drell, 'Cultural Syncretism and Ethnic Identity: the Norman "Conquest" of Southern Italy and Sicily', *JMH* 25 (1999), 198.
98 *Ibid.*, 196.
99 Telese, 37.
100 *Ibid.*, 52–3, 57.
101 *Ibid.*, 62.
102 *Ibid.*, 72; 42.
103 *Ibid.*, 28.

All these things suggest that, if Alexander (and indeed Roger) did not subscribe to a concept of *Normanitas* such as that in circulation in the eleventh century, the cultural symbols that had helped to define the *gens Normannorum* were by no means dead. While Roger might not have been a 'Norman king' in the same way that William the Conqueror was, he still numbered Normans among his subjects, and recognition could still be accorded to their heroic deeds, even when they were his enemies. The dogged resistance (and occasional successes) of Rainulf, the knightly virtues of Robert and Roger de Flenco, and the fit of rage of Richard all have their parallels in the heroes of the Norman tradition who were defined by and represented *Normanitas*.

If Alexander does not criticise these rebels, it is perhaps because they embodied a set of virtues that were still worthy of respect, even in Roger's kingdom; perhaps, also, Alexander had no wish to insult a man whose home at Alife was only a short distance (around 20 km) from Telese, whether through local loyalty or fear of retribution. There may also be a subtext here, that Roger would eventually defeat even such great men as these (though when Alexander was writing, *c*.1136, the outcome between Roger and Rainulf was as yet undecided). If Rainulf and the others are to be considered Roger's 'foil', then this suggests that men still placed value in the attributes that they displayed in a very real sense; the treachery of Tancred is treated far more contemptuously. However, it is difficult to tell whether these virtues can truly be said to be representative of an enduring sense of *Normanitas*, or whether they are simply the product of a chivalric ethos, promoted by (French) vernacular literature. As Amory has noted, the persistence of a given cultural trait does not prove that the possessors constitute an ethnic group any more than the absence of a trait proves that they do not.[104]

It would appear, then, that, while the Normans came to Italy in comparatively small numbers, they were able to maintain their concepts of unity, both among themselves and with their homeland, for some eighty years. However, as the eleventh century drew to a close, the changing emphasis of their society and activities prompted significant changes in the Norman self-perceptions that were the root of *Normanitas*. The result of this was the creation of two slightly differing Norman identities, one basking in the security of victories well won, the other under threat of submergence by the strong and distinctive identities of the surrounding communities. As the first was led to identify with its new homeland, so the second clung to older traditions and thus proved the less resilient of the two. The submission of this latter to a greater unity of cultures in Sicily was paralleled by an integration of its companion on the mainland, and, while the lack of an internal mainland source is regrettable, identity models suggest that the identity of the southern Italian Normans survived in a way that that of the Sicilian Normans did not. The characteristics and behaviour of the mainland rebels in Roger's reign suggest that the concepts that composed the Norman identity of the eleventh century survived into the twelfth, even though the *gens* with which they were associated becomes increasingly difficult to identify. To justify this transformation, we must now look to those external influences that provided for and helped instigate this change.

---

[104] Amory, *People and Identity*, 17.

6

External Identity

Of all Norman identity constructs, the external identity of those Normans in southern Italy and Sicily is the most complicated. The Normans in this area were not, as in France or England, interacting primarily with one *ethnie*, but instead with several groupings, each of which had its own perception of what it meant to be a Norman. As well as local Lombard and papal opinion, we also have records of those ideas of *Normanitas* engendered in the minds of the French and of the Greeks (both within Italy and in Byzantium), in whose empire the Normans interfered. Even though the majority of these opinions are negative, they are all subtly different, and the sheer number of them makes it difficult to gain any sort of unified opinion of the Normans, other than the evident fact that many people didn't like them very much.

While certain of our sources, such as those produced by Falco of Benevento, Anna Comnena and Leo of Ostia, give somewhat wider coverage of the nature of these outlanders, many of the works that provide an opinion of the Normans (either as a people or as individuals) do so incidentally: this contrives to add to the difficulty of this exercise. Thus, the variety and vague nature of our sources makes it unreasonable to attempt an assessment of Norman identity in chronological terms, as a single progression. Rather, the constructs of each individual grouping are best considered in their own terms, and the ramifications of these for *Normanitas* as the Normans saw it addressed in relation to each construct. This approach therefore suffices to provide some idea of the way in which external perceptions of the Normans altered within each *ethnie* / grouping over the period between *c.*1016 and 1154.

French Perceptions

In the first instance, it is clear that the movement of Normans to Italy did nothing to diminish the gradually improving image of the Normans at home in France. Both Adhemar of Chabannes and Rodulf Glaber, whom we have encountered already, record a tradition in which Rodulf of Tosny led a large body of Normans southwards to Italy, where they sought employment under Pope Benedict VIII. Though Glaber's story is more detailed, mentioning the fact that Rodulf fled to Italy from Duke Richard II, 'fearing his wrath', it soon becomes clear in both accounts that these Normans were respected and even famous for their exploits.[1] Neither Adhemar nor Glaber are damning of Rodulf's actions – Glaber even refers to him as '*audacissimus*'

[1]   Glaber, 96–8: '*cuius iram metuens*'.

– and both writers' accounts reflect their attitudes toward the Normans evidenced elsewhere; this is perhaps best evidenced in the arena of battle.[2]

Adhemar recounts a series of four battles in which the Normans won the first three before a final defeat produced the proverb 'the Greeks captured the hare with a four-wheeled carriage'; the Greeks then began to persecute all foreigners that they discovered as a result of their indignation at the Norman attacks.[3] However, in Glaber the Normans are not defeated, but instead the third battle (of three that he records) ends in a draw, and Rodulf then seeks the aid of the German emperor, Henry, who attacked the Greeks when next they advanced.[4] In fact, Glaber shows a far greater distaste than Adhemar for the *gentes* of Italy, observing that 'a mere handful of Normans had triumphed over the arrogance of the Greeks' and that 'the local population was useless in battle'.[5]

Both Adhemar and Glaber provide the impression that, even though the Normans were smaller in number, they were at least militarily superior to the inhabitants of Italy, something that they were, unsurprisingly, less willing to concede with reference to their own *gens*. Yet if they perceived this to be the case, it suggests a certain level of identification with the Normans, not as a separate *gens* that stood apart from the Franks / French, but as part of the *gens Francorum* to a greater or lesser extent; certainly, the Normans were more so than the Lombards or the Greeks. While the Normans were not French in the truest sense, and the usage of the name Norman shows the desire of both Adhemar and Glaber to make this distinction, they were representing France in some way in Italy, and it is also probable that there were some non-Normans among the men who travelled to the south. The attitudes of both writers suggest, however, that from the French perspective the Normans in the south were no different from the Normans of Normandy, at least not by the mid-eleventh century; furthermore, they were not that significantly different from Frenchmen.

Greek Perceptions

This concept of the similarity of Normans and French, and the lack of distinction made between the two, is quite persistent among all the races with whom the Normans interacted in the southern Italian area. Indeed, to the Greeks, the Normans and Franks seem to have been very much one and the same people, and are often not only indistinguishable from one another, but also from other foreign groups with whom the Byzantine Greeks dealt. This disinterest in the difference between non-Greek *gentes* is reflected in the lack of consistency in the names used by the Byzantine writers of the period to refer to the Normans, or those who fought with them. We know, for example, that the term 'Frank' could refer to western Christian

2   *Ibid.*, 96.
3   Adhemar, 178: '*Grecus cum carruca leporem capit*'. Notably, *leporem* can also be translated as 'wit', *carruca* as 'plough'.
4   Glaber, 98–100.
5   *Ibid.*, 98–100: '*paucis Normannorum concessa fuisset de superbientibus Grecis uictoria*'; '*uirosque illius patrie minus belli aptos*'.

peoples in general (much as in the holy land), and its common usage denoted those living or coming from north of the Alps.[6] The vagaries of this term are readily evidenced: John Scylitzes, the Byzantine chronicler, referred to those Normans who served under George Maniaces as Frankish soldiers, and a source from the 1070s makes reference to Robert 'the Frank' when talking of Robert Guiscard.[7] Added to these 'Frank' names (*Phrangoi*, etc.), the Normans could also appear under the headings *Albanoi* (foreigners), *symmachoi* (allies), *symmachikon* (auxiliaries), *ethnikoi* (foreigners) or *misthophoroi / -phorikon* (wage-receivers).[8] Finally, we have Anna Comnena's various uses of Normans, Franks, Kelts and Latins seemingly to describe exactly the same people.[9]

While such variance appears initially dismissive, the wide range of names that could be used to describe the Normans provide us with some valuable insights into the way that the Normans were viewed by their Byzantine contemporaries. Perhaps the best example of this is the term *Albanoi*, which was used by the chronicler Michael Atteliates (who wrote an account of events he had witnessed between 1034 and 1079) to describe one of two groups of people living near the Byzantine territories in Italy; the other group were the *Latinoi*. When this is compared with the terminology of John Scylitzes (written in the second half of the eleventh century), who uses *Phrangoi* and *Italoi* to describe the same people and observes that the *Phrangoi* were led by one Arduin, it becomes clear that the people to whom *Albanoi* referred were the Normans.[10] Yet *Albanoi* is observably not a word that is native to Greek, and nor is it purely an ethnic term, but in fact a common noun – *albanoi* – which corresponds to the medieval Latin *albanus*, meaning 'aliens' or 'men from a different jurisdiction'. As a word of Latin origin, it was no doubt transferred to Greek through the Byzantine administration of their Italian territories.

However, there are, according to Lucio Melazzo, 'good grounds for supposing that when the Normans settled in southern Italy they used the name *albani* for a certain time to refer to themselves'.[11] The basis of Melazzo's argument is one of pronunciation, and the appearance of *albanus* in Greek as ἀλβανοί and not ἀλβᾶνοι. The stress of the final syllable rather than, as one would expect, the penultimate syllable suggests a derivation that stems not from the Latin word *albáni*, consistent with normal Latin accentuation, but from *albaní*. A pronunciation such as this, therefore, must have been the result of the Latin form bearing a particular foreign accent, and this can be explained by the speech of those whose mother tongue was Old French, from which they had transferred the habit of stressing the last syllable.[12] Thus the evidence does seem to support Melazzo's hypothesis, but is it reasonable?

We have seen already that, during the settlement of Normandy, the 'proto-Normans' adopted for themselves the name that they had been given by the Franks, and the situation here is not too dissimilar. The consideration must be made,

---

[6] Jonathan Shepard, 'The Uses of the Franks in Eleventh-Century Byzantium', *ANS* 15 (1993), 277.

[7] Lucio Melazzo, 'The Normans through their Languages', *ANS* 15 (1993), 245; Shepard, 'Uses of the Franks', 277.

[8] Melazzo, 'Languages', 246; Shepard, 'Uses of the Franks', 280–1.

[9] *Alexiad*, 138, 143 and 147 for examples.

[10] Melazzo, 'Languages', 244–6.

[11] *Ibid.*, 246–7, quote p. 247.

[12] *Ibid.*, 247–8.

though, that the new arrivals in southern Italy and Sicily were clearly calling themselves Normans by the end of the eleventh century, as is evident from the writings of Amatus of Montecassino and Geoffrey Malaterra. This makes the used of the appellation '*albani*' rather difficult to understand. Melazzo has suggested that *albani* may relate to the element *wæringi* in 'Varangian', and be part of the maintenance of a Germanic juridical custom concerning the settlement of raiders / mercenaries in new territory; this is added to by the fact that *albanus* has the above-mentioned legal connotations.[13] Yet he observes himself that the Normans must have accepted the name *albani* / *albanoi* 'until their leaders succeeded in gratifying their burning wish to get a piece of land and thus become part of the complicated play of forces'; the term Varangian, however, can be seen to continue in use.[14] This suggests that, rather than explaining the situation, the complex legal parallel (which relies heavily on the Norman remembrance of Germanic custom into the fourth generation and later) is actually too complex: the Normans were simply called foreigners until they ceased to be perceived as such.

This of course raises the question of why the Normans accepted this appellation at all. The answer would seem to lie once again in perceptions, both those of the Greeks and of the Normans themselves. It must not be forgotten that, in the Italian arena, the numbers of Norman mercenaries were actually very small, only a few hundred men. Not only were these few probably split into even smaller groupings, but they lacked recognised leadership from within their own *ethnie*; furthermore, they initially lacked the reputation that they later built for themselves in southern Italy and Sicily, and as newcomers could be easily badged as foreigners by the indigenous inhabitants of the area. The similarities to the settlement of Normandy suggest that, once again, the model best able to explain the interaction between the Normans and Greeks is one of minority situations. Certainly, the treatment of the Normans as aliens or foreigners, embodied in the term '*albani*', fits well with such a model, as does the Norman acceptance of this 'negative' badge as representative of their *gens*.[15]

Obviously, the motivation to accept such a definition requires it to have a use, and the adoption of this term by the Normans themselves would, in these circumstances, serve a number of purposes. In the first instance, it would provide them with a sense of unity, and also a sense of distinctiveness, which had universal recognition in this area – both internal and external. It is hard to represent oneself seriously if the statement 'I am a Norman' is met with the response 'That's nice. What's a Norman?', indicating that the name Norman is without an explicit meaning in the speaker's culture. This result of such a situation would undoubtedly be the perception of the 'Norman' as just another foreign mercenary, a term with value in this environment for its comprehensibility as much as anything else.

For the Normans to build an identity for themselves that the Greeks understood, therefore, it would be reasonable for them to have to do so on the Greeks' own terms; as a minority, the Normans could expect to be defined in terms of the majority group's social framework.[16] It must be remembered that, in the case of the Greeks,

13 *Ibid.*, 249–50; 246.
14 *Ibid.*, 247.
15 Weinreich, 'Operationalisation', 301–5.
16 Barth, *Ethnic Groups*, 31.

the Normans were dealing with a gens only too happy to apply the term 'barbarian / barbaric' to anyone or anything that didn't fit into its prearranged categories of civilised society. Additionally, the process of naming oneself a foreigner detracts from any perception of a threat, which might arise from the realisation that this steady flow of newcomers was primarily of one *gens* that sought not to involve itself in the politics of the area but, in the long term, to control them.

The use by the Byzantines of names such as *symmachoi* (allies), *symmachikon* (auxiliaries) and *misthophoroi / -phorikon* (wage-receivers) to describe the Normans also suggests that they many of their interactions with, and perceptions of, the Normans as a people were military in nature. We know that some Normans served under the Byzantine general George Maniaces as mercenaries, the classical meaning of the term *misthophoros*, and it would seem that there were upwards of 1500 'Franks' stationed in Colonaeia and Constantinople in 1057.[17] The way in which these Normans were employed, and the records of them in the Greek works of the time, show quite clearly that the Normans were respected by the Greeks for their martial qualities. Not only did the Normans become a fixture in ceremonial displays of majesty, as practised by the Byzantine emperor, but heroes appear in the Byzantine sources who display qualities similar to those recorded in the Normans sources, and these men are referred to by the aforementioned ethnic titles.

Both Matthew of Edessa, an Armenian chronicler, and Attaleiates tell the story of a 'Frankish' soldier from the rank and file who was single-handedly responsible for the destruction of a Turkish ballista while pretending to be a courier; he rode '[quick] as an eagle'. As a reward, he received a senior title. Elsewhere, Scylitzes records the deeds of a certain 'Frank' called Randolph, bearing the court title of *patrikios*, who challenged the rebel Nicephorus Botaneiates to single combat after the imperial troops on his own side had been routed. Another passage from Attaleiates recounts the way that Constantine IX, 'despairing of the manliness of his generals' gave command against the Pechenegs to a 'Latin', 'a splendid man in moments of crisis and second to none in realising what must be done' – it is probable that this man was Hervé, the leading Frank in Byzantium at this time.[18]

Such examples of Norman military prowess persisted from the eleventh century into the twelfth, and this is best evidenced by the *Alexiad* of Anna Comnena. It was she who said of her brother-in-law, Nicephorus, that 'on horseback he gave the impression that he was not a Roman at all, but a native of Normandy', and that 'a mounted Kelt is irresistible; he would bore his way through the walls of Babylon'.[19] For Anna, these characteristics of the Norman *gens* are personified in Robert Guiscard, whom she variously describes as 'a brave fighter', 'a man of great intelligence and versatility' and 'a winged horseman'. She comments that 'Robert's manliness, his marvellous skill in war and his steadfast spirit are universally recognised' and that '[his] bellow, so they say, put tens of thousands to flight'.[20] Bohemond, also a heroic figure in her work, 'was the exact replica and living image of his father'.[21] Thus

[17] Shepard, 'Uses of the Franks', 285 & 289.
[18] *Ibid.*, 290–1.
[19] *Alexiad*, 301 & 416.
[20] *Ibid.*, 54, 140, 148, 195–6.
[21] *Ibid.*, 66.

the Byzantine perception of the Normans as great warriors continued into the twelfth century, having become, as Jonathan Shepard has observed, 'almost proverbial'; so much so, in fact, that it prompted a certain cynicism concerning Robert Guiscard: 'if he did pray that his life might be spared, it was only, I suppose, for as long as he could wage war on his chosen enemies'.[22]

Such recognitions of superiority in another gens would have been inconceivable from the Norman standpoint, and this is evidently related to the importance of military ability as an aspect of *Normanitas*. Yet the Greek writers seem happy to acknowledge the Normans' capacity here, and while this may have added to the strength of the Normans' consideration that they were *the* most skilled *gens* in the arts of war, it is fairly clear that such an admission was of little import to the Greeks. For every positive military description, it seems, there is a corresponding denunciation, all of which serve to show that the Greeks regarded the Normans as great military figures who had no place in society off the battlefield. There is a clear perception that the Normans were greedy: John Mauropous refers to people recruited from a barbarian army to the west (presumably Normans, though possibly Flemings) as 'outstandingly fond of money'; Anna Comnena observes, also, that 'all Latins lust after money: for one obol they would sell even their nearest and dearest'.[23] It is interesting to note, additionally, that there is no evidence of trouble between the Normans and Byzantines prior to the Battle of Troina, after which arguments occurred over the division of spoils and the payment of the Normans' 'wage', *siteresion*.[24]

Yet it is not only greed that is used to undermine the Norman *gens*; it is certainly not a tragic flaw here, as it has been suggested to be in William of Apulia's history.[25] Rather, this lust for money was just one of these 'barbarians'' failings, another example being their rebelliousness: we hear of the secession of three prominent Frankish commanders from our Byzantine sources – Hervé, Robert Crispin and Roussel of Bailleu – and commentators such as Michael Attaleiates went so far as to observe that the Franks were 'treacherous by nature'.[26] Perhaps the best examples of Norman failings are, however, those exhibited in the *Alexiad* by Robert Guiscard. As with other Norman leaders, he could be expected to represent the characteristics of his people to the utmost degree, and Anna's complaints against him are quite scathing. He is described as 'the tyrant Robert' with 'a thoroughly villainous mind', whose forcible recruitment of men from Lombardy was 'just as lunatic as the behaviour of Herod, or even worse'. Here was a man who had betrayed his father-in-law and who, revealingly, 'was always careful to observe the customs of his race'.[27]

Interestingly, though, it appears that Attaleiates' comment on Frankish treachery was almost a compliment, given the Byzantine court environment, and that Guiscard's betrayal of his father-in-law was perhaps not the stigmatic event that it at first seems. Indeed, the *Alexiad* in particular seems to reflect a culture of *respect* for the Normans' skills in deception. Emily Albu has drawn attention, in particular, to a ruse executed by Bohemond as a means to escape Antioch for Rome, in order to seek

22 Shepard, 'Uses of the Franks', 290; *Alexiad*, 132–3.
23 Shepard, 'Uses of the Franks', 286; *Alexiad*, 193.
24 Shepard, 'Uses of the Franks', 283–4.
25 Wolf, *Making History*, 137.
26 Shepard, 'Uses of the Franks', 294.
27 *Alexiad*, 53, 54–7, 65, 70, 195.

reinforcements and financial support in 1104.[28] Anna tells us that Bohemond hid himself in a coffin, along with a dead rooster, which provided a suitable smell of foulness and decay. Whenever he and his men encountered anyone, Bohemond remained in the coffin; by these means, he escaped to Rome.[29] Bohemond's ruse was part of an ongoing battle of wits between himself and the Byzantine emperor, Alexius Comnenus, who had previously attempted to deceive Bohemond in order to divide him from his allies by means of forged letters.[30] However, Bohemond was not fooled, and this alongside his 'ruse of death' shows a capacity to outwit the emperor that even his daughter was prepared to acknowledge. Notably, Anna is our only source for this trick of Bohemond's, but she was clearly impressed by the ability of this Norman to play the Byzantine game of trickery.[31]

It is therefore clear that, while the Greeks had a great deal of respect for the military skills and deceptive capacities of the Normans, they were far less impressed with other aspects of Norman culture and society, in particular the qualities of the *gens* that were not, in the Greek mind, associated with prowess in conflict. One is left with impression that the Normans were utilised because they played a vital military role for the Greeks, and that the Greeks were quite willing to endorse the military superiority of the Normans, which was such a significant expression of Norman identity. However, the Normans remained barbarians in essence, and as such were almost expected to behave strangely. There were fundaments of the Norman attitude that the Greeks found incomprehensible, even so; Anna Comnena observes that:

> your Latin barbarian will at the same time handle sacred objects, fasten a shield to his left arm and grasp a spear in his right. He will communicate the Body and Blood of the Deity and meanwhile gaze on bloodshed and become himself 'a man of blood' (as David says in the Psalm). Thus the race is no less devoted to religion than to war.[32]

This comment perhaps exemplifies the Greek attitude towards and perceptions of the Norman settlers of southern Italy and Sicily. They may have been excellent and even unstoppable in battle, but they lacked the culture and stature of their Greek betters. Robert Guiscard, though he and Alexius Comnenus were 'worthy rivals', had various dark aspects to his character that lessened him, and anyway 'the emperor had a certain advantage over Robert, because he was still young and in no way the inferior of his adversary'.[33]

Lombard Perceptions: Montecassino and Benevento

The other major ethnic group with whom the Normans interacted was that of the 'Lombards', the term by which the pre-existing population of the southern Italian areas in which Lombards had settled were known. As we have already seen, at least

---

[28] Emily Albu, 'Bohemond and the Rooster: Byzantines, Normans, and the Artful Ruse', in Thalia Gouma-Peterson (ed.), *Anna Komnene and her Times* (New York, 2000), 157–68.

[29] *Alexiad*, 366–8.

[30] *Ibid.*, 406–8; Albu, 'Bohemond', 160.

[31] Albu, 'Bohemond', 163–5.

[32] *Alexiad*, p. 317, n. 37.

[33] *Ibid.*, 156.

one of the pro-Norman histories in this area was produced by a Lombard author (Amatus of Montecassino), who commemorated the valuable working relationship between the Norman settlers and the abbey of Montecassino, a major source of historical material in this period. However, where we find Amatus' work translated into Old French, and probably accepted by the Normans, other works, such as those of Abbot Desiderius (1058–87) and Leo, later bishop of Ostia, were not. Additionally, the twelfth-century work of Falco of Benevento provides further material, from an area of renowned papal sympathies. These three works between them offer an insight into the local Lombard views of the Normans and, perhaps, those views that the Normans preferred *not* to accept.

Of the three, the earliest work is that of Desiderius, and his *Dialogues on the Miracles of St Benedict* were written between 1076 and 1079.[34] While we only have two-and-a-half books of what was apparently intended to be a four-book work, there are two interesting accounts herein that concern the Normans, in both instances depicted as aggressors from whom Benedict protects the monastery. The two short and anecdotal tales related by Desiderius make up only a small portion of the totality of the work. That, in itself, is unsurprising – the focus, at least in the first two books from which these stories are taken, is on the abbey of Montecassino itself, and it is not a *Historia Normannorum* of any kind; in this, it is similar to all the other external works. From the outset, it is evident that there is no vagueness, as there is in the Greek sources, about the ethnic origin / affiliation of these aggressors: Desiderius uses the term *Normanni* throughout to describe them, and there is no recourse to alternatives such as those used by the Greeks (Gauls, Franks, Kelts, etc.). Importantly, also, the Normans we see depicted here are always judged as a *gens*, and not on the basis of their leaders; in fact, there is no mention of specific leaders here at all, merely the appearance of unnamed Normans as parties hostile to the interests of the monastery.

The first story recounts the protection of the monastery's fisherman (by Benedict) from a Norman who attempted to seize the day's catch. After the nameless Norman had thrown a protesting fisherman into the sea, he began drawing in the nets himself, only to fall overboard and immediately drown, while the fisherman succeeded in swimming to shore. Aside from the immediately obvious moral aspect of this story, that bad things happen to those who prey upon the holy, the depiction of this Norman is extremely revealing of eleventh-century attitudes towards the Normans. The Norman here is 'puffed-up and conceited by pride', 'covetous of the booty of fish' and evidently representative of a race who 'are greedy for plunder, and insatiably anxious to seize the goods of others'.[35] Here, once again, we see the Normans denounced for all-consuming greed by a people with whom they interacted, in the same way as they were by the Greeks.

Furthermore, the same is true in the second story recounted by Desiderius. In this instance, having been installed as protectors of the monastery by Abbot Atenulf, against the potential threat of the count of Aquino, initially, the Normans were well

---

34 Wolf, *Making History*, 73.

35 *Dialogi de miraculis sancti Benedicti auctore Desiderio abbate Casinensi*, ed. Gerhard Schwartz and Adolf Hofmeister, *MGH SS*, Tomus XXX, Pars II (1934), 1124: '*tumidus ac inflatus superbia*'; '*piscium praeda avidus*'; '*sunt ad rapinam avidi, ad invadenda aliena bona inexplebiliter anxii*'.

behaved. 'When they had driven the enemy a long way back all round, they began to defend each of the concerns of the monastery nobly and faithfully in the manner of energetic knights.' However, after the death of Atenulf, so Desiderius writes, 'the Norman company began gradually to be treacherous and hostile to us', becoming 'guided by wicked greed', and took control of the monastery. However, their 'barbarian greed' was eventually overcome, and 'by the will of God many of them were either captured or killed by the people of the city that they had overwhelmed'.[36]

The image of the Normans thus portrayed in Desiderius' *Dialogues* is one of a voraciously greedy race, who will generally stop at nothing to get what they want; thus, when they are kept from their aims, the help of St Benedict is made manifest. The question that remains, though, is to what extent can this collection of miraculous anecdotes be considered a reliable guide to the way in which the Lombards (and Montecassino) perceived the Normans? Certainly, there are significant differences of emphasis between the writings of Desiderius and his exact contemporary Amatus of Montecassino, and yet both were members of exactly the same monastic community. Furthermore, if Amatus was commissioned by Desiderius as he suggests, the likelihood is that the views expressed in the *Dialogues* were in no way a true reflection of Desiderius' (late) opinions.

But this presents a problem. If the behaviour of the Normans in the *Dialogues* was unbelievable to their potential readership, then surely all this would do would be to undermine the veracity of the work as a whole, and cast these 'interventions' by St Benedict in a negative light. One would presumably expect that this was not Desiderius intention, and we must therefore assume that this behaviour was in keeping with people's considerations of the Normans. It is therefore likely that this disparity between Amatus and Desiderius can be explained in the following way.

It must at first be remembered that Amatus' work was commemorative, designed to pay tribute to the good relations between the Normans and Montecassino (above and beyond those between Montecassino and the papacy) and, in particular, to the two Normans who had provided protection to the Church and Montecassino itself within his lifetime, namely Robert Guiscard and Richard of Aversa / Capua.[37] Thus one would expect it to be a highly positive work, full of praise for these men and their *gens*. Not so the work of Desiderius, whose primary interest was to evidence the intervention of St Benedict against the enemies of Montecassino, among whom some Normans were numbered (especially after the plunder of Montecassino by Jordan of Capua in early 1079).[38] Consequently, we are left with a mixture of two extremes: Amatus exaggerates the good qualities of the *gens Normannorum*, as the Lombards perceived them, in the name of continued good relations and protection; Desiderius exaggerates their bad qualities in order to more clearly show the great powers of St Benedict, for who else could stand against something so powerful and renowned as Norman rapacity?

[36] *Ibid.*, 1138–9: '*coeperunt quaeque monasterii pertinentia more strenuorum militum inimicis longe repulsis circumcirca nobiliter fideliterque defendere*'; '*nobis infida atque advera paulatim esse coepit*'; '*sacrilega ducti cupiditate*'; '*nutu Dei a populo civitatis oppressi aliquanti eorum vel occisi vel capti sunt*'. It should be noted that the translation of *barbarica* could be rendered (though not so well) as 'foreign', 'outlandish' or, with a more classical meaning, 'Italian'.

[37] H.E.J. Cowdrey, *The Age of Abbot Desiderius* (Oxford, 1983), 131.

[38] *Ibid.*, 135.

The actual Lombard perception of the Normans in the later eleventh century no doubt falls somewhere between these two: they were acknowledged to be great warriors, generally unparalleled on the battlefield, but people did live in fear of what could appear, to an outsider, to be an all-consuming greed and lust for wealth and power. No doubt the perceptions of the crusader knights in the east were similar – and such reactions are understandable when it is considered that the value system of the Normans was rather opaque to the Lombards in general. They had similarities with one another, of course, as they were both Christian peoples and western Europeans, yet the Norman mix of Germanic and French mannerisms engendered perceptions in the Romanised Lombards that marked the Normans as somewhat alien, and often frightening. Consequently, the Lombard perceptions of the Normans would have served to reinforce the ethnic boundaries between the two groups. Though the Normans were, again, a minority in what were essentially Lombard territories, the reaction here suggests that the ethnic identity of the Lombards was rather weaker and more vulnerable than that of the Greeks.[39]

It is Leo of Ostia's *Chronica Monasterii Casinensis* that provides a control on both Amatus' and Desiderius' works. A monk of Montecassino from *c*.1061, Leo was made cardinal-bishop of Ostia in his later life, commencing his work upon the *Chronica* a short time after both Amatus and Desiderius were writing, after *c*.1098.[40] The original version of the *Chronica* evidenced no knowledge of Amatus' work; however, it was later rewritten up to 1075 to include information taken from Amatus' *Historia Normannorum*, which Leo had since encountered. Leo's work is neither as pro-Norman as Amatus', nor does it depict the Normans as being enemies of the monastery (as does Desiderius); rather, it is a reserved and relatively inexpressive work, reminiscent of that of Flodoard of Reims in its seeming impartiality.

Leo therefore provides a useful middle ground between Amatus' and Desiderius' works. The unfortunate consequence of using such a work is, however, that it expresses very few opinions about the Normans, dealing with the events in a detached and factual way. Yet it is still possible to extract some evidence of the perceptions held of the Normans at the time of writing from the few instances in which Leo uses positive or negative terminology about the Normans or events surrounding them. Indeed, one would expect that, if Leo was trying to show his objectivity, these few instances are very revealing, in that the nature of the work suggests that they were considered factual enough *not* to be regarded as simple opinions, but as generally held perceptions. Within Leo's work, there are four such examples (three of which appear only in the C version of the *Chronica*), which provide insights not only into the Lombard perceptions of the Normans, but also into the acceptability of both Desiderius' and Amatus' works within the wider Lombard community.

The first example is, quite obviously, a simple reiteration of one of those stories appearing in Desiderius' *Miraculi*, namely that concerning the overbearing Norman and the fisherman.[41] The Norman appearing here is no less obnoxious; once again,

---

[39] Weak and vulnerable identities are more likely to perceive newcomers as a threat – see Weinreich, 'Operationalisation', 302.

[40] Dating from Norwich, *Normans in Sicily*, 340.

[41] *CMC*, 294, and see above.

'puffed-up and conceited by pride', he is depicted as attempting to steal the day's catch.[42] Yet, out of context of the other story concerning the Normans that appears in Desiderius' work, the impact of this anecdote is greatly lessened. It does not find itself in company with other denunciations of the Normans' greed or predatory nature, nor is it tied specifically to a theme of saintly protection; rather, it is simply a miraculous occurrence in which the fishing monk is protected from the greed of one man. True, this man is a Norman, but he is, again, unnamed, and serves more to appear as a representative of predatory people in general than specifically as a representative of the behaviour of the *gens Normannorum*. Thus, the application of the term *Normannus* would seem to be fairly incidental here.

Of course, it could equally be argued that the 'Norman' is retained, which signified something of a stereotype of the Normans as a race to which many were capable of subscribing; in modern times, many jokes are altered on a relatively frequent basis to include the group currently in disfavour with that particular identity, or to reflect what are considered distinctive attributes within a race or other identity grouping (i.e. gender). To look at English prejudices, for example, jokes now told with an Irishman as the butt (based upon an English-held stereotype of the Irish) can also be heard told by an older generation with a Frenchman in the same position, again based on a stereotype that has, perhaps, been less-well transmitted to the younger generation. In the instance of the Normans here, the casual use of the name no doubt reflects a stereotype of the rapacious and predatory Norman (as seen in Desiderius) from Leo's own generation, but the lack of other, similar anecdotes or, indeed, judgements of this sort upon the *gens Normannorum* as a whole suggest that this was a transmitted perception, perhaps originally the product of pre-Civitate papal propaganda, rather than one developed from experience (as Desiderius' perceptions seem to have been).

This lack of ethnic judgement is perhaps amplified by Leo's one comment on Robert Guiscard, arguably *the* most distinctive Norman figure in this area, and clearly one who bore these characteristics in abundance. Leo observes that Bohemond was the son of 'duke Robert, of good memory, who was called Viscart'; hardly an insult or judgement, there is no reference to negative qualities.[43] In fact, Leo's other two areas of comment on the Normans suggest that he at least, and doubtless others, perceived them as a thoroughly Christian *gens*. When Guiscard leads his force to Muslim Sicily, he is described as having 'Christ as his guide'; the troops under him, fighting against 'Balchaoth' (Belchus) as Christians, remained unwounded, while it proved hardly possible to count the number of pagan dead.[44] Even at Civitate, where the Normans were responsible for defeating the papal forces in battle, an act seemingly so unchristian, the Normans emerged victorious 'by the judgement of God'.[45]

Unfortunately, these few comments are the limit of the opinions expressed about the Normans in Leo's work, and they do not lend themselves to further conclusions.

---

[42] *Ibid.*, 294: '*tumidus ac inflatus superbia*'; C only.

[43] *Ibid.*, 476: '*Boamundus filius bone memorie ducis Robberti cognomento Viscardi*'; C only.

[44] *Ibid.*, 422: '*Christo duce*'; '*cum ex christianis non equitum vel peditum aliquis vulneraretur vel moreretur, ex paganorum multitudine interfectorum numerus vix colligi potuit*'; C only.

[45] *Ibid.*, 332: '*Normanni Dei iudicio extitere victores*'; CDMS versions.

What can be said with some degree of certainty is that, where Leo has provided a perception of the Normans, this is generally couched in terms that can be found in the works of Amatus and Desiderius. The origins and relevance of the story of the fisherman have already been noted; equally, the concept of the conquest of Sicily as a Christian endeavour can be found in the pages of Amatus' *Historia*. It is, in fact, the case that those perceptions given by Leo are in no way new, being basic continuations of those of the previous generation. What has changed, however, seems to be the conviction with which these opinions were held, and their importance and relevance to the Lombards at the beginning of the twelfth century. For Leo, it appears that though the Normans had some form of a reputation both for predatory behaviour and for the strength of their Christian spirit, these were not excessive, and are not shown as aspects that typified the *gens Normannorum*, merely ones which could be viewed within it.

In fact, Leo's portrayal of the Normans suggests that, rather than an aggressively distinctive *gens*, the Normans were gradually beginning to blend into the background to Lombard eyes. By the time that he was writing, certainly, the Normans' period of conquest was over, the final event in this chain being the completion of the Sicilian conquest in 1091, and Robert Guiscard was already almost fifteen years in the grave. Those cultural features by which the Normans distinguish themselves in Leo's *Chronica*, therefore, are the enduring symbols of a *Normanitas* that was neither threatened nor threatening. The reduction in the visibility of some of the cultural differences that had made the *gens Normannorum* distinct for earlier writers does not, in itself, suggest that Norman ethnicity was any less relevant or that boundaries had disappeared.[46] The Normans were, quite simply, no longer a danger to the status quo; rather, they were the *status quo*, and it was perhaps proving difficult to readily identify a *gens* who were not necessarily sure who they were themselves. For a monastic writer, the events of the First Crusade provided Christian Europe with a far more distinctive and readily identifiable enemy, in the form of the Saracens.

For Falco of Benevento, however, there was only one great enemy, and that was King Roger of Sicily. Writing from before 1127 until 1144 in the province of Benevento (where papal sympathies were often high), Falco is well known for his strong denunciations of Roger. A simple surface examination would thus suggest that Falco was expressing anti-Norman sensibilities that were widely felt in Benevento, but this is perhaps not the case. Falco's work, like that of Alexander of Telese, contains a degree of ambiguity, particularly later on, with regard to the identity of the 'Normans' and their *gens*. Falco's evident support for those who went against Roger provides an interesting and revealing counterpoint to Alexander's criticism of these men. Furthermore, Falco's inconsistent attitude to the major figures in his *Chronicle* has the feel of public opinion, giving the impression that his work may be a close reflection of the beliefs held locally in general, rather than by him alone.[47]

The early pages of his *Chronicle* contain a number of negative portrayals of the Norman *gens*, who are evidently not the heroic or chivalric heroes that one can find in the Normans' own writings. Falco's entry for 1113 records that 'the property of citizens all over the region was every day stolen or plundered by the Normans' and

---

[46] Barth, *Ethnic Groups*, 32–3.
[47] Loud, 'Genesis', 185 for Falco's inconsistency.

that many Lombard lands were 'afflicted' with 'Norman servitude'.[48] These Normans, who 'were convulsed with envy and hatred of the Lombards', were under the leadership of men such as Robert Sclavus, 'an evil man devoted to the study of vice', and were defeated in battle on 12 August by Constable Landulf de Graeca. However, the Normans proved victorious in a subsequent battle, capturing 'twelve noble knights of the city'.[49]

This demonisation of the Normans is a fairly typical (and perhaps even necessary) process for someone in Falco's position. The Normans here are an immediate enemy, and a threat to the Beneventan way of life; there is, therefore, an ongoing ethnic conflict, and Falco's response – a strong, negative representation of the enemy – is wholly expected. It is also unsurprising that, with the advent of peace between the Beneventans and the Normans, Falco suddenly loses interest in the Normans entirely, focusing instead on other events surrounding Benevento.[50] What is more difficult to understand, however, is the fact that, to Falco, it appears that the Normans suddenly ceased to exist as a defined ethnic group. Indeed, he uses the term 'Norman' only once more in the remainder of his *Chronicle*.

This other appearance of the name 'Norman' occurs in Falco's version of a privilege granted to the citizens of Benevento by King Roger I of Sicily in 1137, in which Falco has Roger refer to 'our Norman predecessors'.[51] Whether or not this phrase was part of the original version of the privilege is difficult to say: Falco's version has been identified as a forgery, possibly created to replace the actual privilege, which had been confiscated in 1143. However, the fact that Falco does not, in the surrounding text, denounce the king for this confiscation has led to the suggestion that Falco had composed his version in *c*.1141–2, *before* the confiscation, perhaps because he did not have access to the actual privilege but wished to record its spirit.[52]

Yet the use of the term 'Norman' here, outside the context of the general narrative, does not detract from the point that Falco does not use this name elsewhere in his work beyond the earliest sections, and this creates an obvious difficulty. As with the work of Alexander of Telese, it is difficult to study the perceptions of a *gens* in the *Chronicle* if the existence of the *gens*, and its membership, is either not acknowledged or assumed. The increasing tendency in Falco to discuss individuals on the basis of their personal merits suggests that, largely speaking, ethnic membership is being assumed, but this of course raises the questions of who is being considered to be a member of which grouping, and why. Also, one must also deal with the observed changes in Falco's attitudes to various people throughout his work, which are to a certain extent suggestive of the attitude towards their particular *gens*.

It is evident from his earlier entries that Falco had no particular liking for these *Normanni*, especially not when turning their eyes towards Benevento. The same approach is taken to Roger in the later entries, which show Falco's gradually increasing dislike of him once he had been crowned by Anacletus. Falco, for example, refers to Roger's 'devastation' of Apulia, 'with fire and sword', noting that 'the king behaved towards Christians in a way that had never been heard of in this century'.[53] Roger was a 'wicked king', 'of execrable reputation' who, upon the death of his

[48] Falco, 4–5.
[49] *Ibid.*, 5–8.
[50] *Ibid.*, 15.
[51] *Ibid.*, 127.
[52] Loud, 'Genesis', 188–9.
[53] Falco, 97.

enemy Rainulf 'was filled with vanity and pride and rejoiced more than seemed humanly possible'.[54] And these are only Falco's own opinions as expressed within the main text; the denunciations in those speeches attributed to such as Robert of Capua are even more powerful. Robert says of Roger:

> He greedily desires to plunder all powerful men of their riches, and if they should resist him then he overthrows them and without a trace of compassion reduces their glory to dust. What an evil man, and most worthy of death! He thirsts thus to consume all our glory, to unsheathe his sword and unmercifully expose us all to the peril of death.[55]

Falco even has Roger condemn himself from his own mouth:

> 'I do not want', he said, 'honours of this sort, but if life is granted to me, I shall destroy everything and exile everyone.'[56]

The emphasis here is clearly on Roger's destructiveness and barbaric nature, and these are similar to those aspects criticised in the Normans who, like Roger, directly threatened Benevento and, indeed, Apulia as a whole with violence and conquest. Like the Normans, Roger bears fundamental character flaws, exhibiting the sins of vanity and pride, akin to the Normans' envy and hatred, and thus appears to the reader as a dreadful scourge and tyrant. To Falco, Roger seems to lack even a single good quality once he has become king, remaining up until this event a relatively indistinct figure in the *Chronicle*. Given Roger's Norman descent, and the obvious commonalities in Falco's perception of Roger and the *Normanni*, it is therefore rather surprising that Falco never calls Roger a Norman. Had the Normans, in Falco's (and, most likely, Lombard) eyes ceased to exist as a definable *gens*?

To an extent, Falco's treatment of the heroes of the piece suggests not. Those figures who rebelled against the Rogerian regime, such as Robert of Capua, Rainulf of Alife and Tancred of Conversano, are portrayed by Falco as a sturdy bulwark against Roger's evils. From the point at which Robert and Rainulf are set against Roger (who is, at this point, only a count) by the pope's persuasion, they gradually become more heroic figures in the eyes of Falco, joined later by Tancred.[57] Robert was the speaker who denounced Roger so 'wisely and carefully'; Tancred was 'a man both prudent and high-spirited', 'warlike and energetic', who 'manfully and bravely resisted the king and his army' and for whom Roger 'held a mortal hatred'.[58] But it is Rainulf who receives the most praise, perhaps in his role as the most successful of Roger's enemies. When Roger took his wife and son away from him, Rainulf 'sallied forth with a joyous and intrepid heart, desiring to suffer death before disinheritance and exile in foreign and unknown parts'; he appears as 'a man both prudent and discreet', the 'most warlike and magnanimous of men'.[59] Not only this, but Rainulf is obviously an excellent military leader and warrior, leading his men to victory against Roger's forces on numerous occasions; on his death 'almost the whole of Italy incessantly recounted his probity and his battles'.[60]

What is most notable in all these men, however, is that their bearing and military

---

54 *Ibid.*, 105; 138–9.   57 *Ibid.*, 64, 76.
55 *Ibid.*, 79–80.   58 *Ibid.*, 79, 76, 97, 90.
56 *Ibid.*, 99.   59 *Ibid.*, 78, 121, 138.
60 *Ibid.*, 138. For some of Rainulf's victories, see 84–5, 88, 94, 128–9.

skill are reminiscent of those elements expressed by members of the Norman *ethnie* – the components of *Normanitas*. Yet, once again, we see Falco portraying people who act in an arguably Norman way, but not referring to them as Normans, even though they have a clear connection with the Norman immigrants of the previous century (as do Alexander of Telese's descriptions of the same people). Roger's rapaciousness and Rainulf's military skill and courage are suggestive of descriptions of Normans in eleventh-century works, and notably these specific distinctions were mostly made *only* of Normans in these works. As noted above, it cannot be assumed that the persistence of these elements signifies the presence of a particular ethnicity, but the possibility is worthy of consideration.[61] Certainly, it seems likely that these recognitions are in some way related to *Normanitas*, and it is therefore important to address the question of why Falco does not use the Norman ethnonym to describe these men.

It seems that there are three potential answers to this question. The first is that Falco is praising the heroes of his work in a way that conforms to an aristocratic archetype; this would be a development on the culture introduced into the upper social leve s by the Norman immigration and conquest. The recognition is therefore one of the same good qualities as those appearing in the eleventh-century *gens Normannorum*, but these qualities have ceased to maintain a conceptual connection with that particular *gens*. Given Alexander's equivalent lack of use of the Norman ethnonym, this is initially quite a compelling consideration, but Falco's early usage of the name and its appearance in the forged privilege suggest otherwise. That 'Norman' can appear as an undefined term in the early part of Falco's work and can also be used with meaning in a document as important and formal as a privilege suggests that the concept of the 'Norman' was still very much alive in Apulia and Sicily. Whether the trappings of this concept were positive or negative, one would therefore still expect it to be applicable to one or other of the sides in the *Chronicle*.

The lack of usage thus suggests one of two other (and mutually compatible) explanations. It is possible that Falco recognised the leadership on both sides as 'Norman' to a greater or lesser extent, creating a situation where either praise or criticism of an ethnic nature was firmly invalid. He did not wish to insult the potential liberators of Benevento in his great work, and neither did he wish to dignify a man who he despised above all others. The fact that he uses 'Norman' in such a negative way earlier in his work may also suggest that he saw Roger's enemies as Normans to a greater extent than Roger, once again invalidating Norman as a descriptive term in the latter part of his *Chronicle*. The nature of the earlier passages quite effectively defines 'Norman' as a watchword for a cruel and predatory people, a description more fitting of Roger than of Rainulf, though Rainulf can be seen elsewhere (i.e. in Alexander) to possess more 'Norman' attributes than Roger himself. Certainly, those military skills that distinguish the heroes of Falco's work are equally present in Alexander's *Deeds of King Roger*.

The uncertainty here is of course exacerbated by the changing treatment of the main figures in the *Chronicle* as it progresses – Roger is not, at the outset, the terrible villain that he becomes, and neither are Rainulf and Robert men with entirely unblemished backgrounds (they are seen, for example, to be staunch supporters of

---

[61] Above, p. 84; Amory, *People and Identity*, 17.

the anti-pope Anacletus).[62] The staged construction of the work suggested by Graham Loud goes some way towards explaining the transformation in Falco's approach to the 'Normans'. Loud proposes that the information for the years up to 1122 was compiled *c.*1122, with the entries for 1123–5 being written *c.*1125/6; this accounts for the apparent loss of interest in Benevento's Norman neighbours (and the internal unrest in the province) after the peace of 1120. The entries for 1127–9 were then written before 1132, those for 1130–1 in 1132 or 1133, after which Falco wrote virtually contemporaneously until his exile in 1134; he recommenced writing in 1137, either writing of events as they occurred in the later years, or in one operation in the early 1140s.[63]

What all this evidence suggests is that Falco's primary motivation, when writing about these men who may or may not have been Normans, was to praise his allies and criticise his enemies, as one would expect. As the sides gradually polarised in the years leading up to and after Roger's coronation as king, Falco seems to become more and more definite about the good and bad qualities of the men about whom he was writing. The fact that the terms of praise / abuse conform to the perceptions of Normans in the previous century suggest that these maintain a connection of at least some kind with the internal / external perceptions of *Normanitas* handed down from the previous generation; this, in turn, suggests at least that the concepts that were evident within *Normanitas* were still alive. His use of the term 'Norman' in his work equally suggests that the concept of the *gens Normannorum* remained, even if this was only as a watchword for those who preyed upon their neighbours. Whether he viewed the two as connected ideas, or the major players in the Rogerian rebellions as Normans or not is mostly opaque, though it does seem likely that he was aware of the Norman lineage of both sides and chose, therefore, to omit the term from his narrative.

Papal Perceptions

The final major source of evidence about the Normans in southern Italy and Sicily in this period is the papacy. While we have some amount of earlier evidence of the generally negative perceptions of the Normans held by the papacy, the period most readily studied is that of the pontificates of Leo IX (1049–54) and Gregory VII (1073–85). From this period we have access to a number of letters and acts from Leo and Gregory to a variety of recipients, as well as the works of Wibert of Toul, who wrote a life of Leo IX, and of Bonizo of Sutri and Bruno of Segni, who provide additional evidence of papal feelings about the Normans at the time of Gregory VII (they were both imprisoned in 1082 for their close associations with Gregory).[64] With this evidence at our disposal, an attempt can be made to examine the papal perceptions of the *gens Normannorum*, at least from the eleventh century, and how these differed from the Norman perceptions of themselves expressed by *Normanitas*.

Firstly, unlike in the Greek and later Lombard sources, there is no uncertainty

---

[62] Falco, 75.
[63] Loud, 'Genesis', 190–1.
[64] Wolf, *Making History*, 55.

here as to who the Normans were. The name *Normanni* is used consistently throughout all these sources without fail, evidencing a firm perception that this was one unified and clearly defined *gens* with common characteristics, and this testifies to the regularity and importance of Norman interaction with the papacy in this period: Leo, Gregory and their supporters knew *exactly* who they were talking about. What is therefore surprising is that these writers have so little to say about the *gens Normannorum*; certainly, they express very few either positive or negative opinions about them. While this is understandable to some extent in terms of the wider considerations of the papacy, Leo and Wibert only make one or two observations about the nature of the Normans, and Gregory and his associates make even fewer.

Until the Battle of Civitate (1053) in fact, Leo really does not refer to the Normans at all. His famous letter of January 1054, written from captivity to the Byzantine Emperor Constantine IX Monomachus, is, however, full of negative images of the Normans. He refers to them as 'an undisciplined and strange *gens* with incredible and unheard-of anger', who rose up with 'more impiety than the pagans', attacking the Church, torturing Christians, and committing a variety of atrocities.[65] Yet this letter stands in isolation as his sole judgement on the Normans. His biographer, Wibert, recounts exactly the same description with the alteration of only a few words; however, a few paragraphs later, Wibert makes reference to the Normans both as the 'most evil' *gens* and the 'most warlike' one.[66] It certainly seems rather unusual that it required a direct attack to stir the pope to express an opinion on the *gens Normannorum*, which had been active in the area for some thirty-five years by this point.

The general descriptions of the *Normanni* from the pontificate of Gregory VII are even less critical. Only Bruno, in his single reference to the Normans concerning the Battle of Civitate, is overtly negative. Bonizo contents himself with a reference to the Normans' military strength, calling them the '*Normannorum fortissima gens*', and Gregory himself even speaks positively of them, saying 'I refute [the accusation] that those amongst whom I live, namely the Romans, Lombards and Normans, are, as I often tell them, worse in a way than the Jews and pagans'.[67] However, Bruno's *Libellus de Symoniacis* is clearly damning in his description of Norman behaviour in the time of Leo IX:

> When the blessed Pope Leo was at Rome and ruled the apostolic see in peace, many people came from the territory of Apulia with their eyes put out, noses cut off and hands and feet maimed, pitiably bewailing the cruelty of the Normans.[68]

---

[65] *Sancti Leonis IX, Romani Pontificis, Epistolæ et Decreta Pontificia, PL* 143, c. 778: '*indisciplinatam et alienam gentem incredibili et inaudita rabie, et plusquam pagana impietate*'.

[66] *Sancti Leonis Vita Auctore Wiberto æquali, PL* 143, c. 499; cc. 500–1: '*Pessima gens Normannorum*'; '*Ferocissima gens Normannorum*'.

[67] *Bonizonis episcopi Sutrini liber ad amicum*, ed. Ernest Dümmler, *MGH LL*, Tomus I (1891, repr. 1956), 589; *Das Register Gregors VII*, ed. Erich Caspar, *MGH ES*, 2 vols. (1920–3), I, 189: '*Eos autem, inter quos habito, Romanos videlicet Longobardos et Normannos, sicut sepe illis dico, Iudeis et paganis quodammodo peiores esse redarguo*'.

[68] *Brunonis episcopi Signini Libellus de Symoniacis*, ed. Ernest Sackur, *MGH LL*, Tomus II (1892), 550: '*Cum autem beatus Leo Romae esset et sedem apostolicam in pace rexisset multi ex Apuliae finibus veniebant, oculis effossis, naribus abscissis, manibus pedibusque truncatis, de Normannorum crudelitate miserabiliter conquerentes*'.

A few lines later comes the papal response, in which Leo 'ventured to humble the pride of that *gens*', by raising an army to do battle with the Normans.[69] Still, Bruno's portrait of the Normans here stands very much alone in the papal literature of this period, which is perhaps even more surprising than the relative silence of Leo's pontificate, if only because of Gregory's reputation for vitriol.

The lack of information in the papal sources quite obviously makes an examination of the papal view rather difficult. Clearly, when roused, the papacy could show a strong dislike of the Normans, and Bruno's observation that he wrote about Leo IX from his memories of what he had been told of this man by Gregory himself suggests that it was not only Leo who held these negative opinions of the Normans.[70] However, it is clear from the writings of such people as Desiderius and Falco that the condemnation of the Normans in local sources was not a particular novelty, and the apparent papal restraint can therefore hardly be justified on the basis that it would undermine their support in the peninsula. So how can this seeming silence be explained?

In the first instance, it would be relatively unexpected for the papacy, in general, to make ethnic comments, whether denunciations or not. The papacy was not an overtly ethnic force and, though it had some ethnic connections, the likelihood of papal identity being challenged on ethnic grounds was minimal. On matters that fell within the religious ambit, the papacy might be expected to be more active, and there is extensive historical evidence of the pope acting on a religious level against both individuals – through the medium of excommunication, for example – and ethnic groups who violated the norms of religious behaviour, through paganism and so on. However, the Normans were firmly and even overtly Christian, and while the pope may have had direct and negative dealings with the Norman leadership, it took a direct assault by the *gens Normannorum* as a group to define them as a threat to the papacy in ethnic terms.

Furthermore, it is likely that an element of diplomacy conditioned this restraint. The papal evidence that we possess is closely contemporary, and was produced during the period of Norman expansion and conquest in southern Italy. It is therefore entirely possible that the pope remained largely silent about the Normans because there was always the possibility of the creation of some kind of amicable peace, for which the pope undoubtedly hoped; the existence of a hostile military force in the immediate vicinity of Rome cannot have been a welcome prospect, and the danger of the Normans choosing to support the non-reformers in Rome was very real.

This would go some way towards explaining Leo's sudden outburst, which occurs only *after* the Normans have committed an essentially unthinkable act. For Gregory VII, it was equally unwise to be scathing about the Normans. While his dealings with Robert Guiscard were rather tempestuous, he was often able to rely on the support, explicit or otherwise, of those Normans based at Aversa; negative judgements of the Norman gens as a whole were hardly wise in such circumstances. Additionally, because of the status of the pope as an international figure, any clear statement of his like or dislike of the *gens Normannorum* held repercussions for his dealings with the northern Normans, both in Normandy and in England.

---

[69] *Ibid.*, 550: '*illius gentis superbiam conaretur humiliare*'.
[70] *Ibid.*, 548.

The External Identity

It is quite evident, then, that there is no simple answer to the question of Norman external identity in southern Italy and Sicily. Whether our sources disagree about the good and bad qualities of the Normans or fail to either define or, in some cases, even mention the Normans, there is no general consensus on the external view of *Normanitas*. Perhaps because of the lack of solidarity among (and numbers of) the Normans in the area, many judgements that apply (or seem to apply) to the *gens Normannorum* are made on the basis of the Normans playing a role that was particularly favoured or disliked by a specific writer or group.

To the Greeks, the Normans were useful mercenaries, with admirable military skills; however, they also played the role of the invader, first of the Byzantine possessions in Italy, and later in the Empire itself. For the Lombards, the Normans were often threatening, in their roles as mercenaries, raiders and conquerors; later, the lack of unity in the Norman camp made even the use of the term 'Norman' a rather futile exercise. Finally, to the eleventh-century reform popes, the Normans were potential allies, who were capable of providing an immense amount of protection against the anger of the emperor; their capacity for unconscionable acts, though, rendered them dangerous and untrustworthy.

What we are left with is a *gens* who were not always judged for what they were, and certainly rarely seen in the way that they saw themselves. Evidently, the cultural and behavioural traits that, for the Normans, characterised the *gens Normannorum* were not being validated by these external groups. The Normans often became the subject of changing views, in part because they were generally at war with someone, which would cause alienation in some areas and favour in others, as the identities of the peoples with whom they interacted were challenged and responded. Thus the Normans could be viewed negatively by the monastery of Montecassino one moment, and as firm friends and allies the next.

The consistency in the external views lies not in the fact of positive and negative opinions and perceptions, but in the largely unchanged subject of these things. When they were praised by their adherents, the Normans were generally regaled for their military prowess and knightly virtues; when criticised, they were rapacious, cruel and greedy. That these praises and curses remained largely the same throughout our period suggests that they were attributes that were observable in this *gens* to a greater or lesser extent; there is, for example, no praise of the 'great Norman thinkers', but one would hardly expect there to be in a race 'chosen for conquest'. It speaks highly of the Norman ethnic construct, however, that one of its two most notable features from an external perspective was ego-recognised as well as alter-ascribed. Within common memory, the attributes of the Normans were certainly polarised around these two specific conceptual sets, such that Anna Comena could refer to her brother-in-law as as skilled a horseman as a native of Normandy, and yet Desiderius could employ an unnamed Norman villain in a miracle story without compromising its acceptability. The Normans in southern Italy were, to their neighbours, either great warriors or evil butchers; the choice was simply dependent upon whom they happened to be attacking that week.

PART III

England and Normandy after 1066

7

Sources, 1066–1154

In the preceding chapters, the focus has been on Norman identity at the time of the conquests and settlements in France and in Italy and Sicily. It is easier to examine a conflicted identity than a neutral one, and thus far the study has proceeded on that basis. However, of all the areas this book covers, the period from 1066 to 1154 in England and Normandy is the best documented. The narrative material is plentiful, and there is no period of time for which we do not have at least one narrative history; but while this provides an ideal basis for the study of the development of an identity, it also poses problems.

The very nature of the histories produced during this period means that it rapidly becomes difficult to classify particular works as either 'internal' or 'external' productions. Furthermore, the sheer volume of material means that there is neither time nor space to provide full coverage of all the historical works available, and some amount of discretion has had to be exercised regarding the selection of material presented. The amount of space devoted to 'clearly external' works has been strictly limited, and this chapter will focus in the main on a sample of the works connected more directly with the Normans and English, in the hope of obtaining some understanding of what the *gens Normannorum* had now become. Again owing to limitations of space, the perceptions of ethnicity in England after 1066 are the primary consideration in the following pages; it has proven necessary to put Normandy to one side to an extent. The sources have been thus been set within a purely chronological framework, which allows us to study the continued evolution of the 'Norman', or perhaps 'English', identity.

In the years surrounding the Battle of Hastings of 1066, and the Norman conquest of England, the sources are easily subdivided. The sources we have were written either in England or in Normandy, and therefore maintain a (logical) affiliation to one of the two identities that were in close conflict for the following century. In England, the *Anglo-Saxon Chronicle* runs throughout the whole period, and provides a good deal of information for an external perception of the Normans, from the viewpoint of the conquered and of English speakers. Of three relevant versions of the *Chronicle* (C, D and E), C and D terminate around the time of the conquest (C in 1066, D in 1079) and thus mark themselves as clearly 'external' sources, whereas the E chronicle runs until 1154, giving a good overview of evolving identity trends; this does, however, place it among those sources that cannot reasonably be classified as 'internal' or 'external' views.

Other sources produced in England around the time of the conquest include the *Encomium Emmae Reginae* and the *Vita Ædwardi Regis*. Both the work of anonymous writers (and, arguably, Flemish monks), these are part of the ongoing tradition of panegyric writing throughout the medieval period.[1] The *Encomium* was commissioned by Emma herself and written during the reign of Harthacnut (1040–2), after the return of Edward to England in 1041.[2] It is markedly similar in style and method to Dudo of St-Quentin's *Historia Normannorum*; so much so, in fact, that it has been proposed that Emma may have recommended Dudo's work to the encomiast as a model, and that the *Encomium* echoes something of the 'Norman self-image' that Dudo portrays.[3] Whatever the case, the *Encomium* contains a wealth of anecdotal material, seemingly carefully selected by the author.

The *Vita Ædwardi* is of a different style, yet still clearly the work of a foreigner. Again, though, this is not considered an indictment against the source; on the contrary, it is seen as a fact that supports the writer's honesty and truthfulness.[4] The dating of the *Vita Ædwardi* is slightly more troublesome than that of the *Encomium*. Marc Bloch argued that it was written at Wilton 1103×1120; however, the extant manuscript is datable to *c*.1100, and book I was used by Sulcard of Westminster before 1084–5. Based on the contents of the text, it seems probable that it was written during the lifetime of Queen Edith (d.1075), before the deposition of Archbishop Stigand (1070), giving a 'confident' dating of 1065–6 for book I, and 1067 for book II.[5]

From a Norman perspective, the works of this period are on similar subjects, though great importance is (naturally) placed upon the conquest of England. For the conquest period, we have access to three major works that present a pro-Norman viewpoint: the *Gesta Normannorum Ducum* of William of Jumièges, the *Gesta Guillelmi* of William of Poitiers and the *Carmen de Hastingae Proelio*.

William of Jumièges, whom we have previously encountered, had originally finished his work shortly before 1060, and yet he saw the conquest as significant enough to prompt the addition of eight new chapters to his *Gesta Normannorum Ducum*; he seems to have completed these additions in early 1070, making some minor revisions to other parts of book vii at the same time.[6]

William's work is, as previously observed, in the Norman tradition of leadership-focused history, and that of his contemporary, William of Poitiers, is no less so. Born *c*.1020 and hailing (according to Orderic Vitalis) from Préaux, William was probably the Conqueror's chaplain and therefore well sourced for the writing of his duke's biography.[7] Outside limits of 1071 and 1077 have been suggested for the bulk

---

[1]   The evidence suggests that the *Vita Ædwardi* was written by either a Lotharingian or a Fleming, and Frank Barlow felt that a case could be made for either Goscelin or Folcard, both Flemish monks of St-Bertin, who came to England in *c*.1058 and before 1069 (and probably before 1066) respectively (see *Vita Ædwardi*, xliv–xlv & lix). Neither case is completely convincing, unfortunately, leaving the authorship in doubt. As for the *EER*, there are 'no obvious or decisive clues as to the author's location' (see Simon Keynes in *EER*, xxxix, n. 8). He appears to have been an inmate of either St-Omer or St-Bertin (*EER*, ci & ciii) and, based on the illustration on the frontspiece of the surviving eleventh-century manuscript, Keynes observes 'the likelihood must be that he was a monk' (Keynes in *EER*, xxxix).

[2]   Keynes in *EER*, xxxix; Pauline Stafford, *Queen Emma and Queen Edith* (Oxford, 1997), 28.

[3]   Keynes in *EER*, civ; Stafford, *Queen Emma*, 34.

[4]   *Vita Ædwardi*, lxi.

[5]   *Ibid.*, xxv–xxvii, xxx–xxxii; see also Stafford, *Queen Emma*, 41.

[6]   *GND* I, xxxv.

[7]   *GG*, xv.

of the writing, the terminal date based on the author's writing of Hugh, bishop of Lisieux, as if he were still alive (d. 17 July 1077) and perhaps of the dedication of St-Étienne-de-Caen as already having occurred (13 September 1077).[8] Unfortunately, the work was never completed, and this problem is exacerbated by the state of the extant manuscript, which is missing both the beginning and end, leaving Orderic to provide us with our only information about the author and his purpose.[9]

The author of the *Carmen de Hastingae Proelio* is less readily identifiable than those of the *Gesta Normannorum Ducum* and *Gesta Guillelmi*, however. For a long time, it has generally been assumed to be the work of Guy, bishop of Amiens from 1058 to 1075, and there are good grounds for this accreditation.[10] Orderic Vitalis, for example, mentions that Guy wrote a poem on the 'battle of Senlac', and the style certainly fits Guy's background well. Additionally, the abbreviated greeting in the second line of the prologue, '*L. W. salutat*', can be (and is generally) read as '*Lanfrancum Wido salutat*'.[11] The author's apparent interest in the French contribution to the duke's army supports this, as he probably hailed from northern France; notably, all the heroes of the poem bar William are French.[12] Based on this authorship, the work was dated to the years shortly after the conquest, though there was some doubt as to exactly when it was produced. Catherine Morton and Hope Muntz saw the work as a rush job, possibly intended for the Easter celebrations of 1067, but with a *terminus ad quem* of 1072.[13]

However, following R.H.C. Davis' paper of 1978, in which he suggested that the work was a much later production, being a literary exercise produced in a northern French / southern Flemish school between 1125 and 1135/40, some reassessment was necessary.[14] The resultant debate at the Battle Conference was informative though inconclusive, and L.J. Engels' response to Davis' paper illustrated quite clearly that much work was still required to clarify the issues of authorship and dating; both papers served to highlight a number of discrepancies on both sides of the argument.[15]

More recently (1999), Frank Barlow has provided an up-to-date and compelling argument, placing the composition of the *Carmen* within a narrow period and proposing a start date of early 1067, possibly inspired by the triumphant return of the Conqueror around 21 February of that year – certainly, it was not begun before the return to the continent of the participants from Hastings and the coronation at Westminster (25 December 1066). He further suggests a rough end date of summer 1070 (Lanfranc's elevation to Canterbury), or perhaps as early as May 1068 if Orderic is correct when he says that the poem was already written when Guy ministered to Queen Matilda at her coronation (Whitsun, 1068).[16] Guy's piece is focused

---

8   *Ibid.*, xx; R. Allen Brown, *The Norman Conquest of England* (London, 1984), 15–16.

9   *GG*, xv.

10   *Carmen* (2), xv.

11   *Carmen* (1), xvii & xxv.

12   *Ibid.*, xxiv–xxv.

13   *Carmen* (2), xxi & lxx.

14   R.H.C. Davis, 'The Carmen de Hastingae Proelio', *EHR* 93 (1978), 261.

15   R.H.C. Davis, L.J. Engels et al., 'The *Carmen de Hastingae Proelio*: a discussion', *ANS* 2 (1980), 1–20.

16   *Carmen* (1), xl.

entirely on the Battle of Hastings and the events immediately surrounding it, and the fact that it was written so soon after the battle makes the information it provides extremely useful, though Guy's loyalties make it occasionally a little suspect.

From this point on, though, it becomes increasingly more difficult to badge a given source as 'internal' or 'external'. For the latter part of the eleventh and very early twelfth century, when Baudri, abbot of Bourgeuil and later bishop of Dol, wrote the majority of his *Carmina* (during his abbacy of 1079–1107; his famous *Adelae Comitissae* dates from *c.*1102), and Eadmer of Canterbury his *Historia Novorum in Anglia* (probably commencing the 1090s, and completed in 1122), it would be unreasonable to name sources arbitrarily pro-Norman or -English on the basis of their place of composition, or on the perceived 'racial' affiliation of their author.[17] Both were ranking members of the Church hierarchy, though of different 'racial' origin, and this element of unity muddies the water of their identification with either *gens* from the perspective of any simple, surface examination.

The same difficulty applies to John of Worcester's *Chronicon ex Chronicis*. Though it was originally regarded merely as the continuation of Florence of Worcester's work (d. 1118), Orderic Vitalis implies that the *Chronicle* was compiled by John alone. The work was begun at Worcester on the order of Bishop Wulfstan II, who died in 1095, and for the earlier period seems to draw heavily on a version of the *Anglo-Saxon Chronicle* that was similar to D, but is probably now lost.[18] However, there is no sign that the *Chronicle* was written year by year, and it is possible that the entries for 1128–40 were written 1140×1143.[19]

Once we enter the twelfth century, this difficulty is even more pronounced, undoubtedly the result of a new generation of writers who did not have the experience of a separate England and Normandy within their memories, and who therefore wrote within a newer framework. Of these twelfth-century authors, the first to appear is Orderic Vitalis, who was born in 1075, schooled in Shrewsbury from 1080, and was sent to St-Évroult in Normandy in 1085. The son of father who was 'of Orléans', and an English mother, he became involved in the writing of the *Annals of St-Évroult* from 1095, and it seems to be around this date that he also commenced his interpolations in the *Gesta Normannorum Ducum*.[20] The last datable section of this work suggests an end date of *c.*1113 – he refers to the length of office of Matilda, abbess of Ste-Trinité (Caen) as 47 or 48 years, presumably from the dedication of the

---

[17]   For Baudri: *Les Œuvres Poétiques de Baudri de Bourgeuil (1046–1130)*, ed. Phyllis Abrahams (1926), xxii; Shirley Ann Brown and Michael W. Herren, 'The *Adelae Comitissae* of Baudri of Bourgeuil and the Bayeux Tapestry', *ANS* 16 (1994), 56. Baudri became bishop of Dol in 1107, having previously failed as a candidate for the bishopric of Orléans in 1096. Shirley Ann Brown, *The Bayeux Tapestry: History and Bibliography* (Woodbridge, 1988) gives the date of *Adelae Comitissae* (1 & 29). For Eadmer: *The Chronicle of John of Worcester*, ed. R.R. Darlington and P. McGurk, OMT (Oxford, 1995), vol. 2, lxxii. Eadmer appears to have initially completed his work *c.* 1115, but then taken it up again in 1119 (R.W. Southern, *Saint Anselm and his Biographer* (Cambridge, 1963), 298–9).

[18]   Brown, *Norman Conquest*, 52.

[19]   *John of Worcester*, ed. Darlington and McGurk, lxix.

[20]   Orderic's father was called Odelerius of Orléans, a name that 'indicates that he was either born or educated at Orléans. He may have been French by birth; but in the mid-eleventh century, when the Norman schools had not yet grown in learning and reputation, most Normans went to schools in France for anything more than the rudiments of learning' (Marjorie Chibnall, *The World of Orderic Vitalis* (Oxford, 1984), p. 8). For his work on the *GND*, see Orderic, vol. I, 2–6, 29; *GND* I, lxviii.

monastery in 1066. However, earlier sections suggest that the main part of the redaction was complete by 1109, the year in which St Anselm died (whom Orderic mentions as still living in book vii); these revisions included two new chapters dealing with the exploits of the Normans in southern Italy.[21] We have no idea of his motivation for producing this redaction, however.

Orderic's additions to the *Gesta Normannorum Ducum* are not the only relevant sections of his work, though. His *Historia Æcclesiastica*, written at the request of Abbot Robert of Le Sap (1091–1123), initially focuses on the cloister, before suddenly embarking upon an account of the conquest of England; from this point, it appears that Orderic was writing a much wider work than his title suggests – both a church history, and a history of the Normans.[22] He seems to have begun work on the *Historia* by 1114 (probably after his revision of the *Gesta Normannorum Ducum*), commencing with earliest chapters of book III, although this was not completed until 1123 or 1124. The majority of the work was written between 1123 and 1137, and was finally completed in 1141.[23] Both his redaction of the *Gesta Normannorum Ducum* and his *Historia Æcclesiastica* provide a great deal of information about Normandy and England in the first half of the twelfth century.

In this, Orderic is ably supported by his contemporary, William of Malmesbury. William's three major works, the *Gesta Regum Anglorum*, *Gesta Pontificum Anglorum* and *Historia Novella*, are all invaluable for the study of England and Normandy in this period. William, like Orderic, was a Benedictine monk, and was probably librarian at the monastery of Malmesbury in England.[24] His life and work have been much discussed by historians and have seen many differences of interpretation. He is usually considered to have been born *c.*1095, though it has been noted that a date of *c.*1090 would seem preferable.[25]

His *Gesta Regum* was first taken up at the invitation of Matilda, Henry I's queen, who died in 1118; he appears to have worked in the Canterbury archives between 1115 and 1120 collecting material for both this and his *Gesta Pontificum*.[26] William also used a wide range of other sources, notably Eadmer's *Historia Novorum*, which provided his information for much of book V of the *Gesta Regum*.[27] Both *gesta* works appear to have seen their first completion in 1125, and were then subsequently revised; two further editions of the *Gesta Regum* appeared after 1134, and the *Gesta Pontificum* saw revision until *c.*1140.[28] The *Historia Novella* was commissioned by Robert, earl of Gloucester and written between October 1140 and early 1143, ending with the escape of the empress from the siege of Oxford of December 1142.[29] A number of other works are attributed to William, such as his *Vita Wulfstani*, all from the 1120s and 1130s.[30]

---

[21] *GND* I, lxviii, lxxi.

[22] Orderic, vol. I, 58; vol. II, xvi.

[23] *Ibid.*, I, 31–2, 112.

[24] Rodney Thomson, *William of Malmesbury* (Woodbridge, 1987), 3.

[25] *Ibid.*, p. 2. William of Malmesbury, *Historia Novella*, ed. Edmund King, tr. K.R. Potter, OMT (Oxford, 1998), xviii; *GRA*, vol. 2, xxxvi, n. 41.

[26] *Historia Novella*, xviii.

[27] *Ibid.*, xxiv.

[28] Thomson, *William*, pp. 4–5; *Historia Novella*, xxii.

[29] *Historia Novella*, xxix–xxxiii.

[30] For a full bibliography of William's work, see Thomson, *William*, 3–5 and *GRA*, vol. 2, xlvi–xlvii.

One other source from this period that must be mentioned is the so-called 'Hyde Chronicle'.[31] Written between 1128 and 1134, the chronicle recounts the history of the Norman dukes from 1035 to 1120, though in a comparatively abridged format (only 39 pages of printed text).[32] The author is unidentifiable, however, and his ethnicity is presumed, through his comment that *Sudsexia* was a name 'in their language', to be Norman or Anglo-Norman.[33] It seems clear that the author was attached to the Warenne family, from the attention shown to the earls of Surrey and the area around Mortemer. This has influenced the belief that he may have been a monk at St Pancras, Lewes (a Warenne foundation).[34] However, John Gillingham has pointed out that the latter part of the chronicle, dealing with the author's own time, focuses more and more on France, and is suggestive of an author writing in Normandy, not England.[35]

And thus we come to those writers who take us up to the end of our chosen period. Henry, archdeacon of Huntingdon, possibly the most significant of these, appears to have written only a single work, his *Historia Anglorum*. Commissioned by Alexander, bishop of Lincoln, Henry began writing some time after April 1123. The *Historia Anglorum* evolved through six versions, with endings at 1129 (versions 1 and 2), 1138 (version 3), 1146 (version 4), 1149 (version 5) and 1154 (version 6). Version 1 was not finished until after October 1131, with the copy on which version 2 was based not seeing completion until after March 1133. Version 3 was written in or after 1140, and version 4 includes a list of clergy (added to *De contemptu mundi*) datable to between 1146 and May 1147.[36] The last chapters, especially from 1151, chapter 31, were written after the Treaty of Westminster of December 1153, and we can conclude that Henry completed his work between this date and the accession of Henry II a year later. He eventually died between 1156 and 1164.[37]

During the time in which Henry of Huntingdon wrote, various other authors set quill to parchment: notable among these were Geoffrey of Monmouth, Geffrei Gaimar, Robert of Torigni and Richard, prior of Hexham. Geoffrey was probably born in Monmouth (hence the epithet), and likely a teacher (*magister*) at the college of St George's, Oxford. His famous *History of the Kings of Britain* was completed in 1136 (his death occurring much later, *c*.1155), around the same time that Gaimar embarked upon the production of his great *Lestorie des Engles*, composed 1135×1147.[38] It seems evident from his frequent mistranslations of the *Anglo-Saxon Chronicle* that Geffrei was not of English descent, and the likelihood is that he was Norman-born.[39] Robert de Torigni's redaction of the *Gesta Normannorum Ducum*

[31] 'Chronicon Monasterii de Hida iuxta Wintoniam', in *LMH*, 284–321.

[32] C.P. Lewis, citing Elisabeth van Houts' tentative dating, 'The Earldom of Surrey and the Date of Domesday Book', *Historical Research* 63 (1990), 330–1 & n. 12.

[33] *Ibid.*, 332; *LMH*, 288.

[34] John Gillingham, 'Henry of Huntingdon and the Twelfth-Century Revival of the English Nation', *Concepts of National Identity in the Middle Ages*, ed. Simon Forde, Lesley Johnson and Alan V. Murray, Leeds Texts and Monographs, New Series 14 (Leeds, 1995), 90; Lewis, 'Domesday Book', 332.

[35] Gillingham, 'Revival', p. 91.

[36] Huntingdon, lxvi–lxvii, lxx, lxxv.

[37] *Ibid.*, lxvii & lxxvi.

[38] Dates for Geoffrey from Geoffrey of Monmouth, *The History of the Kings of Britain*, tr. Lewis Thorpe (Harmondsworth, 1966), 13.

[39] Gaimar, vol. 2, ix–x.

appeared around this time also, with the last datable passage being written between January 1138 and July 1139, though he did make corrections to his work as late as 1159; Richard of Hexham is his contemporary, writing c.1140.

Furthermore, this was a period during which significant sections of the *Liber Eliensis* were composed. Though the second book was not completed before 1154, and the third not before 1169, the first book is likely to have been written within the latter part of our period (begun after 1131, but enough before the commencement of book 2 to 'warrant an apology for the delay').[40] The first 49 chapters of the second book, additionally, are a version of an earlier work, the *Libellus quorundam insignium operum beati Æthelwoldi episcopi*, translated from a vernacular source between 1109 and 1131.[41] However, authorship of the *Liber Eliensis* is uncertain, though Richard, author of an *historia* about the litigation over Stetchworth, is considered a strong claimant.[42]

The last work to be examined brings the cycle full circle – another anonymous piece. The *Gesta Stephani* was written seemingly in two sections, the first twelve years c.1148, and the subsequent work during or shortly after 1153.[43] While the piece cannot be attributed to any author with certainty, evidence from the text suggests that he was from the West Country, and he shows a particular interest in Bath; this has led to the consideration that it was the work of Robert of Lewes, bishop of Bath from 1136 to 1166.[44] The *Gesta Stephani* tells of the life of the ill-fated King Stephen, whose reign occupies the closing years of the period 1066–1154.

In closing, it should be noted that the work of certain significant writers has been excluded from this study, in the main because the constraints of space force a very tight rein on those sources that cross the period boundaries. As already noted, only certain elements of the *Liber Eliensis* are considered, as the later sections were written after 1154. The same proves true of the majority of the work of Robert of Torigni. His update of the annals of Mont-St-Michel, while covering the years 1135–73 would not, one would imagine, have been undertaken before his election to the abbacy there in 1154 (from the position of claustral prior of Le Bec); his redaction of the *Gesta Normannorum Ducum* has already been mentioned. Even his continuation of the *World Chronicle* (318–1111) of Sigebert of Gembloux is extremely derivative until the entries for 1145 and beyond.[45]

Aelred of Rievaulx, again, wrote mostly during the last decade before his death, in 1167, while disabled by arthritis.[46] Certainly, he did not start writing historical works until 1153, and even then wrote with an eye to the future – the focus of his first work is on the future Henry II, as duke of Normandy, in order to extol his Englishness.[47] Though his writing includes many interesting perspectives, such as his

---

[40] *LE*, xlviii.

[41] *Ibid.*, ix.

[42] *Ibid.*, xlvii.

[43] *GS*, xx–xxi.

[44] *Ibid.*, xxvii & xxxiv.

[45] For Robert's works, see *GND* I, lxxvii–lxxix and *The Chronicle of Robert of Torigni*, ed. R. Howlett, *Chronicles of the Reigns of Stephen, Henry II, and Richard I*, vol. IV, RS (London, 1889), xvi, xviii, xxiv, xxx.

[46] *Aelredi Rievallensis Opera Omnia*, ed. A. Hoste and C.H. Talbot, Corpus Christianorum Continuatio Medievalis, I (Brepols, 1976), vi.

[47] Ann Williams, *The English and the Norman Conquest* (Woodbridge, 1995), 184. Antonia Gransden,

depiction of Henry as 'the corner-stone which bound together the two walls of the English and Norman race', the ramifications of such comments stretch far beyond 1154.[48]

Perhaps most unfortunately, the work of Gerald of Wales, though a major and 'highly innovative' contribution to ethnographic writing, has also to be set aside – the most significant passages date from 1188 and later, when the world of the 'Normans' was a rather different place.[49]

The following chapters will, therefore, investigate the identity of the Normans within the aforementioned constraints, studying the changes and transformations it underwent as it bore the rigours of yet another conquest.

Historical Writing in England c.550 to c.1307 (London, 1974) gives a probable date of 1155–7 for the *Relatio de Standardo*, which she calls Aelred's 'only historical work' (pp. 213–14).

[48] Walter Daniel, *The Life of Ailred of Rievaulx*, tr. Maurice Powicke (Oxford, 1950, repr. 1978), xlvii.

[49] For Gerald's ethnographic work, see Robert Bartlett, *Gerald of Wales, 1146–1223* (Oxford, 1982).

8

The Conquest of England

At the commencement of such an examination, it seems only reasonable to justify the choice of period under scrutiny. The start date, 1066, is almost self-justifying, so well-known is it within English history – that such an event as the Norman conquest can still shout out its importance almost a millennium later can only be the result of a deep-rooted presence in English culture. Certainly, the Battle of Hastings itself has been analysed, examined and studied to an unparalleled degree, and 1066 is one date known to perhaps every member of the English populace.

But 1154, it must be said, is rather less of a cultural landmark; so why this date and no other? The answer lies in part in the convenience of such a date in the context of Norman history, and in part in the significance of the events of this year in the history of *Normanitas*. As to convenience, the date marks not only the death of King Stephen of England, but also of King Roger of Sicily, whose reigns both represented transitional phases for the *gens Normannorum*. The significance of these deaths, in context of *Normanitas*, is clear when the strong emphasis placed on leadership by the Normans is recalled. In 1154, the capacity to call oneself Norman did not disappear – evidently not, in fact, when one considers that people in the twenty first century continue both to call themselves and be called Normans. Yet the changes in royal dynasties around this time were highly important: neither Roger nor Stephen were truly 'Norman' in the ways of their predecessors – Roger in no way reflected the Norman knight so easily seen in his father, and Stephen was of Blois, not Rouen. Their successors were even further removed from *Normanitas*, and those elements recognisable as Norman – Stephen was succeeded not by a Norman, but by a Plantagenet; Roger's successor can, quite reasonably, be called a 'Sicilian'.

Changes of such great importance do not negate those that came before, however. Between 1066 and 1154, the identity of the *gens Normannorum* was transformed significantly. In Italy, as we have seen, the two major turning points in the evolution of *Normanitas* were the 'conquest event', and the rise of the new generation of Italian-born 'Normans'. Back at home, in the duchy of Normandy itself, similar things were occurring – the conquest of England, following victory at Hastings in 1066, instigated many changes in the identity of the Normans, from both internal and external perspectives; they struggled to control their new acquisitions, much as their forefathers had struggled to hold Rouen in the early part of the tenth century. Also, in England and Normandy, as in Italy, the rise of a new generation in the early part of the twelfth century, of 'Normans' born often of mixed parentage, or simply in England, created a shift in the defining ideas of the *gens*. The purpose of the following chapters is to investigate these changes, to find out just how *Normanitas* changed during these times and, if possible, why it did so.

External Identity

Prior to the Norman invasion of England, there is little information in Anglo-centric sources to inform us as to the 'English' perception of the *gens Normannorum*. Having achieved seeming acceptance in France in the earlier part of the eleventh century, they had come to be viewed as militarily successful and pious in their own right, rather than the collection of uncultured barbarians they had been considered to be in earlier years.[1] In the context of French ethnic groups, the Normans had achieved some sort of equilibrium, and is it apparent from this that the other ethnicities in France had ceased to see the Normans as threatening: they were no more exciting, stupid, violent, etc. than any other French sub-group. The earlier 'English' sources certainly seem to bear this out, even though two of them (the *Encomium Emmae Reginae* and *Vita Ædwardi Regis*) were written by foreign (Flemish) authors. As with Dudo of St-Quentin's *Historia Normannorum*, these works cannot be dismissed on these grounds – the author had a readership and patron to please, and therefore the work is likely to reflect their views in the main and not his own. Indeed, as Frank Barlow notes:

> A foreigner composing under those conditions is very dependent on others. He can misunderstand and he can suppress; but he cannot, unless he is dishonest, pass off his own conjectures or embroideries for fact.[2]

Some element of trust must therefore be given to those views expressed in these two works.

The *Encomium Emmae Reginae* certainly contains subject matter worthy of note, in particular the author's use of names. He was writing to appeal to both Norman and English viewpoints: Emma herself was of Norman extraction, but symbolised 'Englishness' in England during a period of Danish rule.[3] The author's description of Emma's origins is revealing. He describes her as living 'within the bounds of Gaul, and to be precise in the Norman area' and comments that 'she derived her origin from a victorious people, who had appropriated for themselves part of Gaul, against the wishes of those of French descent and their prince'.[4] While this use of the idea of 'Gaul' as opposed to France may be simply an attempt to bring a classical quality to his work, this term seems also to provide an ideal balance between the two views that the author is trying to encompass. To the English, the term Gaul would be as comprehensible as 'France / Francia', though some of the significance of the distinction may have been lost; one might expect the English to interpret *Gallia* in a classical sense, as distinct from *Francia* (referring to those lands north of the Loire). From

---

[1]   See above, Chapter 3.
[2]   *Vita Ædwardi*, lxi.
[3]   Stafford, *Queen Emma*, 213; also, 251 for the development of perspectives of Emma over time.
[4]   *EER*, 32: '*In confinitate Galliae et praecipue in Normandensi regio*'; '*Erat oriunda ex uictrici gente, quæ sibi partem Galliæ uendicauerat inuitis Francigenis et eorum principe.*'

Emma's standpoint, however, distinctions of this sort would be much more important. The Normans are portrayed as inhabitants of Gaul and yet as a *gens* both distinct and separate from the French, also inhabitants of Gaul. They had 'appropriated' part of Gaul 'for themselves', and while Normandy was '*in confinitate Galliae*', it was not '*in confinitate Franciae*'.

The English element in the readership is more strongly represented a little later, when the author observes:

> Gaul rejoiced, the land of the English rejoiced likewise, when so great an ornament was conveyed over the seas. Gaul, I say, rejoiced to have brought forth so great a lady, and one worthy of so great a king, the country of the English indeed rejoiced to have received such a one into its towns.[5]

Such praise of the king would only be expected, yet there is no lack of worth depicted on either side; the standpoint is, again, clearly both pro-Norman *and* pro-English.

Within the *Vita Ædwardi Regis*, we encounter again this apparently neutral attitude towards the Normans; little comment is made upon them at all. The author notes that he was informed of Edward's miracles in Normandy by the '*Franci*', a term that associates the Normans with the other inhabitants of France, and Frank Barlow has suggested that these *Franci* 'may have considered healing a normal ornament of kingship'.[6] Certainly, healing powers were apparently manifested by Robert the Pious (996–1031), Philip I (1060–1108) and Louis VI (1108–37), though it is notable that parallel claims were never made for the Norman kings of England.[7] The English attitude towards such things comes across in the author's statement that 'this seems new and strange to us'.[8]

Yet, in the subsequent years, the English view of the Normans changed drastically. In the aftermath of Hastings, as the Normans subdued England and gradually took power, the 'native' view becomes increasingly negative, and this progression is most easily seen in the *Anglo-Saxon Chronicle*. The three versions that cover this time period, C, D and E, provide a very useful insight into the changes in identity structures within England. As the work of 'Englishmen', the *Chronicle* often takes a rather partisan line, and such expression provides precisely the sort of information that allows for the study of the identity of the *gens Normannorum* – the alter-ascribed structures that inform the ego-recognised beliefs. The fact that the three versions end at different points (and can, arguably, be seen as the work of different periods) provides even more information about the way in which the external viewpoint was changing and, in doing so, representing the changes within the society.

The earliest version of the *Chronicle*, C, terminates in 1066, and retains the neutrality that we have come to expect of the pre-conquest sources. The one notable mention of the Normans concerns the pending invasion: the chronicler tells us that Harold had been told that William from Normandy, 'King Edward's kinsman, meant to come here and subdue this country'.[9] This statement is, if anything, positive about the Normans, if only through the association of William with King Edward,

5   *Ibid.*, 33.
6   *Vita Ædwardi*, lxxii & n. 292; lxxii–lxxiii.
7   Frank Barlow, *The Feudal Kingdom of England, 1042–1216*, 4th edn (London, 1988), 236–7.
8   *Vita Ædwardi*, 94: '*Licet nobis nouum uideatur.*'
9   *ASC (C)*, 120: '*Eadwardes cingces mæg, wolde hider cuman ꞽ þis land gegan*'; *ASC (tr.)*, 141.

who the other pre-conquest sources praise highly. Not so version D, which ends in 1079 and has, for the same entry, 'William the Bastard', significantly more negative terminology.[10] As a whole, indeed, D is anti-Norman in a way that earlier sources are not. For the author of this version of the *Chronicle*, the Normans are French, and in no way deserve the neutrality accorded them to this point. The true enemy, however, appears to be William himself.

The first mention of the Normans and, more specifically, William in D refers to a visit to England prior to the conquest: 'Count William came from overseas with a great force of Frenchmen, and the king received him and as many of his companions as suited him, and let him go again'.[11] There is nothing particularly positive in this statement and, throughout, a certain disdain for the Normans is in evidence – the king's reception sounds ('and let him go again') to have been frosty, or so the chronicler would have us believe. The Normans are referred to as 'Frenchmen'; distinguishing the precise *gens* is clearly not the author's concern here.

The account of the Battle of Hastings a few entries later is in the same mould, with the chronicler recording that the Norman forces came upon Harold 'by surprise before his army was drawn up in battle array . . . there were heavy casualties on both sides. There King Harold was killed and Earl Leofwine his brother, and Earl Gyrth his brother, and many good men, and the French remained masters of the field.'[12] As one would expect in such a 'native' text, the record is of the noble English dead, with no praises for the Norman victors; indeed, the chronicler mentions the great losses on *both* sides, to show the valour of the English defence.

Yet it is the end of this entry that is perhaps of greatest import, the consideration that, as the text records, 'God granted it [victory] to them because of the sins of the people.'[13] For here, once again, we see the conquering Normans depicted as a scourge of God, His punishment for a wayward, sinful people. Strongly reminiscent of the early Frankish sources and their references to the *Normanni*, this reference shows quite clearly that the chronicler cannot understand why the Normans were victorious, and a punishment is his justification of the loss. This is not to say that he believed the Normans to be pagans – quite the contrary, one would imagine, from his comment that 'God *granted* it to them' – simply that God had taken the side of the Normans in battle, and from the later entries in D, that the Norman victory was considered a punishment was nowhere in doubt. As the chronicler comments, 'Bishop Odo and Earl William stayed behind and built castles far and wide throughout this country, and distressed the wretched folk, and always after that it grew much worse.'[14]

This negative depiction of both the Normans and their leader continues until D comes to an end. When Edgar Aetheling came to York with a force of Northumbrians, we see that 'King William came on them by surprise from the south

10   *ASC (D)*, 79: '*Wyllelm Bastard*'; *ASC (tr.)*, 141.

11   *ASC (D)*, 71: '*Com Willelm eorl fram geondan sæ mid mycclum werode frencisra manna, ⁊ se cyning hine underfeng, ⁊ swa feola his geferan swa him to onhagode, ⁊ let hine eft ongean*'; *ASC (tr.)*, 120–1.

12   *ASC (D)*, 80: '*Unwær, ær his folc gefylced wære . . . þær weard micel wæl geslægen on ægðre healfe*'; *ASC (tr.)*, 143.

13   *ASC (D)*, 80: '*Heom God uðe for folces synnon*'; *ASC (tr.)*, 143.

14   *ASC (D)*, 81: '*Oda biscop ⁊ Wyllelm eorl belifen her æfter ⁊ worhton castelas wide geond þas þeode, ⁊ earm folc swencte, ⁊ a syððan hit yflade swiðe*'; *ASC (tr.)*, 145.

with an overwhelming army and routed them, and killed those who could not escape, which was many hundreds of men, and ravaged the city, and made St Peter's minster an object of scorn, and ravaged and humiliated all the others.'[15] Even when the Danes joined with Edgar to retake York, 'before the shipmen got there the Frenchmen had burned the city, and has also thoroughly ravaged and burnt the holy minster of St Peter'. William's response to the attack was hardly more acceptable: 'he went northwards with all his army that he could collect, and utterly ravaged and laid waste that shire'.[16] And it was not only this treatment of the English that was worthy of condemnation; the Norman treatment of Breton traitors resulted in the verse lines:

> Some of them were blinded
> And some banished from the land
> And some were put to shame.
> Thus were the traitors to the king
> Brought low.[17]

Additionally, the chronicler is only too happy to highlight 'French' defeats, such as the storming of York, in which the Danes and Edgar's men razed the castle, killed many hundreds of 'Frenchmen' and took many others as prisoners.[18] When the Bretons held Dol in the face of Norman attack, 'King William went away and lost there both men and horses and incalculable treasure.'[19] Further, during William's conquest of Maine, the English contingent appear as somewhat overzealous in their attack upon the French: 'they destroyed vineyards and burned down cities, and damaged the country severely, and made all the country surrender to the king. And afterwards they went home to England.'[20]

Version E of the *Chronicle* is, however, a rather different source from D. While it covers the same period, it terminates much later (1154), and is never as critical of the Normans as D is. Indeed, as a whole, the source is fairly indifferent towards the Normans' early exploits, after the same fashion as C, and reports even the invasion itself in a most impartial way. Notably, also, the entry for 1091 refers to the 'good men who guarded the country'.[21] It is not until the Norman attack on Edgar at York that they are cast in a bad light, and even here the description is less graphic and terrible than that in D. For here, 'King William came from the south with all his army and ravaged the city, and killed many hundreds of men.'[22] The chronicler's

---

[15] *ASC (D)*, 83–4: 'Wyllelm kyng com suðan on unwær on heom mid geotendan here, 7 hi aflymde, 7 þa ofsloh þa þe ætfleon ne mihton, þæt wæron fela hund manna, 7 þa burh forhergode, 7 sancte Petres mynster to bysmere macede, 7 ealle þa oðre eac forhergode 7 forhynde'; *ASC (tr.)*, 149.

[16] *ASC (D)*, 84: 'Ær þan þa scypmenn þider comon, hæfdon þa frenciscan þa burh forbærned, 7 eac þæt halie mynster sanctus Petrus eall forhergod 7 forbærned', 'For he norðward mid ealre him fyrde þe he gegaderian mihte, 7 þa scire mid ealle forhergode 7 aweste'; *ASC (tr.)*, 150.

[17] *ASC (D)*, 87–8: 'Sum hi wurdon geblende, 7 sume wrecan of lande, 7 sume getawod to scande. Þus wurdon þæs kyninges swican genyðerade'; *ASC (tr.)*, 158.

[18] *ASC (D)*, 84; *ASC (tr.)*, 150.

[19] *ASC (D)*, 88: 'Wyllelm cyngc þa þanon for, 7 þær forleas ægðer menn 7 hors 7 unarimede gærsaman'; *ASC (tr.)*, 158.

[20] *ASC (D)*, 86: 'Wingeardas hi fordydon, 7 burga forbærndan, 7 þæt land swiðe amyrdon, 7 eall þæt land gebegdan þan kyninge to handan, 7 hig seoððan ham gewendan'; *ASC (tr.)*, 155.

[21] *ASC (E)*, 19: 'Þa gode mæn þe þis land bewiston'; *ASC (tr.)*, 169.

[22] *ASC (tr.)*, 149.

description of William's response to the Danish threat is also restrained: 'King William went into the shire and ruined it completely.'[23] Even the defeats are less strongly highlighted – while the account of the treatment of the Bretons is much the same as in D, the events at Dol are slightly less catastrophic, William losing only 'much of his treasure'.[24]

Strangely enough, the most damning commentary against the Normans in E occurs shortly after D ends, in the record of events at Glastonbury. Here, the chronicler records that

> the Frenchmen broke into the choir and threw missiles towards the altar where the monks were, and some of the retainers went up to the upper story and shot arrows down towards the sanctuary, so that many arrows stuck in the cross that stood above the altar, and the wretched monks were lying round about the altar, and some crept under it, and cried to God zealously, asking for his mercy when they could get no mercy from men. What can we say, except that they shot fiercely, and others broke down the doors there, and went in and killed some of the monks and wounded many there in the church, so that the blood came from the altar on to the steps, and from the steps on to the floor. Three were killed there and eighteen wounded.[25]

This graphic description of 'French' cruelty and violation of a sacred place is, very much, a indictment against the conquerors. Unlike D, however, the E chronicler does not associate the king with this kind of atrocity, and this event strikes the reader as unusual in the context of E, whereas it would almost seem expected in the context of D.

In fact, William I is surprisingly well represented in E. In his epitaph in the *Chronicle*, he is described as 'a very wise man, and very powerful and more worshipful and stronger than any predecessor of his had been. He was gentle to the good men who loved God, and stern beyond all measure to those people who resisted his will.' The chronicler praises his provision of security in the country against robbers and rapists, his survey of the land, his subjection of Wales, Scotland and Maine, and nearly of Ireland.[26] Of course, William was not perfect, and pains are taken to point this out – an equal amount of space is spent on bewailing his avarice and forest and game laws, in which he was perceived to 'exalt himself and reckon himself above all men'.[27] Yet, in all, it almost seems as if the chronicler has accepted William as a king of his race, rather than a conqueror.

23 *Ibid.*, 150.
24 *ASC (E)*, 6: '*Feola his gersuma*'; *ASC (tr.)*, 158.
25 *ASC (E)*, 7–8: '*Þet þa frencisce men bræcen þone chor ꝛ torfedon towærd þam weofode þær ða munecas wæron. ꝛ Sume of ðam cnihtan ferdon uppon þone uppflore ꝛ scotedon adunweard mid arewan toweard þam haligdome swa þet on þære rode þe stod bufon þam weofode sticodon on mænige arewan. ꝛ Þa wreccan munecas lagon onbuton þam weofode – ꝛ sume crupon under – ꝛ gyrne cleopedon to Gode, his miltse biddende ða þa hi ne mihton nane miltse æt mannum begytan. Hwæt magon we secgean? – buton þet hi scotedon swiðe, ꝛ þa oðre ða dura bræcon þær adune ꝛ eodon inn, ꝛ ofslogon sume þa munecas to deaðe ꝛ mænige gewundedon þærinne, swa þet ðet blod com of ðam weofode uppon þam gradan ꝛ of ðam gradan on þa flore. Þreo þær wæron ofslagene to deaðe ꝛ eahteteone gewundade*'; *ASC (tr.)*, 160.
26 *ASC (E)*, 11: '*Swiðe wis man, ꝛ swiðe rice, ꝛ wurðfulre and strengere þonne ænig his foregenga wære. He wæs milde þam godum mannum þe God lufedon, ꝛ ofer eall gemett stearc þam mannum þe wiðcwaedon his willan*'; *ASC (tr.)*, 163–4.
27 *ASC (E)*, 13: ' *Hine sylf upp ahebban / ꝛ ofer ealle men tellan*'; *ASC (tr.)*, 165.

However, the divide between 'French' and English still remains, as is evident from the events recorded in the reign of William II.[28] This is most pronounced when referring to events that concern people other than the English, notably the Scots and Welsh. For Scotland, after William lent troops to Duncan in order that he might restore himself to the kingship, the chronicler records that the Scots 'came to an agreement, to the effect that he (Duncan) would never again bring Englishmen nor Frenchmen into the country'.[29] As for Wales, the entry for 1094 runs as follows: 'In this year the Welshmen gathered together and started a fight with the French who were in Wales or in the neighbourhood and had deprived them of land, and they stormed many fortresses and castles, and killed the men.'[30]

Additionally, while the chronicler may have shown some degree of acceptance of William I, based perhaps on his perceived good qualities as king, no such respect was forthcoming for William II. Suffering from the avarice of his father, for which reason 'he was always harassing this nation with military service and excessive taxes', he was also considered unjust ('in his days all justice was in abeyance, and all injustice arose both in ecclesiastical and secular matters') and 'very terrible'.[31] When William I died, the chronicle read 'May Almighty God show mercy to his soul'; William II, on the other hand, received the following comment: 'All that was hateful to God and just men was customary in this country in his time; and therefore he was hateful to nearly all his people, and odious to God, just as his end showed, because he departed in the midst of his injustice without repentance and any reparation.'[32]

So, by the end of the eleventh century, there was still a clear divide between French and English within England, at least from the viewpoint of the 'native' English. The Norman kings, while they were able to exhibit good qualities (in the case of William I, for example) could also evidence the vices of the worst conquerors – in the *Anglo-Saxon Chronicle*, William II comes across as a despot. If the wording of the *Chronicle* is to be believed, also, there was a distinction between French and English that could be and was made by outsiders: in the Scottish example above, Englishmen and Frenchmen are specified separately. Notably, however, there is never any distinction made within this concept of Frenchmen in England to take account of the different sub-groups (i.e. Normans, Bretons, etc.), and after the conquest, 'Frenchman' seems to have become synonymous with the concept of 'otherness'. This issue is addressed more fully after the consideration of the internal evidence.[33]

What can be said with some certainty is that the Battle of Hastings and its

---

[28]   *ASC (E)*, 17; *ASC (tr.)*, 167–8, for example.

[29]   *ASC (E)*, 21: '. . . *wurdon sehte on þa gerad þet he næfre eft englisce ne frencisce into þam lande ne gelogige*'; *ASC (tr.)*, 170.

[30]   *ASC (E)*, 22: '*On þisum ylcan geare þa wylisce menn hi gegaderodon, ꝺ wið þa frencisce þe on Walon oððe on þære neawiste wæron ꝺ hi ær belandedon gewinn up ahofon, ꝺ manige festena ꝺ castelas abræcon ꝺ men ofslogon*'; *ASC (tr.)*, 171.

[31]   *ASC (E)*, 27: '*He æfre þas leode mid here ꝺ mid ungylde tyrwigende wæs*'; 28: '*On his dagan ælc riht afeoll ꝺ ælc unriht for Gode ꝺ for worulde up aras*'; 27: '*Swiðe ondrædendlic*'. *ASC (tr.)*, 176.

[32]   *ASC (E)*, 14: '*Se ælmihtiga God cyþæ his saule mildheortnisse*'; *ASC (tr.)*, 165. *ASC (E)*, 28: '*Eall þet þe Gode wæs lað ꝺ rihtfulle mannan, eall þet wæs gewunelic on þisan lande on his tyman; ꝺ forþi he wæs forneah ealre his leode lað ꝺ Gode andsæte, swa swa his ænde ætywde, forþan þe he on middewardan his unrihte buten behreowsunge ꝺ ælcere dædbote gewat*'; *ASC (tr.)*, 176.

[33]   Below, pp. 131–3.

aftermath were both a crisis point for English identity and the immediate cause of a stark transformation in English attitudes to the Normans – the ethnic conflict instigated a redefinition of English identity. That this change occurred is hardly surprising – people who like being conquered do not seem to be common in the historical record – but the nature of the crisis for the *gens Anglorum* is hard to assess. While kings would be expected to play a highly significant role within an identity, as the central focus for their people, the resilience evidenced by Englishness stands as a reminder that this was not always the case.[34] One can, in fact, hypothesise that the leadership figure was less important to the English than to the Normans entirely because of the nature of English society. Looking back over only the previous hundred years, we see the English monarchy replaced by Danish rulers, only to re-emerge again relatively intact. While David C. Douglas has suggested that there was an absence of national sentiment at the time (justifying this with the examples of 'Englishmen' on both sides at Stamford Bridge (1066) and fighting under William against Exeter in 1068), which would explain this to some extent, it seems more likely that the identity of the *gens Anglorum* was possessed of something that the *gens Normannorum* lacked.[35]

One element of Hugh Thomas' work perhaps reveals to us what this was. Thomas notes that, within Englishness, it was possible for the link between *rex* and *regnum* to be broken, and for English territorial loyalties to transcend loyalties to kings.[36] Although the significance of territories to the identities of *gentes* at this time is hard to estimate, the *gens Anglorum* never found themselves detached from their homeland in the same way that the *gens Normannorum* frequently did, at first by distance (England, Italy) and then, later, by the disassociation of Normandy from England during the reign of William II and some of that of Henry I. Additionally, the identity of the English had a far longer tradition than that of the Normans, and one built up from a slow process of settlement and unification, rather than one forged in relatively recent fires of conquest. As a result, pre-conquest Englishness was very strong indeed.[37]

Internal Identity

To truly understand what was happening to *Normanitas* at this time, however, we have also to look at the Norman internal sources, which have rather more to say on the matter. Though the English sources express an unsurprising negativity, the Normans still clearly had a positive self-image, such that Roger de Montgomery could proudly declare himself 'Norman, [born] of Normans' in the early 1080s.[38] Indeed, such a sign of individual *gens* association is rare, and a reassuring sentiment for students of identity. For the period around the time of the conquest, we have three main Norman narrative sources with which to work: William of Jumièges'

---

34 Goetz, et al., 'Conclusion', 624–5; above, pp. 6–7.
35 Douglas, *Norman Achievement*, 11.
36 Thomas, *English and Normans*, 24.
37 *Ibid.*, 31.
38 *RRAN*, no. 281: '*ex Northmannis Northmannus*'. Also van Houts, *Normans in Europe*, 12.

Gesta Normannorum Ducum, William of Poitiers' *Gesta Guillelmi*, and Guy of Amiens' *Carmen de Hastingae Proelio*. Additionally, some other sources, such as the Bayeux Tapestry, provide invaluable information about the identity of the *gens Normannorum* by their alternative forms of expression. These sources also provide a certain insight into the period before the conquest when, to use Frank Barlow's words, 'William was a young prince of note, yet had not achieved such distinction as to disquiet the Anglo-Danish nobility'.[39]

Of primary interest are the differences in the way that the Norman writers perceived the ethnic boundaries around them, which can be seen through their use of ethnic titles. We have noted above how the conquerors of England were repeatedly classified as part of a monolithic *Franci*; unsurprisingly, they themselves saw things as a little more complicated. Certainly, historians generally agree that the distinctions made between the different groups of '*Franci*' are significant and worthy of remark (though rarely explaining exactly *why* this is the case).[40] Once again, it is a question of perception. Within William of Poitiers' work, for example, there is no room for iden-tifying the Normans as French – any account of the life of William of Normandy cannot avoid the Battle of Mortemer, where the *Gesta Guillelmi* would have us believe that the French army was made to look small by the huge Norman host.[41]

William also uses the terms Francia and Gaul interchangeably to describe 'France' (in the modern sense), or so it at first appears. With a closer reading, though, he does appear to make a distinction: when talking of Duke William's youth, he observes, 'Our duke . . . was armed as a knight. The news of this spread *fear* throughout Francia. Gaul had not another man who was reputed to be such a knight at arms.'[42] The meaning here necessitates that Francia *does not* include Normandy, but that Gaul *does* – the men of the duchy would not be expected to fear their duke being armed as a knight, but their neighbours would. Equally, a statement extolling the prowess of the duke by comparison to others would necessarily involve the men of his own duchy.

With regard to the conquest of England, however, both William of Poitiers and William of Jumièges are quite happy to have their readership believe it was, to all intents and purposes, a Norman venture: 'historical narratives represented the way in which the Normans wanted their endeavours to be regarded'.[43]

Guy of Amiens has a rather different perspective on this, doubtless owing to his French (and therefore non-Norman) origins, recognising various 'national' entities within his work. To Guy, *Gallia / Francia* are, as for the English, the same place; but this is not to say that he has no interest in their inhabitants. In Guy's *Gallia / Francia* live not only the *Galli / Franci*, but also the *Normanni*, *Cenomanni* (men of Maine) and *Britanni*, and his attitude to the title *dux Normannorum* is an unusual one at this time: for Guy, this is a territorial title, expressing perhaps his greater connection with the wider *Gallia / Francia* and the territorial nature of that particular claim.

[39] Barlow, *Feudal Kingdom*, 64.
[40] See, for example, David C. Douglas, 'The Norman Conquest and English Feudalism', *Time and the Hour* (London, 1977), 163; Davis, *Normans and their Myth*, 105.
[41] *GG*, 14.
[42] *GG*, 6–8: '*Dux noster . . . arma militaria sumit; qui rumor metum Franciae detulit omni. Alium non habebat Gallia qui talis praedicaretur eques et armatus.*'
[43] Douglas, *Norman Achievement*, 16.

Conversely, Guy does not include an *Anglia* among his recognised territories, merely a racial grouping of *Angli*.[44]

Some mention should also be made in this context of the Bayeux Tapestry. In the inscription, prior to the Battle of Hastings, William is referred to as '*dux Normannorum*', and Harold as '*rex Anglorum*'.[45] Yet, once battle has been joined, we find the Normans and their allies referred to as '*Franci*', in contrast to the enemy '*Angli*'.[46] Given the works of William of Jumièges and William of Poitiers, this seems somewhat unusual, and it is no surprise to discover that the general consensus has been that the inscription was of English origin. While Francis Wormald suggested that we only have a single instance of 'Ð' to betray an acquaintance with English lettering, this association is further supported by the forms of certain names, which are clearly non-Norman representations: '*Willem*', '*Ælfgyva*' and '*Hestengaceastra*', to give a few examples.[47]

However, recent work by Ian Short has provided good evidence to suggest that the underlying language of the inscription is French and not English.[48] Though the execution of the piece is still considered by art historians to be firmly English, and the English word-forms do represent an English input, Short's argument indicates that the Tapestry not only had Norman patronage, but a Norman designer. His conclusion is, therefore, that it is 'a truly Anglo-Norman artefact', and this perhaps explains the relative neutrality of the inscription: the only weighted comment appears towards the end, as William 'exhorts his soldiers that they prepare themselves manfully and wisely for battle against the English army'.[49]

Such a comment is simply proof of a Norman element within the audience for the piece, however. The Normans evidently had no doubt of their own greatness, as is apparent from the symbolic expressions of Norman identity in the pages of narrative histories. William of Jumièges, in fact, has nothing new to say on the *gens Normannorum* as a whole, but the account of the conquest occurs towards the end of his work, which contains quite enough pro-Norman sentiment in its earlier pages to last the distance.

William of Poitiers' Normans are, quite predictably, the valiant warriors who we have previously seen them to be. William even manages to make adjectives such as 'violent' sound positive when speaking of them.[50] These men were heroes in the making, as he observes of one young knight who, 'while fighting that day in his first battle performed a praiseworthy deed that deserves to be immortalised; charging with the battalion he commanded on the right wing, he laid the enemy low with the greatest audacity'.[51] Even the reverses at Hastings itself are explained away; he brushes off a near-collapse of the Norman line, 'if such a thing can be said of the

[44] *Carmen* (1), xxiii. For discussion of the royal titles, *rex Anglorum* and *rex Angli(a)e*, see p. 157, n. 187.
[45] Francis Wormald, 'The Inscriptions with a Translation', in F.M. Stenton, *The Bayeux Tapestry* (London, 1957), 178: 15–16; 179: 34.
[46] *Ibid.*, 180: 66–7, 69–71 & 72–3.
[47] *Ibid.*, 177; 178: 19–21, 178: 19 & p. 179: 50–1.
[48] Ian Short, 'The Language of the Bayeux Tapestry Inscription', *ANS* 23 (2001), 267–77.
[49] Wormald, 'Inscriptions', 180: 59–62; Short, 'Language', 277.
[50] *GG*, 24: '*Feruentissimaque*'.
[51] *Ibid.*, 130: '*Praelium illodie primum experiens, egit quod aeternandum esset laude: cum legione, quam in dextro cornu duxit, irruens ac sternens magna cum audacia.*'

unconquered people of the Normans', and his attitude to the first rout of the cavalry is similarly one of justification: 'The Normans believed that their duke and lord had fallen, so it was not too shameful to give way to flight; least of all was it to be deplored, since it helped them greatly.'[52]

The attitude of Guy of Amiens to the Normans is equally positive but, though he praises all the invaders present at Hastings, the most importance and prestige appears to be accrued by the *Franci*. Observing that the attack force was composed of Normans, Frenchmen and Bretons, the speech of exhortation attributed to Duke William characterises Guy's approach:

> You warriors who France, renowned for its nobility, has bred, soldiers without malice, famed youth chosen and beloved by God, whose enduring renown as invincible in war flies through the four quarters of the world; you nation of Bretons, who excel in arms and for whom, unless the earth itself should flee, there is no such thing as flight; you illustrious men of Maine, who glory in battle with the help of your valour; you Normans, accustomed to heroic deeds, and to whom the Apulians, Calabrians, and Sicilians are slaves.[53]

Guy, like William of Poitiers, can also find a ready explanation for reverses. The flight of the cavalry is justified as a trick – the *Franci*, 'versed in stratagems, skilled in warfare, pretended to fly as if defeated' – yet it seems likely that this was a genuine rout.[54] The fact that the duke reveals himself here and entreats the *Franci* to return to the battle supports this: ' "Where are you off to?" he cried. "Where do you want to die? France, the noblest of the earth's kingdoms, how could you, when you had been the victors, allow yourself to appear the vanquished?" '[55] Once again, the failing of morale is used as an opportunity for praise.

As a conflict between *ethnies*, it is only to be expected that these narrative histories would further emphasise the strength of the Norman (French) contingent by positive comparisons with the ill-fated English. Thus, to William of Jumièges, the Norman invasion was a divine punishment for the English, 'God's retribution for their unjust murder of Alfred, King Edward's brother'.[56] William of Poitiers provides a classical allusion, comparing the Norman invasion to that of Caesar: 'The horsemen of the Britons and their charioteers inflicted no little damage on Caesar, bravely fighting against him on level ground; the English, by contrast, trembling

---

[52] *Ibid.*, 128: '*Quod cum pace dictum sit Normannorum inuictissimae nationis*'; '*Credidere Normanni ducem ac dominum suum cecidisse. Non ergo nimis pudenda fuga cessere; minime uero dolenda, cum plurimum iuuerit.*'

[53] *Carmen* (1), 16: '*Francia quos genuit, nobilitate cluens, / Belligere sine fella uiri, famosa iuuentus, / Quos Deus elegit uel quibus ipse fauet, / Fama uolat quorum per climata quatuor orbis / Inuictusque manens milicie titulus: / Gensque Brtiannorum, quorum decus extat in armis, / Tellus ni fugiat, est fuga nulla quibus: / Viribus illustres Cenomanni, gloria quorum / Bello monstratur per probitatis opem: / Apulus et Calaber, Siculus quibus incola seruit, / Normanni faciles actibus egregiis.*' There is some disagreement as to the translation of this passage – presented here is Barlow's version; Morton and Muntz have 'Apulians and Calabrians, whose darts fly in swarms: Normans, ripe for incomparable achievements!' (*Carmen* (2), 18).

[54] *Carmen* (1), 26: '*Artibus instructi . . . bellare periti, / Ac si deuicti fraude fugam simulant*'; *Carmen* (2), 28.

[55] *Carmen* (1), 28: ' "*Quo fugitis? Quo iuuat ire mori? / Que fueras uictrix, pateris cur uicta uideri / Regnis terrarum Gallia nobilior?*" '; *Carmen* (2), 28–30.

[56] *GND* II, 170: '*Christo illis uicem reddente ob Aluredi, fratris Hetwardi regis, necem ab eis iniuste perpetratem.*'

with fear, waited for William on a hill. The Britons often gave battle to Caesar, whereas William crushed the English so thoroughly in one day that afterwards they could not muster the courage to fight him again.'[57] Guy of Amiens was no less damning of the English; he records that 'a blazing comet with outstretched tail informed the English of their destined ruin' and refers to them as 'unskilled in the art of war'.[58] Even when the *Franci* are running from them, the English are still considered weak, and William cries after the retreating French, 'it is not from men but from sheep that you run. Your fear is mistaken.'[59] Indeed, this rallying speech is echoed in Harold's inspirational speech to his men, where he debases the enemy rather than praising the English, claiming William to have 'great renown, but a fearful heart'; Guy suggests here that the English need to be rallied before the battle has even begun.[60] Even after William's coronation, the English did not behave as the Normans would have hoped, and it was possible to find 'many Englishmen whose fickle minds had turned away from loyalty by sinful conspiracy'.[61]

For all that the English are portrayed as weak and disloyal, though, they never come across as 'evil'. They may be seen as poor warriors, but it appears that they are not bad people, suggesting that the negativity about them is purely a product of the short-term identity conflict. Harold, on the other hand, is thoroughly demonised in the Norman sources, in a way which holds kinship with the depiction of William in version D of the *Anglo-Saxon Chronicle*. William of Jumièges records that Harold perjured the faith he had made to William and seized England for himself; when he was subsequently slain in the first assault at Hastings, the English broke and ran.[62] William of Poitiers provides far more vocal denunciation of Harold, with regard to his coronation:

> This mad Englishman could not endure to await the decision of a public election, but on the tragic day when the best of all men was buried, while all the people were mourning, he violated his oath and seized the royal throne with acclamation, with the connivance of a few wicked men. He received an impious consecration from Stigand, who had been deprived of his priestly office by the just zeal and anathema of the pope.[63]

But regardless of the level of criticism, it is clear that both 'Norman' sources considered Harold's kingship to be an illegitimate one, and this fact underlies their criticisms of him.

<hr/>

[57] *GG*, 170: '*Equitatus Britannorum et essedarii cladem illi non paruam intulerant, aequo loco audacissime cum eo confligentes, Angli uero Guillelmum pauidi in monte operiebantur. Caesarem praelio saepius adorti sunt Britanni; Anglos adeo Guillelmus die uno protriuit, ut post secum dimicandi fiduciam nullatenus reciperent.*'

[58] *Carmen* (1), 8 & 22: '*E celo fulgens, extenso crine, cometes / Anglis fatatum nunciat exidium*', '*Nescia . . . belli*'; *Carmen* (2), 10 & 24.

[59] *Carmen* (1), 28: '*Non homines set oues fugitis, frustraque timetis*'; *Carmen* (2), 30.

[60] *Carmen* (1), 12: '*Nomen . . . magnum; cor tamen est pauidum*'; *Carmen* (2), 12.

[61] *GND* II, 178: '*Plurimos eiusdem gentis . . . quorum leuia in corda ab eius fidelitate preuaricatrix conspiratio aduerterat.*'

[62] *Ibid.*, 160 & 168.

[63] *GG*, 100: '*Sustinuit uesanus Anglus quid electio publica statueret consulere; sed in die lugubri quo optimus ille humatus est, cum gens uniuersa plangeret, periurus regium solium cum plausu occupauit, quibusdam iniquis fauentibus. Ordinatus est non sacra consecratione Stigandi, iusto zelo apostolici et anathemate ministerio sacerdotum priuati.*'

This is not, however, true of the presentation of Harold in Guy of Amiens'
Carmen. There is little or no criticism of Harold's kingly claims; instead, he is shown
to be genuinely evil. Describing Harold as 'the king, the abode and heir of dark
deception, active in the craft of the thief', Guy considers William as an arbiter of
justice: 'He who subjected the realm which was owed to you ordained all these things
so that you would go to avenge that violent crime.'[64] The crime in question here was
Harold's fratricide at Stamford Bridge, recorded with evident disgust by Guy:
Harold, 'the wicked king, was preparing treacherous weapons for a brother's destruction at the farthest end of the land . . . Harold did not fear to do his brother to death
. . . That envious Cain hewed off his brother's head, and thus he buried head and
body in the earth.'[65] Thus are events brought full circle, as Harold is treated in the
same way by William – his mother is refused his body, and it is buried in the earth in
an apparently Scandinavian fashion.[66]

It has also been suggested that Harold is given a negative treatment in the border
pictures of the Bayeux Tapestry. It is generally accepted that these border pictures
represent animal fables, which tell a tale with the predominant theme of the 'hidden
danger present to the unwary by the crafty and deceitful'.[67] Thus Harold is represented as a wily fox, a voracious wolf, etc. However, it has equally been suggested that
the images 'invite viewers to take a stand on the justice of the Norman claims to
England', and a viable case has been advanced for identifying the Normans as synonymous with the wolves of the borderwork.[68] In this instance, the border pictures
carry a pro-English subtext, at odds with the official versions of Norman justice
espoused by documents such as the *Gesta Guillelmi*. Yet, while the case for deceitful
Normans is the more compelling of the two, neither version seems to comfortably fit
all the instances, though this is doubtless the product of the same ambiguity that
allows for such opposed interpretations in the first place. In any case, it is most probable that the intention of the Norman designer (above) was not to include
anti-Norman sentiment, and we must therefore assume that the intended function of
these pictures was to demonise Harold, not to vindicate him.

Such negativity concerning the enemy leader is not really a surprise, given the
central importance of the leadership aspect in Norman ethnicity. It must be remembered that Harold is not being examined here solely in his own right, but that he is
being portrayed in opposition to (and therefore in comparison with) William
himself. Thus, whereas Harold is treacherous, deceitful and a fratricide, William is
'the most valiant duke', 'the very fortunate war-leader', 'most noble conqueror and

---

[64] *Carmen* (1), 18: '*Sedes fuscate fraudis et heres, / Nocte sub obscura, furis in arte uigens, / Rex*'; *Carmen*
(2), 18. *Carmen* (1), 10: '*Hec tibi preuidit qui debita regna subegit: / Criminis infesti quatinus ultor eas*';
Carmen (2), 10.

[65] *Carmen* (1), 8–10: '*Rex Heraldus enim sceleratus ad ultima terra / Fratris ad exicium perfida tela parat /
. . . Heraldus . . . / Non timuit fratris tradere membra neci / . . . Inuidus ille Cain fratris caput amputat ense, /
Et caput et corpus sic sepeliuit humo*'; *Carmen* (2), 10.

[66] *Carmen* (1), 34; *Carmen* (2), 36–8.

[67] Albu, *Normans in their Histories*, 91, quoting H.E.J. Cowdrey. Albu provides an excellent and interesting discussion of the fable argument, with an examination of each of the nine fables that appear –
Normans in their Histories, 88–105.

[68] *Ibid.*, 90.

hereditary lord' and 'our most illustrious duke'.[69] William of Jumièges records the election of this 'great warrior' as king, and comments: 'I wish for our devout and orthodox king himself, protected by angels, to rule the English in happiness, to subdue the English with courage and to reign in justice,' making reference to William's 'most noble and excellent merits'.[70] William of Poitiers is even more full in his praise of William, doubtless owing to the nature of the work he is writing. From the moment that William can bear arms, William of Poitiers depicts him as a Christian hero:

> As he stood out in beauty when wearing the garments of a prince and at peace, so also the adornments which are put on against the enemy suited him perfectly. From this time a virile spirit and valour shone in him. From this time he began with the utmost zeal to protect the churches of God, to uphold the cause of the weak, to impose laws which would not be burdensome, and to make judgements which never deviated from equity and temperance. He especially prohibited slaughter, fire, and pillage.[71]

William is even shown to restrain himself when in the position to take vengeance, and as to his people: 'when they consider whom they have as a defender . . . their fear is tempered with hope and their suffering is eased by confidence'.[72] Guy of Amiens, too, joins the cavalcade of praise, describing William as a 'blessed king, guardian of justice, giver of peace to the fatherland, a foe to it foes, and protector of its church', 'a fearless knight and full of valour', and as 'another Caesar'.[73] He even has an English native refer to William as 'more beautiful than the sun, wiser than Solomon, readier than Pompey, and more bountiful than Charles'.[74]

From all this information, the myth / symbol complex of *Normanitas*, at least as expressed in these texts, appears to have undergone few changes since the early eleventh century. In the 'internal' narrative histories, there is no real change in the treatment of the Normans themselves, and the portrayal is still one of a victorious people who are destined to conquer, as one might find in the tenth- and early eleventh-century histories of the Normans or, indeed, in the eleventh-century Italian histories.

---

[69] *GND* II, 170: '*Fortissimus . . . dux*'; '*Felicissimus . . . belli ductor*'; '*Nobilissimo uictori suo hereditario domino*'; '*Dux noster inclitarum uirtutum.*'

[70] *Ibid.*, 170 & 178: '*Magni debellatoris*'; 182–4: '*Ipsum autem pium atque ortodoxum regem sub angelorum tutela Anglis feliciter dominari Anglos fortiter perdomare iuste gubernare exopto*'; '*Nobilissima . . . probissimaque merita.*'

[71] *GG*, 8: '*Uti pulchritudine praestabat cum indumenta principis gestaret aut pacis, ita ornatus qui contra hostem sumitur eum singulariter decebat. Hinc uirilis in eo animus et uirtus enitescebat egregia claritudine. Hinc namque summo studio coepit ecclesiis Dei patrocinari, causas impotentium tutari, iura imponere quae non grauarent, iudicia facere quae nequaquam ab aequitate deuiarent. Imprimis prohibere caedes, incendia, rapinas.*'

[72] *Ibid.*, 26; 46: '*Cum reminiscuntur quem habeant propugnatorem . . . spe timorem leniunt, afflictionem fiducia consolantur.*'

[73] *Carmen* (1), 4: '*Iusticie cultor, patrie pax, hostibus hostis, / Tutor et ecclesie, rex benedicte*'; *Carmen* (2), 4. *Carmen* (1), 14: '*Pondus uirtutum, miles et intrepidus*'; *Carmen* (2), 16. *Carmen* (1), 4: '*Iulius alter*'; *Carmen* (2), 4.

[74] *Carmen* (1), 44: '*Pulchrior est sole, sapientior et Salomone; Promptior est Magno, largior et Carolo*'; *Carmen* (2), 46. There is some disagreement as to whether *Magno* and *Carolo* refer to two different people (Pompey and Charles), or are simply both parts of the name Charlemagne. See *Carmen* (1), p. 44, n. 1 and *Carmen* (2), p. 47, n. 6 for the reasoning behind each translation.

The enemies of the Normans are still criticised, notably for military inadequacy, and the Norman leader appears as a great conqueror and warrior.

Yet it is also evident that a significant change occurred in the identity of the *gens Normannorum*, typified by the particular qualities attributed to the Norman leader, William, and to their allies and enemies – the 'other'. Thus, some explanation and investigation of this change is necessary, in order to understand the state of the *gens Normannorum* by the end of the eleventh century.

Marjorie Chibnall has said that, for the Normans in England, the English were 'the other', and that the non-Normans on the Norman side received similar treatment to the Normans once William became king.[75] While this may be true for the twelfth century and, equally, true from the perspective of non-Normans (such as Guy of Amiens, for example), it is apparently untrue for the Normans themselves in the first years after Hastings. As already noted, the conquest is considered both by William of Jumièges and William of Poitiers as a 'Norman' venture, borne out yet further by William of Poitiers' description of the Battle of Hastings itself. He describes how 'the loud shouting, *here Norman, there foreign*, was drowned by the clash of weapons and the groans of the dying', and this is representative of the Norman attitude at this time.[76] The English did not become 'the other' – they did not need to, because they already were.

True, the identity of the *gens Anglorum* was the one that was in primary opposition to that of the *gens Normannorum*, doubtless explaining the harsh treatment that the English received in the conquest narratives, but for William of Poitiers there was a single, clear division, between the *gens Normannorum* and *everyone else*.[77] Though *barbaricus* could be taken to refer to the English alone, this seems unlikely. William was happy to use the term 'English' to refer to the 'enemy' at Hastings, and it would be strange if, at that moment when the two sides clashed in earnest, he chose to use a less specific term. Furthermore, this is not the first instance in which William makes reference to the 'foreign' nature of the Normans' allies. Though in this passage and shortly afterwards, William writes firstly of 'Breton knights', and then of 'men of Maine, French-born, Bretons, Aquitanians', during the preparations for the invasion he tells how 'foreign knights flocked to help [William] in great numbers'.[78] There is a realisation here that shows the Normans' awareness of the fact that, though they fought against the English as one *gens* among many, this did not make these other *gentes Normanni* any more than it made the *Normanni Franci*, say, or *Britanni*. The force arrayed against the English was not, therefore, united along ethnic lines, but along lines perhaps similar to those who travelled east on the First Crusade.[79] To serve its purpose, such a unity would stem from a commonality among the invaders that served to distinguish them from those against whom they

75 Marjorie Chibnall, *The Debate on the Norman Conquest* (Manchester, 1999), 128.

76 *GG*, 128, my italics: '*Altissimus clamor, hinc Normannicus, illinc barbaricus, armorum sonitu et gemitu morientium superatur.*'

77 To clarify, here: William of Poitiers took his name from the Poitevin schools in which he was educated; he was Norman by birth, from Préaux (*ibid.*, xv).

78 *Ibid.*, 128: '*Equites Britanni*'; 130: '*Cenomanici, Francigenae, Britanni, Aquitani*'; 103: '*Conuenit etiam externus miles in auxilium copiosus.*'

79 Above, pp. 73–4.

fought – in this instance, perhaps *Franci* expressed a unity of territorial origin.[80] In ethnic terms, *Normanitas* was being challenged by Englishness, and thus it is against the English that our sources react; but the English are not the only 'other' here, merely the one in opposition.

With that said, the Norman treatment of the English in the narratives is surprisingly gentle. There is no aggressive criticism of the *gens Anglorum* at all from either William of Jumièges or William of Poitiers, but instead a sense of faint derision at the 'outdated' English infantry tactics, which cannot stand against the superior Norman cavalry. There is an element of divine support for the Norman venture, making it a destined victory, but the English are no epic foe; there is an overwhelming sense of defensiveness and desperation in the English side at Hastings. William of Poitiers even goes so far as to praise the English regnal line, referring to Edward the Confessor as the 'best of all men', though it must be noted that the legitimacy of Edward's reign was crucial to William I's claim to the throne.[81]

Perhaps the most revealing comments, however, are those of William of Jumièges that the English were turned against William by Harold, and of Guy of Amiens, that the English were 'sheep'.[82] It seems quite clear that the blame for English behaviour and opposition to the Normans is being placed not on the English themselves, but on their leader, Harold, and 'a few wicked men'.[83] It must be remembered that these accounts were all being written after the fact, once the battle had been fought and won, and the conquest was under-way. While the Normans evidently did not trust the English, there is still a suggestion of hope here, that the English could be set on the right path under the right leadership as, it is implied, they had been under Edward the Confessor.[84] Additionally, it appears that certain commonalities were perceived between the Normans and the English by the conquerors: the use of Germanic initiation ceremonies for knighthood, and Odo's threat of *nithing* against those refusing to respond to his military summons for the siege of Rochester suggest that the Normans 'understood' the English after a fashion.[85]

If they understood the English, though, they were not prepared to understand Harold, if the sources are taken at face value. Given the importance of leadership within *Normanitas* (and one cannot deny the intense focus of the sources on the two leaders at Hastings), it is unsurprising that Harold is seen as the key to English defeat. Certainly, William of Poitiers was quite happy to justify a Norman flight on the grounds that they thought William was dead; a similar occurrence on the part of the 'fearful' English was only to be expected.[86] Yet the criticisms of Harold, especially those in the *Carmen*, seem to go far beyond the usual criticism of enemy leaders; indeed, though usually burdened with once vice or another, the Normans are generally seen to face leaders who had at least *some* good qualities and, of course, Harold's predecessor is praised, not scorned. Harold appears to have no positive attributes. It is not even as if criticism of Harold is required to shed a better light on William, such

---

[80] See Thomas, *English and Normans*, 33 for a discussion of similar ideas.

[81] *Ibid.*, 100: '*Optimus*'.

[82] *GND* II, 160; *Carmen* (1), 28: '*Oues*'; *Carmen* (2), 30.

[83] *GG*, 100: '*Iniquis*'.

[84] William of Jumièges considered the English to have 'fickle minds' (*GND* II, 178: '*Leuia corda*').

[85] Barlow, *Feudal Kingdom*, 118 & 144.

[86] *GG*, 128.

is the glorification of the new king in the Norman works. Why, then, do the pro-Norman sources seem to despise Harold quite so much?

In the first instance, it is evident that this move to discredit the English leader is in some way connected with the significance that the Normans attached to that particular role. We have seen, above, that Englishness was less dependent on leadership than *Normanitas*, but such an assault on the English leader seems perfectly logical in a Norman context. This underlying identity clash helps to explain the two more immediate aspects of the Normans' treatment of Harold. Firstly, there was a perceived need to discredit Harold's claim to the English throne. The dispute regarding who was to inherit on the death of Edward is well known to historians, and shall not be recounted here, but it is evident from the Norman sources that there was no doubt that Harold was a usurper. Chibnall notes that William of Poitiers records what can be described as the 'official' Norman case for the conquest, used to obtain papal support for the venture against England; 'the narrative behind the panegyric is a clear statement of what many contemporary Normans believed'.[87]

In both William of Jumièges' and William of Poitiers' works, therefore, there is a strong focus on the fact that Harold had perjured himself under oath, and gone against divine will in so doing. The account in the *Carmen* takes this a step further, expressing little concern regarding legitimate claims but making it clear that Harold is, basically, a monster, and that his defeat and death was, in fact, a deed of greatness. However, this still all seems a little excessive, until it is recalled that William himself was not legitimate, and therefore a standard justification of his claim was simply not enough. William not only had to have even more of a right to the throne than anyone else, he also had to represent something good and holy (in contrast to his sinful birth) against someone variously described as a 'mad Englishman' and an 'envious Cain'. Therefore, the Normans are not only justifying the conquest of England, but also the fact that they follow this man at all: this justification is of core importance. As the very representation of all that was Norman, William had to be the best Norman that there had so far been; correspondingly, his enemies had to be the worst.

In the course of all this, though, there remains a core Norman identity that is not, at first glance, dissimilar from that of the Normans in Normandy in the early eleventh century. Things *were* changing, however, and the conquest of England was part and parcel of that change; indeed, as it prompted such an ethnic clash, it is likely to have been a significant cause of redefinition for Norman ethnicity. The Normans, as we have seen, still called themselves Normans, but they were aware that others didn't. The English, in particular, saw all their conquerors as part of the *Franci*, and this is highly significant, if only because it marks a trend that continues onwards into law, where we find writs addressed *omnibus fidelibus francis et anglis* (and variants thereof). Yet why did the English call the Normans *Franci* and not *Normanni*? This issue is a difficult one, and not something that can be easily laid to rest. The two main arguments for the use of *Franci* are that either there were multiple *gentes* at Hastings, and this is explicit recognition of that fact, or that all the incomers spoke French, and that this distinguished them from the English settlers in a simple and clear manner.

In reality, there were probably multiple elements at work. The realisation that these people were all connected to the *gens Francorum* perhaps guided the choice of

---

[87] Chibnall, *Debate*, 9.

ethnonym in some cases, but both the *Anglo-Saxon Chronicle* (version D) and the *Vita Ædwardi* refer to the Normans as *Franci* when describing earlier events.[88] Though these sections may have been written rather later than the events that they recount, the authors must surely have realised that the *Franci* in question were actually *Normanni*, the author of the *Vita Ædwardi* (as, potentially, a Fleming) in particular.

With regard to the common language, we enter a more complex area. To say that the difference of speech caused post-conquest annalists to write of the Normans as *Franci*, but explained why they noticed separately both Bretons and Flemings, is perhaps going too far – the majority of English speakers would have been monolingual.[89] People could certainly pick out a 'foreign' language, though, and if they had been led to expect French, then they could learn to recognise the 'sound' of French. Naming, also, may have helped with such a definition initially, but the abandonment of Anglo-Saxon names in favour of Norman names in the aftermath of the conquest would soon have rendered this differentiation increasingly inaccurate.[90] Further possibilities also exist, and Hugh Thomas has recently drawn attention to the potential ambiguity of the name 'Norman' for the English, given its similarity to the terms used for Vikings or Norsemen.[91] Lastly, it may have been the case that such a blanket term was chosen and used because the exact specifics of the *gentes* did not matter to the English – they were all invaders, all the 'other', and the term *Franci* would communicate this breadth of meaning to a writer's audience.

The use, in legal documents, of the term *Franci* requires additional explanation. According to Barlow, the king saw all his non-Norman vassals as *Franci*, while baronial documents would often differentiate between Bretons, Flemish, etc.[92] Significantly, though, we have those documents that differentiated between conquerors and conquered: *Franci et Angli*. One such was the *murdrum* law, enacted in order to protect the conquerors from death at the hands of their very large number of new subjects; interestingly, this law only applied to newcomers, and excluded those *Franci* who were already resident in England at the time of the conquest.[93] That the term *Franci* included the Normans is beyond doubt; that the Normans chose to use it is a sign of typical Norman pragmatism regarding their ethnonym.[94] We have seen

---

[88] Above, pp. 117 & 118.

[89] D.J.A. Matthew, 'The English Cultivation of Norman History', in David Bates and Ann Curry (eds), *England and Normandy in the Middle Ages* (London, 1994), 2; Ian Short, '*Tam Angli quam Franci*: Self-Definition in Anglo-Norman England', *ANS* 18 (1996), 159.

[90] For changes of name see Short, 'Self-Definition', 160–1; Emma Cownie, *Religious Patronage in Anglo-Norman England* (London, 1998), 135; Cecily Clark, '*Willelmus rex? vel alius Willelmus*', in *Words, Names and History: Selected Writings of Cecily Clark*, ed. Peter Jackson (Cambridge, 1995), 280–91, and 'Onomastics', in *The Cambridge History of the English Language*, vol. II: *1066–1476*, ed. Norman Blake (Cambridge, 1992), 551–4 & 558–63.

[91] Thomas, *English and Normans*, 33–4.

[92] Barlow, *Feudal Kingdom*, 113.

[93] George Garnett, ' "*Franci et Angli*": the Legal Distinctions between Peoples after the Conquest', *ANS* 8 (1986), 118. For the English origins of the *murdrum* law, and similar legal mechanisms, see Bruce R. O'Brien, 'From *Morðor* to *Murdrum*: the Preconquest Origin and Norman Revival of the Murder Fine', *Speculum* 71 (1996), 321–57, and *God's Peace*, 14–16.

[94] Garnett, '*Franci et Angli*', 114 suggests that the basic French / English division was at least partly a matter of practicality. For further mentions of Norman pragmatism, see Thomas, *English and Normans*, 40 & 370.

elsewhere that the Normans accepted the name *Franci* as a method of expressing their unity with their allies.[95] Furthermore, as they had accepted the term *Albani* in Italy because it meant more to the local population than *Normanni*, so in England they accepted *Franci* on the same grounds – these laws were, after all, *for* the English, and were therefore couched in English terminology. The English were, apparently, already calling them *Franci* anyway and there was nothing to stop the Normans and their allies from accepting the title on the basis of their common language.[96]

The presence of a simple linguistic divide was also likely to have been reinforced by the oral nature of the shire courts. Though the writs addressed to these courts would have been written in Latin in the main, the languages in which they would have been read were French and English. This is only one sign of the beginnings of the slow Norman acceptance of English society. The Normans had begun to appropriate the English past, not least by their regard for Edward the Confessor, 'the last "legitimate" English king'.[97] This is evidence of a change in the bases of the Norman historical myth, one of the significant elements of *Normanitas*. Furthermore, R.H.C. Davis noted the importance of the amount of time that the Normans spent in England and, though many families apparently made a swift division in their holdings in the next generation, the interests of the ruling family and the aristocracy were unifying forces that bridged the Channel.[98] For the conquering generation, Normandy was inalienably their *patria*, but England was their newly promised land.

Changes are not only evident in the Norman attitude to society, though. The cultural elements of *Normanitas* can also be seen to be changing, and moving even further away from the militant ideologies of the Scandinavian warriors who first settled Normandy. The emphasis on the religious aspect of *Normanitas* is, here, stronger than ever. The 'crusading' aspect of the conquest of England, combined with the basic dechristianisation of Harold, who 'received an impious consecration from Stigand', show the Normans as God's servants and, of course, his 'retribution' against the murderers of Alfred and the avengers of Harold's 'violent crime'.[99] William, as the Norman leader, personifies this religious element, as 'protector of the church' and a 'devout and orthodox king'; unsurprisingly, perhaps, as the son of a renowned pilgrim.[100] Yet it is in the other aspects of William's character that the most significant changes show themselves, as the 'ideal' (the leader) diverges from the 'norm' (the people) and the face of a much changed *Normanitas* is revealed, maintaining even so the same sort of duality that could be witnessed in Richard I.

---

[95]   Above, pp. 129–30, 73.

[96]   Short, 'Self-Definition', 163–4. This division in law appears to become fossilised in formulaic charters, however, and can still be seen to appear much later; one can find charters from the end of the reign of Henry I addressed from the king '*omnibus . . . fidelibus suis Francis et Anglis, salutem*' (see *Regesta* ii, 386 (no. 308) and 387 (no. 316) for examples; also Short, 'Self-Definition', 163 and Garnett, '*Franci et Angli*', 135).

[97]   Barlow, *Feudal Kingdom*, 74.

[98]   Davis, *Normans and their Myth*, 122; John Le Patourel, *The Norman Empire* (Oxford, 1976), 191 & 222. David Crouch has observed that the second generation would have been less interested in Normandy 'unless it retained estates in Normandy to confuse its sense of identity' ('Normans and Anglo-Normans: A Divided Aristocracy?', in Bates and Curry (eds), *England and Normandy*, 61).

[99]   *GG*, 100: '*Ordinatus est non sancta consecratione Stigandi*'; *GND* II, 170: '*Reddente*'; *Carmen* (1), 10: '*Criminis infesti*'; *Carmen* (2), 10.

[100]   *Carmen* (1), 4: '*Tutor et ecclesie*'; *Carmen* (2), 4; *GND* II, 184: '*Pium atque ortodoxum regem*'.

As always before, the Normans remain great and renowned warriors, the 'unconquered people'.[101] The individuals who make themselves known in the histories do so for their great exploits in battle; the valiant display of the young knight at Hastings, mentioned by William of Poitiers, is a classic example.[102] As the Norman leader, William is expected to manifest exceptional martial skills, and this he does: hence William of Jumièges' characterisation of him as 'the most valiant duke', 'the great warrior'.[103] We have already seen William of Poitiers' glowing description of him as a young knight at arms, but anecdotes such as that told of William in battle against the French, where he sought combat at every turn, and his loss of two horses at Hastings, where he fought on foot with the 'strength of Hercules', add colour to this depiction of a great warrior.[104] Additionally, he makes rousing speeches to his men, rallies them in their flight, and does all those things expected from a good general; he 'excelled all in intelligence, assiduity and strength', and 'crushed the English so thoroughly in one day that afterwards they could not muster the courage to fight him again'.[105]

However, William was not only a warrior. As William of Poitiers records, he was as comfortable 'wearing the garments of a prince and at peace' as he was in 'the adornments which are put on against the enemy'.[106] It is this aspect of William's character that led William of Jumièges to attribute to him 'most noble and excellent merits', and Guy of Amiens to refer to the 'noble ancestors' of this 'great duke'.[107] William of Poitiers records, almost with astonishment, his duke's self-control: 'he knows that it is characteristic of wise men to temper victory, and that the man who cannot restrain himself when he has the power to take vengeance is not really powerful'.[108] Such a collection of valour and virtue are, in truth, highly reminiscent of those descriptions of Richard I appearing to us in the works of Dudo of St-Quentin and serve to show that William was, in the eyes of the Normans, a knight in the truest sense, 'admirable in his constancy and shaken by no fear'.[109] The description of Robert, his son, is along similar lines: he is seen 'brilliantly shining in the blossoming flower of his handsome body and his advantageous age', possessing 'noble virtue'.[110] A far cry indeed from the gritty Scandinavian warriors of one hundred years before.

Thus, those elements that defined an individual as a member of the *gens Normannorum* had undergone, during the course of the eleventh century, an evolution from the simple warrior virtues of the first Norman dukes to those attributes considered to befit a knight, and that were personified for the conquering Normans

---

101 *GG*, 128: '*Inuictissimae nationis*'.

102 *Ibid.*, 130.

103 *GND* II, 170 & 178: '*Fortissimus . . . dux*'; '*Magni debellatoris*'.

104 *GG*, 14; *Carmen* (1), 28: '*Uiribus Herculeis*'; *Carmen* (2), 30.

105 *GG*, 14: '*Inter cunctos . . . excelluisse ingenio, industria, manu*'; 170: '*Die uno protriuit, ut post secum dimicandi fiduciam nullatenus reciperent.*'

106 *Ibid.*, 8: '*Indumenta principis gestaret aut pacis*'; '*Ornatus qui contra hostem sumitur.*'

107 *GND* II, 184: '*Nobilissima . . . probissimaque merita*'; *Carmen* (1), 20: '*Nobilium . . . patrum*', '*Dux magne*'; *Carmen* (2), 22.

108 *GG*, 26: '*Nouit esse prudentium uictoriae temperare, atque non satis potentem esse qui semet in potestate ulciscendi continere non possit.*'

109 *Ibid.*, 46: '*Admirandae constantiae . . . nulla perculsus formidine.*'

110 *GND* II, 184: '*Pulcherrimo tam decentissimi corporis quam gratissime etatis flore uernans in iuuentutem enitescat*'; '*Ingenua . . . uirtute*'.

by their leader, William. There had, however, also been a certain change in the way that the Norman leader was perceived in relation to the Normans as a whole, not least because he was no longer simply *dux Normannorum* but now also *rex Anglorum*, for while the new title may have had no tangible significance on the Norman political stage, it positively radiated ideological change. Always before, the Norman leaders had had to fight for their supremacy. William himself had to fend off those who would disinherit him, both as a child and an illegitimate son, and we can see similar troubles for Richard I in his earlier years, or William Longsword when Riulf rebelled against him.

Yet there was now something more to William's power over the Normans, which could even be seen by non-Normans, and showed itself at Hastings. When the first rout occurred, we have seen how the *Franci* had to be exhorted to return to the battle, yet Guy notes that William simply 'glared' at the Normans, and they returned to the fray.[111] Literary motifs aside, it is clear that Guy perceived a certain loyalty in the Normans that was not present in their allies, and which set them quite clearly apart from the treacherous English. This is not, of course, to say that William met with no revolts within his Norman followers, but rather that they were more surreptitious; the position of *dux Normannorum* had evolved to be a truly powerful one within *Normanitas*, and even the duke's enemies within the *gens Normannorum* respected this fact.

In the years leading up to the conquest, the English and Normans showed themselves to be relatively disinterested in one another; certainly, we lack evidence of significant ethnic conflict. The Normans, as we have already seen, had become 'members' of the *Franci* as far as any outsiders were concerned, and indeed affected much of the symbolism associated with Frankishness. However, when the matter of battle once again reared its head, the Normans proceeded to emphasise their separateness, both on the battlefield and off it, in opposition not only to those *Franci* who accompanied them to England, but also to the *Angli* already there. The ideals expressed as *Normanitas* had changed in a number of ways since the earlier part of the eleventh century, mostly in order to accommodate the concept of knighthood, but also to accept this external badge of *Franci*; they had to change still further when their vaunted leader became something entirely new to them.

Though the Norman leaders had, for generations, effectively been kings within Normandy itself, William became a king in actuality: he held a kingdom, even if that kingdom was *Anglia* and not *Normannia*. William was, to the Normans, a model knight and a great king; to the English, he was something less than either, though by the time of his death he had become mostly acceptable to the native Englishmen, in a way that his son, William Rufus, never quite managed. Unfortunately, there are no Norman sources from the very end of the century with which to compare the English attitude, but we can see that William of Jumièges looked with hope at the promise of the young Robert Curthose. Whether or not his hopes were recognised by the *gens Normannorum*, or whether the criticisms of the *Anglo-Saxon Chronicle* found an echo in the next generation of writers will be examined in the next chapter.

---

[111] *Carmen* (1), 26–8: '*Vultum*'; *Carmen* (2), 28.

9

The Twelfth Century

From the beginning of the twelfth century (and, indeed, slightly before) the narrative histories available for England and Normandy are the product of a new generation of English and Norman historians. During the years from the 1090s until 1154, some of the best-known historians of England produced their works – men like William of Malmesbury, Orderic Vitalis and Henry of Huntingdon – and there is no shortage of histories to examine. A source environment of this type should, therefore, be highly conducive to identity study, allowing for not only a large variety of individual perspectives, but also for a close examination of the changes that *Normanitas* underwent – the abundance of sources leave us with no point in time at which there is no-one writing, and few years where there are not at least two works in progress.

It is, however, no longer possible to pigeonhole these works into 'external' and 'internal' groups, as has been done in previous chapters. As in Apulia, the gap between the conquerors and conquered in England was rapidly disappearing, and the new generation of writers are the product of this collision of societies: often of mixed-blood, certainly of mixed sympathies, they cannot be simply divided. It is best, therefore, to study each source in its own right, as opposed to as part of a group, and compare the various aspects of each source with its contemporaries. These difficulties of division, between 'internal' and 'external' reflect in many ways the difficulties of classifying *Normanitas* as these societies collided. Therefore, in the following chapter, much importance has been attached to an understanding of our sources and their authors, from an identity perspective – definitions of 'self' and 'other' have taken precedence over those elements covered in previous chapters.[1] This treatment of the source material should hopefully provide the most useful information towards an understanding of the perceptions of the *gens Normannorum* and *Normanitas* in this period. Furthermore, a clear understanding of the 'others', which certain writers saw as important, helps us comprehend the framework within which these writers defined their own people.

As has been seen in earlier chapters, perhaps one of the most revealing aspects of any narrative historical source is the way in which the writer uses ethnonyms and, in relation, personal pronouns (us, them, etc.) – the sense of 'we' and 'they' that modern anthropologists believe to form the basis of distinction between such groups.[2] Our

---

[1]   Hugh Thomas has noted the importance of the study of 'otherness' in post-conquest England: *English and Normans*, 27 & 307–22.
[2]   Florin Curta, 'Slavs in Fredegar and Paul the Deacon: medieval *gens* or "scourge of God"?', *EME* 6 (1997), 142.

historians are not always partisans for either the 'Norman' or 'English' side of a debate, but this does not mean that they did not know who they were – the strength of the hold an inherited identity exerts on an individual is very much a situational factor.[3] The responses of some of our writers were conditioned by their religious background, and the dual-socialisation of a number of others, born as they were of mixed-blood, does not create for them a crisis of identity.

Many modern historians, when attempting to define the writers behind the histories, have tried to decide whether a given writer was 'English' or 'Norman' in his sensibilities, affiliations, or whatever else. Yet the fact remains that, as with the earlier Norman leaders, these men did not have to be *either* Norman *or* English: they were quite capable of being both. Indeed, Hugh Thomas has suggested that medieval people were quite capable of holding multiple ethnic identities.[4] This new generation of historians knew what they were, and were merely exploring, through their work, exactly what it was that this meant. The use of ethnonyms in these histories is thus highly representative of which ethnic group(s) these historians felt themselves to be a member of, and the attitudes that were associated with this membership; also, they provide evidence of the way in which such terminology was used to identify other people.

The earliest of the twelfth-century sources are the works of Baudri of Bourgueil (later of Dol) and Eadmer of Canterbury; Baudri wrote his *Carmina* throughout his life, with a particular focus on the period of his abbacy at Bourgueil (1079–1107),[5] while Eadmer commenced the writing of his *Historia Novorum in Anglia* in the 1090s. The first works with a political / historical element in them to appear 'after a generation of silence', both these sources approach the world from what is very much a religious standpoint, undoubtedly in an attempt to avoid the sensitive subject that politics apparently was at this time.[6] The writings of both Eadmer and Baudri lack the sense of a strong tie to a given *ethnie*; however, their use of names still reveals something of the way in which they saw the world.

It is apparent that Baudri, writing from Bourgueil (and France, to be more specific), saw things very much in terms of territory. While he refers to the *gentes* of the *Normanni* and *Angli*, where possible he utilises toponyms: *Normannia* and *Anglia / regna Anglica*.[7] Distinctions of place are further employed within his concept of France – he refers to Maine (as distinct from Guy of Amiens' '*men* of Maine'), *Francia* and *Gallia* – and classical allusions to '*Roma*' and '*Britannia*' are also present, in keeping with the poetic nature of his works (along with Hector and Achilles, the Greeks and Troy).[8] Whether or not his references to *Francia* and *Gallia* have a

---

3   Heather, *Goths*, 5.
4   Thomas, *English and Normans*, 71.
5   Bourgueil is situated in the Pays de Loire, to the south-east of Angers.
6   Quote from Gransden, *Historical Writing*, 136.
7   Baudri, *passim*.
8   Baudri, 157: '*In Cenomannenses audax Normannia uires / Extulit atque ipsos funditus edomuit*'; 84: '*Francia natalis sibi sorduit . . .*'; 115: '*Gallia tunc etiam studiis florebat opimis / Florebatque tuo Gallia plus studio*'. See above, 123, for Guy of Amiens' '*Cenomanni*'. Baudri, 158–9: '*Imperii iussu ceduntur milia patrum / Rome Roma suis ignibus occubuit*'; 157: '*Quid referam Gallos uos debellasse feroces / Et totiens enses uos hebetasse suos? / An portuit uobis obstare Britannia tota?*'; 160–1: '*Non Hector tantus Grecos nec tantus Achilles / Strauit Troianos, fortis uterque tamen.*'

difference of meaning is, unfortunately, unclear given the paucity of evidence either way; however, of his three uses of *Gallia*, two seem to be in a context that necessarily includes 'principalities' of France as well as the simple core of *Francia*.[9] Finally, something of the concerns of Baudri's audience are revealed, in his account of the Battle of Hastings as presented in *Adelae Comitissae*. The poem contains strong pro-Norman overtones throughout, and though Baudri never refers to *nostri Normanni*, his consideration of the English as '*hostes*' reflects the Norman heart of Adèle, the daughter of William the Conqueror and the person to whom his poem was offered.[10]

Eadmer, on the other hand, is even less explicit concerning the *gentes* with which he was involved – he was, as Southern said, 'not greatly interested' in the world around him.[11] The focus of the work on the activities of Anselm ties it strongly to the religious sphere, and it is clear that a religious perspective is uppermost in Eadmer's mind throughout the piece. His references to England are unusual – though it was, apparently, his home, he does not reveal this in the *Historia*, and the only deviation from simple references to it as 'England' is one instance when he calls it 'the King's land'.[12] However, some historians have highlighted a sense of pride in England in some areas of Eadmer's work, perhaps in his unusually long anecdote concerning the cope of the archbishop of Benevento (which was of English workmanship), or in his references to the greatness of St Wulfstan, as 'the one sole survivor of the old Fathers of the English people'.[13] Certainly, this sense is present again in Eadmer's hagiographical writings, but it is clear that, as Sally Vaughn has said, there were 'other factors in Eadmer's life more significant than his Englishness'.[14]

Notably, Eadmer almost never uses ethnonyms to describe people, and his only uses of 'us' refer to himself and Anselm, and whoever happened to be travelling with them. Even when ethnonyms are used, they reveal little about Eadmer's ethnic affiliation. St Gregory, the 'Apostle of the English', is mentioned at one point, but this was long-standing Canterbury usage (though perhaps reflecting Eadmer's loyalty to the community of Canterbury, and its English saints).[15] Elsewhere, in a letter from Anselm to Pope Paschal, which Eadmer records, Henry I of England is referred to as 'the King, who rules the English and the Normans'.[16] Prefixed as this is by a comment regarding accomplishments in 'England and Normandy', there is little to

---

[9]   Baudri does not use both *Francia* and *Gallia* in the same piece at any point, and uses either only occasionally: Baudri, 84, 86 & 246 for *Francia*; 57, 85 & 115 for *Gallia*. Abrahams notes (*Œuvres Poétiques*, 87) that, on the death of Godefroi de Reims, 'la France tout entière se lamente', and it is in this context that the first of Baudri's uses of *Gallia* appears. The second is in the phrase '*Gallia congaude*'.

[10]   Baudri, 159–61. See also Michael W. Herren's translation of lines 207–578 in Brown, *Bayeux Tapestry*, 167–77. For discussion of the relationship between this poem and the Bayeux Tapestry, see Brown and Herren, '*Adelae Comitissae*' and Brown, *Bayeux Tapestry*.

[11]   Southern, *Saint Anselm*, 302.

[12]   Eadmer, 110: '*Terram suam*'; Eadmer (tr.), 115.

[13]   Eadmer, 107–10 & 46; Eadmer (tr.), 111–14 & 46–7; Southern, *Saint Anselm*, 231–2; Williams, *English*, 166–8.

[14]   Sally N. Vaughn, 'Eadmer's *Historia Novorum*: A Reinterpretation', *ANS* 10 (1988), 260.

[15]   Eadmer, 212: '*Beati Gregorii Anglorum apostoli*'; Eadmer (tr.), 227. For Eadmer's role as a spokesman for the needs of the community of Canterbury, see Southern, *Saint Anselm*, 275–7.

[16]   Eadmer, 191: '*Rex qui dominatur Anglis et Normannis*'; Eadmer (tr.), 204.

suggest that Eadmer felt that there was any significance at all to a distinction between Normans and English other than one of where they lived.

There are only two comments by Eadmer that suggest that there was even any tension between the two groups. The first concerns Robert, count of Meulan, who 'had no love for the English and could not bear that any one of them should be preferred to any position of dignity in the Church'.[17] The second deals, again, with ecclesiastical preferment, with Eadmer complaining that, if a candidate was English, 'no virtue that was judged worthy in some other office could help him'. In foreigners, he continued, 'the mere appearance of virtue, vouched for by their friends, was sufficient for them to be judged worthy of the highest office'.[18]

Generally, the limited interest in the either the *gens Normannorum* or *gens Anglorum* is at least partially the product of our writers' religious nature and the political sensitivity of the subject matter. The division of Normandy and England after the death of William I created problems for the historian of the period that were, evidently, best avoided, and this is probably why there are no narrative histories from the period shortly after the Conqueror's death. Certainly, Baudri could write an account in which the Normans were his chosen 'side', and the English were the enemy, but this is an account of Hastings, not one of things that were, for him, current events.

For both Baudri and Eadmer, the concepts of 'Norman' and 'English' were arguably not even useful to their descriptions of events; certainly, they were sensitive terms. In the climate of hostility between Robert Curthose and William Rufus, as duke of Normandy (1087–1106) and king of England (1087–1100) respectively, to call someone 'Norman' or 'English' was, perhaps, to suggest their affiliation to one side or the other, and this included our writers themselves. Once Henry I had control of both England and Normandy, once he had become 'the King, who rules the English and the Normans', then ethnonyms were a more useful resource, but until this point one cannot help but suspect that our writers did not use ethnonyms because they felt that they could not.

A 'tiered' identity model provides a good explanation of the forces at work in such cases as this. Consider, first, that the identity of an individual does not consist solely of the structures produced by and surrounding this membership of one particular group. Personal identity notwithstanding, the sense of self is bound up in a variety of group identities, including (but not limited to) ethnicity, gender, family, socioeconomic class and community, and all these are aspects of a totality.[19] These aspects are layers within the identity of an individual, and each layer exerts a different level of attraction upon that individual, an attraction that is often of varying strength depending upon circumstances.

---

[17] Eadmer, 192: '*Nec Anglos diligere, nec aliquem illorum ad ecclesiasticam dignitatem provehi patiebatur*'; Eadmer (tr.), 205.

[18] Eadmer, 224: '*Nulla virtus ut honore aliquo dignus judicaretur eum poterat adjuvare*'; '*Solummodo quæ alicujus boni speciem amicorum testimonio prætenderent illi ascriberentur, honori præcipuo dignus illico judicabatur.*' The latter translation is from Williams, *English*, 168. Thomas notes that Eadmer's complaints about preferment applied only to the very highest ecclesiastical offices (*English and Normans*, 213).

[19] Geertz, in Hutchinson and Smith, *Nationalism*, 30; Weinreich, 'Operationalisation', 308; Heather, *Goths*, 6.

In late eleventh-century England and Normandy and, more specifically, in the cases of Eadmer and Baudri, what we are seeing is the result of a change in this structure, as a non-ethnic identity layer exerts the strongest hold on them and is thus at the top of the tier. During the conquest period, the ethnic identity can be reasonably perceived as being uppermost, because it is this identity that is uniting the attacking force and the defending force against each other, providing the sense of 'we' and 'they' that is so significant in the distinction between identities.[20] After the conquest, these identities continued to be ranged against one another, but the advent of a new generation altered this state of affairs.

The most significant sign of this change was the division between England and Normandy, which could no longer be considered to be part of the same entity, as they looked for governance to two separate rulers.[21] Against this backdrop were born and raised many men who were no longer sure what their personal affiliation to the *gens Normannorum* or *gens Anglorum* truly meant. What did it mean to be Norman if you lived in England and had less (or even no) contact with the Norman *patria*? If you were *Angli*, were those who your fathers perceived as *Franci* but who now lived in *Anglia* part of your 'us' or your 'them'? Thus, the meaning of the ethnonyms and membership of the associated ethnic identities had come to mean rather less, simply because of the lack of clarity of this definition. Clearer definitions were therefore sought, and the most obvious were those that had been politically created and had, indeed, caused the confusion of *ethnies*: the divisions of territory.[22] England and Normandy as territorial areas had a significance and provided a definition that ethnicity did not, even if the boundaries of these areas were disputed. The landward bounds of Normandy and England were not relevant to this distinction, as the *gentes* within the *Franci* had not been relevant to Anglo-Saxons before the conquest. Normandy and England were clearly divided by the English Channel.

While these definitions provided our writers with a way of making certain distinctions of place, however, there was still an unavoidable difficulty in narrating the political events of the day. The fact that the output of both writers focused on religious matters primarily, and that the historical tradition sees a break here, suggests

---

[20] Curta, 'Slavs', 6 proposes that this sense is the basis of distinction between ethnic groups. However, it is, also, the basis of distinction between *all* groups.

[21] Of course, it could be argued that they never were. The extent to which England and Normandy could be regarded as a single structure has been the subject of much debate among historians, though the idea of 'Norman unity' has proven persistent (for example, Douglas, *Norman Achievement*, 110–12). John Le Patourel's *The Norman Empire* concentrated on the close links created by the interests of the ruling and aristocratic families, and advanced the term 'Norman Empire' as a description of this 'complex of dominion and lordship' (p. 354). Warren Hollister, equally, saw a strong connection between Normandy and England, but noted that this was at its height under Henry I, and that we must be wary of making too much of the cohesion under William I (C. Warren Hollister, 'Normandy, France and the Anglo-Norman *Regnum*', *Speculum* 51 (1976), 202–42). David Bates has also attempted to advance the debate somewhat, drawing attention to the weaknesses and instabilities in this cross-Channel structure (David Bates, 'Normandy and England after 1066', *EHR* 413 (1989), 851–80). Furthermore, Emma Cownie's examination of religious patronage has highlighted the tendency of continental newcomers to give English lands to English religious houses (as opposed to bridging the Channel) (Cownie, *Religious Patronage*, 195). For further, useful discussion, see Chibnall, *Debate*, 115–22.

[22] Thomas has noted that England could provide a locus for collective identity when Englishness proved controversial (*English and Normans*, 268–9).

that religion could acceptably take the place of ethnicity within the identity structures of such men.[23] Adrian Hastings sees religion as a constructor both of ethnicities and nations, a restrainer, and a challenger, through its capacity to create alternative communities.[24] To join a religious community in this period was to forgo local (community, family) ties, and it is possible that the affiliation of religious men and women to their *ethnic* identity might also be challenged by the pull of the Church, allowing them to look past ethnic differences – the regularity of conflicts in the medieval period, however, suggests very much that this was the exception rather than the norm. The power that religion held over people can be seen in the Crusades, when the sensibilities and motivations of ethnic and religious identities were aligned in the same direction – the result was impressive.

In the instance of Baudri and Eadmer, the lack of overriding ethnic ties and the affiliation of both these men to religious communities is clearly evident. While there had been both a religious and an ethnic element to the conquest of England (as the Norman force had papal support for the venture), ethnic distinctions had, by this time, become muddled. Religious matters had not, however – the Normans, in the aftermath of the conquest, were able to adopt English saints, for example – and this allowed both Baudri and Eadmer to avoid the confusion of writing as 'Normans' or 'Englishmen', and instead to write simply as churchmen.[25] This was not a phenomenon solely limited to these two writers either, as it is clear that religious ties superseded ethnic ties for, among others, Lanfranc, Anselm and Wulfstan of Worcester.[26] To these men the people around them were not, in any significant sense, 'Normans' or 'Englishmen' either – these terms are doubly meaningless, both because of the political confusion and because they were *all* Christians. Therefore, while people could be grouped by the territory in which they lived (hence the widespread use of toponyms), ethnic qualifiers are replaced by a religious outlook.

The strength of this religious element is evidently enhanced, in Eadmer's work, by the fact that the problems of investiture in England saw a direct challenge of the spiritual by the temporal, and identities are always at their most apparent when in conflict. This, when attached to his innate Englishness (which is present but not so explicit), is what generates his ethnically orientated comments regarding preferment. The fact that the latter of these two statements appears in the later section of his *Historia* (written after 1119) makes a good amount of sense – it is more ethnically sensitive than the first and, it would appear, the product of a time when the sensitive, transitory stage had passed.[27]

[23] Though Baudri wrote many personal letters / poems, he also produced much religious / spiritual verse, as well as the following works: *Historia Hierosolimitana, Vita Sancti Hugonis Rhotomogensis Episcopi, Vita Sancti Samsonis, Vita Beati Roberti de Arbrissello, Acta Translationis Capitis Sancti Valentini Martyris Gemmeticum in Gallia, Itinerarium sive Epistola ad Fiscannensis, De Vistatione Infirmorum, De Scuto et Gladio Sancti Michaelis, Gesta Pontificum Dolensium* (see *Œuvres Poétiques*, ed. Abrahams, xxiv).

[24] Hastings, *Construction*, 184.

[25] Though there is a 'myth' of Norman scepticism, it appears that the Normans adopted the English saints for the health of the religious community, rather than as any sort of PR exercise. The consequent need for a fully documented history and publicity produced a good deal of hagiographical work (see S.J. Ridyard, '*Condigna veneratio*: Post-Conquest Attitudes to the Saints of the Anglo-Saxons', *ANS* 9 (1987), 204–6).

[26] Thomas, *English and Normans*, 215 & 221.

[27] For the dating, see Southern, *Saint Anselm*, 299.

Orderic Vitalis

The same is apparently true for the majority of the sources written after 1100, adding weight to the suggestion that it was the product of the political climate of the later eleventh and very early twelfth century. The redaction of the *Gesta Normannorum Ducum* produced by Orderic Vitalis from *c.*1109 to *c.*1113 is perhaps a signal that this period was ending. By its nature as a *gesta*-type history, the subject matter of the *Gesta Normannorum Ducum* is political history. Yet, though Orderic added substantial material to William of Jumièges' original work, he at no point extended the work to include the events of 1087–1109. Indeed, Orderic's only extension is to regularise the work by bringing the final book to its logical conclusion, with the death of William I; he does not recount the complex period in which England and Normandy are divided. Thus, he is far freer with his use of ethnonyms here than Baudri and Eadmer could afford to be, and uses far fewer territorial identifiers as a consequence.

Within Orderic's *Gesta Normannorum Ducum* we find Normans, English and French as we would expect, but also Flemings, Bretons and Norwegians. Indeed, Orderic evidences a far clearer perception of the nature of the *gentes* around him than previous authors; the Hastings campaign, in Orderic's *Gesta Normannorum Ducum*, is a venture of not only the Normans against the English, but of the Normans, Flemish, French and Bretons.[28] However, during the course of his redaction, he reveals little of his own affiliation, remaining silent as to exactly who, from his perspective, he sides with in this engagement.

Orderic's later work, the *Historia Æcclesiastica*, is both fuller and more revealing. Though commenced as a church history, it rapidly grew to resemble the Norman *gesta* histories that had preceded it, notably those of William of Jumièges and Dudo of St-Quentin, and Orderic was well aware of his position in this historical tradition.[29] As the major historical source in the Anglo-Norman world for those events which occurred during the period in which it was written (*c.*1113–41), and to some extent for those things that had come before, the *Historia Æcclesiastica* provides a wealth of information. Orderic was of mixed heritage, part English, part Norman, though he was Norman by domicile. His account raises a number of issues to do with Norman perceptions of their own ethnicity, and that of the various *ethnies* that were involved in the history of Normandy and England up to the middle of the twelfth century.

Orderic's pronouncements on the *gens Normannorum* are well known and oft-cited; his (indeed *the*) classic description of the Normans, attributed to the dying King William I, bears recitation:

> If the Normans are disciplined under a just and firm rule they are men of great valour, who press invincibly to the fore in arduous undertakings and, proving their strength, fight resolutely to overcome all enemies. But without such rule they tear each other to pieces and destroy themselves, for they hanker after rebellion, cherish sedition, and are ready for any treachery.[30]

---

[28] *GND* II, 164–6.

[29] Orderic, vol. III, bk VI, p. 306.

[30] Orderic, vol. IV, bk VII, p. 82: '*Normanni si bono rigidoque dominatu reguntur strenuissimi sunt, et in*

This tempered approach to the *gens Normannorum*, as a people who could both achieve the greatest heights of military skill and yet also commit the worst of treacheries, pervades the *Historia Æcclesiastica* from beginning to end. We see Norman magnates who, Orderic tells us, 'had inherited the warlike courage of their ancestors and excelled in judgement and wise counsel' and who 'would have yielded nothing to the Roman senate in talents or experience'; yet these men ruled a *gens* who could be seen to be 'a turbulent people, always ready to cause disturbances'.[31] Of the Norman leaders themselves, Orderic is just as positive, and as damning.

Yet such observations are of little merit without context, and these observations are made more valuable by the fact that they are given the perspective and context of *gens* membership. Though Orderic was clearly aware of his mixed origins, and refers to his place of birth as England, his work was apparently intended to represent a non-English viewpoint.[32] At the end of book IV of his *Historia Æcclesiastica*, Orderic expresses his intention to 'fully and truly describe the fortunes of *our* people in war and peace', qualifying this reference early in book V with the comment that he 'endeavoured by God's grace to commit to writing an account of the deeds of the Normans for Normans to read'.[33] It is evident from these remarks that Orderic here was presenting himself as a Norman and, also, that he thought that the opinions and perspectives in his work would be acceptable to a Norman reader and thus represented, with fair accuracy, the precepts of *Normanitas*.

What is interesting, however, is that Orderic portrays a *gens* not only aware of its greatness, but also of its flaws. The long tradition of Norman rebelliousness and violence appears, in Orderic, as an ego-recognised element, and this is reminiscent of the comments of the eleventh- and twelfth-century sources from the area of Italy.[34] If the acknowledgement of an ego-recognised quality by external writers was a mark of the strength of *Normanitas*, as was the case in Italy, Orderic's explicit acceptance of an external criticism evidenced weakness. But to whom did he feel this weakness applied? As he was writing from Normandy, it is natural to assume that Orderic wrote of the *Normanni* among whom he lived – the populace of Normandy. Indeed, Orderic is to a degree, more informative about the identity in Normandy than about that in England. Yet his conservative mindset, evident in his well-known diatribes against the fashion of long hair and 'pulley-shoes', and rigid respect for tradition had a direct effect on his approach to the *gens Normannorum*.[35]

The *Normanni* of whom he wrote were not simply those people who lived in Normandy, but also those who had since left it. For Orderic, the deeds of those

---

arduis rebus inuicti omnes excellunt, et cunctis hostibus fortiores superare contendunt. Alioquin sese uicissim dilaniant atque consumunt, rebelliones enim cupiunt, seditiones appetuntm et ad omne nefas prompti sunt.' See also Orderic, vol. V, bk IX, p. 24.

[31] Orderic, vol. II, bk III, p. 140: *'militari stemmate feroces, sensuque sagaci consilioque potentes qui Romano senatui uirtute seu maturitate non cederent'*; vol. III, bk V, p. 98: *'semper inquieti sunt et perturbitiones ardenter sitiunt'*.

[32] For discussion of the meaning of Orderic's use of *angligena*, and Orderic's sense of Englishness, see Orderic, vol. I, 2; Chibnall, *World of Orderic*, 8–11; Thomas, *English and Normans*, 81–2, 153–4 and p. 153, n. 51.

[33] Orderic, vol. II, bk IV, p. 360: *'Casus guerræ pacisque nostratuum ueraci stilo copiose dilucidabo'*; vol. III, bk V, p. 6: *'Inspirante Deo Normannorum gesta et euentus Normannis promere scripto sum conatus.'*

[34] Above, p. 103.

[35] Orderic, vol. IV, bk VIII, pp. 186–90; vol. VI, bk XI, pp. 64–6.

Normans who had gone to live in Italy or to England were as much a part of *Normanitas* as those Normans living in Normandy.[36] Even though he was writing in the twelfth century, he considered the movements to England and to southern Italy and Sicily to be expansions of the *gens Normannorum*, rather than divisions into new kingdoms; if some of those who went were guilty of 'forgetting Normandy', they still received a place in Orderic's account of Norman deeds.[37] Orderic was writing from the 'centre of a political vortex', and certainly by the time that he finished his work, his world was collapsing around him.[38] His 'inclusive' attitude to the *Normanni* and the vulnerability of the *Normanitas* that he portrays, therefore, reflect the uncertainties of his environment and his position in the traditional *patria* of the *gens Normannorum*.

With such a strong focus on the Norman homeland, it is unsurprising to discover that Orderic's clearest idea of 'otherness' occurs in relation to Normandy itself. In book V, he records the vision of 'a certain good and holy hermit', which foretells great disaster for Normandy under Robert Curthose.[39] The dream is akin to that of Rollo, as recorded by Dudo, and requires interpretation by a guide, who observes:

> . . . the unbridled horse portends William king of England, under whose protection the holy order of dedicated men and women fights undistracted for the King of angels. But the greedy animals who ring them round are the French and Bretons, the Flemings and Angevins, and other frontier peoples, who are jealous of the prosperity of Normandy, and are eager to seize some of its riches as wolves their prey, but are held at bay by the invincible might of King William.[40]

Evidently, the identification of the 'other' here is, primarily, a military one: the neighbours of Normandy provided a threat of conquest, and therefore a challenge to the basic combative nature of *Normanitas*. The French, Bretons, Flemings and Angevins had all been military opponents of the Normans in the past, and thus are mentioned by name; they are the prevalent 'others'. The presence of these other *gentes* in close proximity to the Norman *patria* makes it entirely unsurprising that they are used as referents for the definition of what was considered non-Norman; also, this listing makes clear the maintenance of a division in the Norman mind between *Franci*, *Normanni* and various regional groups. Orderic's mention of 'other frontier peoples' reflects those who were, as noted, simply not Normans, but against whom the Normans had no particularly strong case – the Normans were aware of them, but were not challenged by them.

The significance of the *Franci* to the process of Norman self-definition goes far beyond this simple awareness of their status as enemies within Orderic's own lifetime, however. When Orderic writes of the history of the Normans, and of their origins under Rollo, it becomes clear that the otherness of the *Franci* is not something that is

---

[36] See Davis, *Normans and their Myth*, 15 and above, pp. 67–8.

[37] Orderic, vol. II, bk III, p. 126: '*Normanniam oblitus*'.

[38] Chibnall, *World of Orderic*, 219 & 41.

[39] Orderic, vol. III, bk V, pp. 104–6: '*Quidam anachorita uir bonus et sanctus.*'

[40] Orderic, vol. III, bk V, p. 106: '*Effrenis caballus portendit Guillelmum regem Anglorum, sub cuius defensione sacer ordo deuotorum, secure militat regi angelorum. Auida uero animalia quæ circumstant sunt Franci et Britones, Morini et Andegauenses, aliæque gentes collimitaneæ, quæ nimis inuident felicitati Normanniæ, et paratæ sunt uelut lupi ad prædam opes eius inuadere, sed Guillelmi regis penitus repelluntur inuincibili fortitudine.*' For Rollo's dream, above, p. 25.

short-lived. Whether looking back only to the ancient dispute between the Normans and the French over the Vexin, or further to the time that 'Rollo led a strong force of young Danes into Neustria and strove with all his might to annihilate the Gauls', it is evident that enmity between the Normans and the French is presented as a fundamental tradition.[41] Rollo may also have defeated the 'king of Denmark' and 'forced the Frisians, crushed in bloody battles, / To offer fealty and pay him tribute', but it was the French who they had to live beside and who therefore challenged their identity more than most.[42] Indeed, Orderic sees a divine element in this conflict, blaming Satan for creating 'great enmity between the French and the Normans'.[43] For Orderic, Normandy was ringed around with enemies, all of them longstanding, and each therefore clearly defined by name and nature. The distinctiveness of *Normanitas* in Normandy, therefore, was maintained in part by reference to these well-known and clearly defined alternate structures.

In the south and east, from Orderic's standpoint in Normandy, the enemies were rather more vague, and certainly less important. The Normans in Italy had to contend with the Greeks and Lombards, the former in battle and the latter because of their inherently treacherous nature.[44] Yet there appear to be two levels of 'otherness' here: the Normans seem not to want to fight the Greeks and, indeed, appear to be more interested in working *with* them, whereas the Lombards have, in Orderic's narrative, the same attributes as can be seen in the Norman histories written in the Italian area: they are perfidious, and desert their leaders in battle. The more positive attitude towards the Greeks is perhaps a product of the First Crusade, which for Orderic is even less complicated: there are Christians and non-Christians. Ethnically, these see representation in the events at Tarsus, where Orderic reports the citizens shouting:

> 'Franks, conquerors and rulers of the world! The Turks have gone, the city is open, enter! Hurry, unconquered Franks, to receive the city'.[45]

This reveals the ethnic perceptions that underlay these religious identities. The non-Christians are 'Turks', the Christian soldiery 'Franks'; those subject people who invite the Franks into their city can only be Greeks. Therefore, the Greeks and Franks, holding Christianity in common, are united by a religious identity that reaches above and beyond even the largest divisions of doctrine, when faced with the challenge of the Muslim 'Turks'. When talking of the Franks, the divisions of the Norman perspective once again find themselves in evidence – we see men of France, of Normandy and of Flanders, for example – and there is still discord among these people, but they are united against a common enemy. Unsurprisingly, the 'Turks' are just that: there is no distinction for Orderic within this monolithic unchristian entity. Those who are Christian are seen to desert their leaders and join the crusaders

---

41 *Ibid.*, vol. IV, bk VII, p. 74; vol. II, bk III, p. 6: '*Rollo dux cum ualida Danorum iuuentute Neustriam ingressus est, et Gallos . . . uehementer attere nisus est.*'
42 *Ibid.*, vol. III, bk V, p. 90: '*Regem . . . Daciæ*'; '*Fresios per plurima uulnera uictos / Vt sibi iurarent atque tributa darent.*'
43 *Ibid.*, vol. II, bk III, p. 78: '*Nimia inter Francos et Normannos seditio.*'
44 *Ibid.*, vol. IV, bk VII, pp. 26 and 32, for example.
45 *Ibid.*, vol. V, bk IX, p. 66: '*Franci triumphatores orbis et dominatores; Turci recesserunt, urbs patet, accedite! Currite Franci inuictissimi recepturi ciuitatem.*'

in at least one instance.[46] On another note, while the only apparent distinction here is one of religion, Orderic was not averse to using skin colour as a signifier. His depiction of the Devil as 'an Ethiopian, black as soot, with a flowing beard, breathing sparks of fire from his mouth' says much of the Norman perspective of the associations of colour, religion and evil.[47]

For the purposes of this chapter, though, our most significant focus is, of course, England. It is evident from Orderic's use of language that he sees a clear divide between the Normans and the English, and the only other *gentes* mentioned – the Welsh and the Norwegians – are viewed fairly dismissively. As with the Normans elsewhere, the Normans in England are, for Orderic, part of that expansive *gens Normannorum* of which he himself is a member. But this is not to say that the situation in England is necessarily clear-cut; on the contrary, while the view provided of the Normans is consistent, that of the English is not entirely what one might expect. That there was opposition between the Norman and English *gentes* was only to be expected, as one had conquered the other; what *is* unusual is Orderic's consideration that it was possible for the conquered people to have a reasonable grievance against their conquerors. He records an event in which some guards overreacted and burnt some buildings – 'the English, after hearing of the perpetration of such misdeeds, never again trusted the Normans who seemed to have betrayed them, but nursed the anger and bided their time to take revenge' – and mentions that the Normans hated the English abbots, apparently without good reason.[48] The suggestion is, therefore, that the English in some way differ from the usual 'other', and this is reinforced by the fact that Orderic finds himself able to praise their achievements. When the English defeat the Norwegians, for example, he describes them as 'relentless'.[49] It appears, therefore, that Orderic is elevating the English to some degree, perhaps from 'non-Normans' to 'almost-Normans'. Certainly, he seems to show some awareness of a Germanic commonality when he notes the following derivation of the ethnonym 'Norman':

> In the English language 'aquilo' means 'north' and 'homo', 'man'; Norman therefore means 'man of the north'. . .[50]

The choice of English here, rather than Norse, is suggestive of a traditional connection between Normandy and England, perhaps even that tradition recorded by Dudo of St-Quentin, wherein Rollo was granted half of the English kingdom in return for the aid he rendered to the king.[51]

This is not to say that Orderic considered the English and Normans to have a direct connection in the contemporary world, however. He continues to distinguish

[46] *Ibid.*, vol. V, bk X, p. 364.

[47] *Ibid.*, vol. III, bk V, p. 40: '*Æthiops, niger ut fuligo barbam prolixam habens; et scintillas igneas ex ore mittens.*'

[48] *Ibid.*, vol. II, bk III, p. 184: '*Angli factionem tam insperatæ rei dimetientes nimis irati sunt; et postea Normannos semper suspectos habuerunt, et infidos sibi diiudicantes ultionis tempus de eis peroptauerunt*'; vol. II, bk IV, p. 344.

[49] *Ibid.*, vol. II, bk III, p. 168: '*Instantibus*'.

[50] *Ibid.*, vol. V, bk IX, p. 24: '*North . . . anglice aquilo; man uero dicitur homo. Normannus igitur aquilonalis homo interpretatur . . .*'.

[51] Dudo, p. 159; Dudo (tr.), 40.

between *Franci* (used, when writing on England and perhaps linguistically, to differentiate between those of native and continental origin) and *Angli* throughout his work, and an example can be seen as late as book XII.[52] Additionally, in his account of the rebellion of Robert of Bellême, in which Robert 'strengthened the ramparts and walls of his castles everywhere, and called on his fellow Normans, the alien Welsh, and all his neighbours to assist him', the English are notably absent.[53] The same account reveals something of his perceptions of territory, also; when the Normans are defeated by Robert, 'the more spirited Normans were overcome with shame because, after triumphantly conquering foreign peoples in barbarous regions, they were now themselves conquered and put to flight *in the heart of their own land* by one of the sons of Normandy'.[54]

Clearly, Orderic considered England to be part of the Norman homeland, but did not consider the English to be any true part of the *gens Normannorum*. That he held some respect for the English is unsurprising, given that he was half-English himself; that he was happy to include such ambivalence towards the English in 'an account of the deeds of the Normans for Normans to read' suggests that he believed that this would be readily accepted by his readership.[55]

William of Malmesbury

Orderic's contemporary, William of Malmesbury, also appears to have felt free to expresses his particular *gens* affiliation. That he wrote extensively on England, in his *Gesta Regum Anglorum*, *Gesta Pontificum Anglorum* and various saints' lives is in itself suggestive of an Anglocentric standpoint, and the declaration of intent at the outset of the *Gesta Regum* would seem to support this:

> It was therefore my design, in part moved by love of *my country* and in part encouraged by influential friends, to mend the broken chain of *our history*, and give a Roman polish to the rough annals of *our native speech*.[56]

And it is not only in this one sentence that William ties himself to England. He tells (in II.207) of a portent appearing on the borders of Normandy and Brittany, of

> a woman, or rather pair of women, with two heads, four arms, and everything else double down to the navel; below that two legs, two feet, and everything else single.

---

52 Orderic, vol. VI, bk XII, p. 194.
53 *Ibid.*, vol. VI, bk XI, p. 20: '*Castella sua uallis et muris undique muniuit, et a cognatis Normannis extraneisque Gualis et a cunctis affinibus suis adminicula petiuit.*'
54 *Ibid.*, vol. VI, bk XI, p. 34: '*Animosiores Normanni uehementer erubuerunt, quod illi qui exterarum uictores gentium in barbaris regionibus floruerunt, nunc in suæ telluris sinu ab uno filiorum uicti et fugati sunt*'; my italics.
55 *Ibid.*, vol. III, bk V, p. 6: '*Normannorum gesta et euentus Normannis.*'
56 *GRA*, vol. I, bk I, p. 14: '*Vnde michi cum propter patriae caritatem, tum propter adhortantium auctoritatem uoluntati fuit interruptam temporum seriem sarcire et exarata barbarice Romano sale condire.*' The inclusion of the pronouns (after Mynors' translation) italicised above is not an entirely accurate rendering of the Latin into English, as these words do not appear in the Latin itself. However, without pronouns, the passage makes no sense and, as William has already declared his love (*caritatem*) for the country in question, the addition of these particular pronouns seems reasonable.

One of them laughed, ate and talked; the other cried, fasted and said nothing. There were two mouths to eat with, but only one channel for digestion. In the end one died, and the other lived; the survivor carried round her dead partner for nearly three years, until the heavy weight and smell of the corpse were too much for her also.[57]

William's discussion of the meaning of this portent is not, in itself, suggestion of his affiliation; though he gives the interpretation that it represented the fact that 'Normandy, dead and nearly sucked dry, is supported by the financial strength of England', he adds the disclaimer that 'the idea was even published'.[58] However, his subsequent comment on England – 'if the moment ever comes when she can breathe the air of that freedom whose empty shadow she has pursued so long!' – reveals rather more of his perceptions, and adds to the evidence for an Anglocentric perspective.[59]

Yet, while William quite clearly considered himself to be 'of England', it would appear that he didn't consider himself to be 'English' in a true sense. While his focus was on England, and England was evidently where his heart was, William makes a comment at the beginning of book III that cannot be ignored. When talking of King William I, he notes that he has been overpraised by Norman writers and ravaged by English writers, after which he observes:

> For my part, having the blood of both nations in my veins, I propose in my narrative to keep a middle path.[60]

He was, evidently, conscious of his mixed heritage, and was not averse to admitting to it and, indeed, allowing it to condition his outlook (where William I was concerned, for example). With that in mind, it cannot be said with conviction that William was writing a genuinely Anglocentric history, and certainly it is impossible to agree without qualification with the statements of historians such as John Gillingham that William thought of himself to be 'English'.[61]

William's attitude towards the 'other' adds at least something to our understanding of his affiliation. In the context of England, we see his somewhat negative depiction of the Welsh, 'in constant revolt' and what may be a positive portrayal of the Scots.[62] He tells us that Matilda was 'a daughter of the king of the Scots . . . descended from an ancient and illustrious line of kings', but the later comment may refer to her 'exalted rank as a great-great-niece of King Edward, through his brother

---

[57] *Ibid.*, vol. I, bk II, p. 384: '*In una uel potius duabus mulieribus due erant capita, quattuor brachia, et cetera gemina omnia usque ad umbilicum; inferius duo crura, duo pedes et cetera omnia singula. Ridebat comedebat loquebatur una, flebat esuriebat tacebat altera; ore gemino manducabatur, sed uno meatu digerebatur. Postremo una defuncta superuixit altera; portauit pene triennio uiua mortuam, donec et mole ponderis et nidore cadaueris ipsa quoque defecit.*'

[58] *Ibid.*, vol. I, bk II, p. 386: '*Mortuam et pene exhaustam Normanniam uigens pecuniis sustentat Anglia*' and p. 384: '*Litteris etiam traditum*'.

[59] *Ibid.*, vol. I, bk II, p. 386: '*si umquam in libertatem respirare poterit, cuius inanem iam dudum persequitur umbram*'.

[60] *Ibid.*, vol. I, bk III, p. 424: '*Ego autem, quia utriusque gentis sanguinem traho, dicendi tale temperamentum seruabo.*'

[61] John Gillingham, 'The Foundations of a Disunited Kingdom', *The English in the Twelfth Century* (Woodbridge, 2000), 99. Gillingham is, of course, aware that William was of mixed-blood (Gillingham, 'Revival', 89).

[62] *GRA*, vol. I, bk V, p. 726: '*Semper in rebellionem surgentes.*'

Edmund', which William mentions elsewhere.[63] Additionally, he was obviously aware that the newcomers in England are not solely Norman in origin – he mentions the Flemings who 'were lying low in England in such numbers as actually to seem a burden on the realm itself'.[64] Even though he can be seen to use the distinction of *Franci et Angli*, it is clear that he saw the French and Normans as separate people (he refers to '*Francis et Normannis*', for example).[65]

Further revealing information appears concerning the first crusade when, after his recitation of the call to crusade, William comments that:

> The central areas were not alone in feeling the force of this emotion: it affected all who in the remotest islands or among barbarian tribes had heard the call of Christ. The time had come for the Welshman to give up hunting in his forests, the Scotsman forsook his familiar fleas, the Dane broke off his long drawn-out potations, the Norwegian left his diet of raw fish.[66]

Evidently, for William, the 'barbarians' here listed were those who constituted important 'others' and all of whom had a direct bearing on the history of the English.

Perhaps the most important definitions here, however, are those of English and Norman. Is it possible, through William's work, to see either a particular affiliation to either one of these ethnicities? There are three occasions on which direct comparison of the two reveal something of William's views on the qualities of each *gens*. Two of these surround Hastings, as might be expected, the first being a comparison of the actions of the two *gentes* prior to the battle itself. In the *Gesta Regum*, both sides drew up their lines 'each in the traditional manner' – the English 'spent a sleepless night in song and wassail, and in the morning moved without delay against the enemy'; the Normans 'spent the whole night confessing their sins, and in the morning made their communion'.[67] Elsewhere, the English appear as drunkards, rash and hot-blooded, 'hair short, chin shaven, arms loaded with gold bracelets, skin tattooed with coloured patterns, eating till they were sick and drinking till they spewed'.[68] The Normans, conversely, are bellicose, ambitious and pious, 'well-dressed to a fault, and particular about their food, but this side of any excess'.[69]

The Normans are, it would appear, the superior of the two *gentes*, at least from William's viewpoint, by dint of their piety if nothing else. Evidently, the Normans

---

63   *Ibid.*, vol. I, bk V, p. 754: '*Ex antiqua et illustri regum stirpe descendit . . . filia regis Scottorum*'; vol. I, bk V, pp. 714–16: '*Genere sullimis utpote regis Eduardi ex fratre Edmundo abneptis.*'

64   *Ibid.*, vol. I, bk V, p. 726: '*Occultabat Anglia, adeo ut ipsi regno pro multitudine onerosi uiderentur.*'

65   In the *GRP*, William records Aldred's exaction of an oath from King William to dispense the same law to the French and the English ('*aequo jure Anglos quo Francos tractaret*': *GRP*, 252). Yet throughout the *GRA*, he makes distinctions between French and Norman (for example, see *GRA*, vol. I, bk III, p. 458).

66   *GRA*, vol. I, bk IV, p. 606: '*Nam non solum mediterraneas prouintias hic amor mouit, sed et omnes qui uel in penitissimis insulis uel in nationibus barbaris Chrisi nomen audierant. Tunc Walensis uenationem saltuum, tunc Scottus familiaritatem pulicum, tunc Danus continuationem potuum, tunc Noricus cruditatem reliquit piscium.*'

67   *Ibid.*, vol. I, bk III, p. 452: '*Patrio quique ritu*'; '*Totam noctem insomnem cantibus potibusque ducentes, mane incunctanter in hostem procedunt*'; p. 454: '*Nocte tota confessioni peccatorum uacantes, mane Dominico corpori communicarunt.*'

68   *Ibid.*, vol. I, bk III, p. 458: '*Crines tonsi, barbas rasi, armillis aureis brachia onerati, picturatis stigmatibus cutem insigniti; in cibis urgentes crapulam, in potibus irritantes uomicam.*'

69   *Ibid.*, vol. I, bk III, p. 460: '*Uestibus ad inuidiam culti, cibis citra ullam nimietatem delicati.*'

were also felt to be militarily superior, as is shown by events surrounding Robert Curthose's invasion of England in the reign of Henry I. Though many Normans had joined Robert's cause, the English widely remained loyal to Henry, and he,

> grateful for his subjects' loyalty and careful for their safety, went constantly through their ranks, teaching them how to counter fierce cavalry attacks by holding their shields before them and returning blow for blow. As a result, they lost all their fear of the Normans, and actually demanded to be allowed to fight.[70]

It would appear that William saw the *gens Anglorum* as cowed by the *gens Normannorum*, aware that their martial technique was lacking, and this is yet another instance in which William portrays the Normans as superior to the English when the two *gentes* are directly compared.

In William, then, we see a writer who evidently thought of England as his home: he was a patriot, and England was his *patria*.[71] That the idea of the *patria* was important to him can be seen when he writes, critically, of Robert Curthose in the *Gesta Regum*: 'For at that time [of his father's death] Robert, the eldest son, was in France, making war on his fatherland.'[72]

However, in William's perceptions, there is an unusual discontinuity. One would expect that, in identifying himself with England, William would also identify himself with the English, as the product of this *patria*. Yet there is no evidence that held the English themselves in anything like the same esteem as England itself. Conscious as he was of his mixed-blood, he quite clearly saw the *gens Normannorum* as the superior of the two *gentes* from which he originated, not only in matters of piety, but also in matters of war, conduct and dress; it was the 'rough' English annals that required a 'Roman polish'.[73] From his comments on the Welsh and Scots, he evidently didn't consider the English to be interlopers or anything of that sort, and the dedication of the work to Robert, earl of Gloucester, while perhaps promoting praise of the conquerors, does not in itself explain the negative attitude taken towards the *gens Anglorum* in general.

In short, then, what was William up to? There was obviously a clear distinction in his mind between territory and people, between *patria* and *gens*, and his affiliations in these two areas bear witness to this separation. What is difficult to explain, however, is how the idea that one's *patria* and one's favoured *gens* could be, in turn, the conquered and the conqueror. The territorial affiliation is perhaps most easily explained, in that England was not only William's *patria*, but also his home, and his attachment to the country itself is therefore entirely reasonable. His apparent attachment to the conquering *gens Normannorum* is, with due consideration, not quite as simple as it seems. In his statement of intention, mentioned above, William makes reference to 'our country' and 'our native speech', neither of which can be said to be comments on his territorial affiliation, and must therefore suggest a *gens*

---

[70] *Ibid.*, vol. I, bk V, p. 716: '*Prouintialium fidei gratus et saluti prouidus, plerumque cuneos circuiens docebat quomodo, militum ferotiam eludentes, clipeos obiectarent et ictus remitterent; quo effecit ut ultroneis uotis pugnam deposcerent, in nullo Normannos metuentes.*'

[71] **Patriot**: 2. a. One who disinterestedly or self-sacrificingly exerts himself to promote the wellbeing of his country (*Oxford English Dictionary*, vol. XI, p. 349).

[72] *GRA*, vol. I, bk III, p. 512: '*Nam tunc Robertus primogenitus in Francia contra patriam bellebat.*'

[73] Above, n. 56.

membership, which can be assumed, from the context, to be 'English'. Yet elsewhere, William's refers to his mixed-blood, suggesting that the 'our' here is not necessarily straightforward, especially as he proceeds to denigrate the English throughout his work, and praise the Normans.

The significant issue here would seem to be the fact that William is writing a history, and therefore is, in the main, writing of events in the past from a contemporary perspective. William is 'Anglo-Norman': he states his intention to judge William I from this very standpoint, which is evidently neither strictly 'Norman', nor strictly 'English'.[74] At the time William was writing, it was the descendants of the Norman conquerors who set the standards of the day in England; Norman values were those that predominated in society, and it is these values that doubtless conditioned William's upbringing. Thus, when William looked on the past, he saw the Norman exemplifying the values of his own day, while the English were different, and therefore worthy of criticism. Furthermore, the 'our' of William's intention is *not* one of Englishness. That this referred to the English could only ever be assumed, as there is nothing in the text itself that actually states this. William refers to 'my country', which we can see from the context of the work itself was England, and therefore the group to which the 'our' refers is one of 'inhabitants of England'; 'our native speech' is evidently English, as the language of the natives of England.

Therefore, as a *Gesta Regum Anglorum*, written in the twelfth century, could happily include those Norman kings of the English who came after the conquest, so the 'inhabitants of England' could include those who lived in England in William's day – his people. William saw himself as neither Norman, like William of Jumièges, nor English, like the Anglo-Saxon chronicler, but as a product of two *gentes*, two cultures and one country.

A last remark should be made concerning William's religious affiliations, by dint of their great significance within his outlook. As he was a monk, religion was evidently a significant element within his community identity, but was never responsible for replacing his ethnic / territorial identity, though these may well have been informed by his strong religious ties. Certainly, when he compares the *gens Normannorum* and *gens Anglorum*, much significance is given to religious degeneracy among the English, and to the Normans' great piety.[75] Prior to Hastings, the difference in the importance of Christianity to the two peoples is again evident, the English spending the night singing and drinking while the Normans prayed.[76] Though some of the people were less Christian than he might have hoped, however, he was aware that some of the *gens Anglorum* still trod 'the narrow path of holiness', and he continued to praise the strong tradition of hagiolatry in England:

> Does not the whole island gleam with so many relics of its own natives, that you can scarcely pass through any town of note without hearing the name of a new saint? And think of the many whose memory has perished for want of historians![77]

---

[74] *GRA*, vol. I, bk III, p. 424.

[75] *Ibid.*, vol. I, bk III, pp. 456–60.

[76] *Ibid.*, vol. I, bk III, pp. 452–4. The papal support for the Norman invasion is doubtless relevant here, also.

[77] *Ibid.*, vol. I, bk III, p. 458: '*Uia semitam sanctitatis*'; vol. I, bk III, pp. 456–8: '*Nonne tota insula tantis reliquiis indigenarum fulgurat ut uix aliquem uicum insignem pretereas ubi noui sancti nomen non audias?*

That these factors may have guided his identification with England (as the home of so many saints) and the values of the *gens Normannorum* cannot but be suspected, and once again we see the concept of religion, as a constructor of identities, at work.[78]

The Hyde Chronicle

In contrast to both Orderic and William, the so-called Hyde Chronicle, though written during the same time period, is a relatively uncomplicated source in many ways. The author clearly did not consider himself to be English, as he refers to Sussex as a name 'in *their* language', and the probability is that he was either Norman or Anglo-Norman.[79] Generally, however, there is little to see in the way of ethnically charged language with regard to any of the *gentes* to which the author refers. Though Harold is mentioned as usurping the English kingdom, the chronicler goes on to call him king, both of the English and of all England, in subsequent passages.[80] Even the 'unusually hostile view of Hereward the Wake' may be blamed more on the attachment of the author to the Warenne family (as Frederick, William de Warenne's brother-in-law, was killed by Hereward) than on his *gens* affiliation.[81]

The interesting and, indeed, unique element within the Hyde Chronicle is the formulation *Normananglorum*, and variants thereof. The 23 usages, in such forms as *rex Normanglorum* and *regnum Normananglorum,* are the only instances in any contemporary source of such a hybrid term.[82] The question is, of course, what does this term signify? Apparently, modern historians are not the first people to have asked it, as the expression appears to have confused the thirteenth-century scribe who produced our surviving manuscript; he was led to write *Norma=n=anglorum* on the first occasion, then became somewhat erratic with his abbreviation marks before settling on *Normanglorum*. The hyphens in the printed edition ('*Norman-Anglorum*') exacerbate the problem for the modern reader, as they are not represented in the manuscript. [83]

Both John Le Patourel and Warren Hollister considered this term to be important, and Hollister went so far as to suggest that it bore 'the weight of a calculated political theory'.[84] However, more recent work has sounded a note of caution: David Bates, for example, considers the term to be simply 'one which draws attention to the coming together of two peoples under a single ruler and / or ruling class and within a single Church'.[85] Ian Short, equally, advises against reading into the term 'any

---

Quam multorum etiam periit memoria pro scriptorum inopia!' For more on the post-Conquest saints cults, see Ridyard, '*Condigna veneratio*'.

[78] Hastings, *Construction*, 184.

[79] *LMH*, 288: '*Regio quæ lingua eorum dicitur Sudsexia*'; also Lewis, 'Domesday Book', 332 & n. 28, 331.

[80] *LMH*, 290: '*Haroldus . . . regnum Anglorum . . . usurpavit*'; 291: '*Haroldus, rex Anglorum*'; 292: '*Haroldus vero, rex totius Angliæ*'.

[81] Gillingham, 'Revival', 90; *LMH*, 295.

[82] *LMH*, 297 & 300, for example.

[83] Bates, 'Normandy and England', 877.

[84] Le Patourel, *Norman Empire*, 231; Hollister, 'Anglo-Norman *Regnum*', 231–2.

[85] Bates, 'Normandy and England', 880.

specific ideological or political subtext'.[86] Certainly, the application of the term does not suggest that it signified the unity of Normandy and England: we see them mentioned separately in the same sentence on various occasions, even when there was an ideal opportunity to use *regnum Normananglorum* in a territorial sense, and William II appears as *rex Normananglorum* on four occasions (and, of course, was never Duke of Normandy).[87]

Bates sees the term as an adaptation of Anglo-Saxon formulations such as *AngolSaxonum* and *Angulsaxonum* (used in charters, Asser's *Life of Alfred* and the second English Coronation Ordo, for example), used in circumstances 'where Normans and English were ruled by a single *rex*', and much of the evidence seems to support this.[88] However, the assertion is undermined by the passage concerning the death of Matilda, queen of Henry I. The Latin in question relates to the date of Matilda's death, '*adventus vero Norm-Anglorum in Angliam anno circiter liii°*', and it is hard to see how this 'can only refer to the two peoples in England', when it seems to point to the invading Normans alone.[89] The use, on the occasion of William I's death, of the similar construction '*adventus vero Normannorum in Angliam anno circiter xxii°*' suggests that *Normannorum* and *Norm-Anglorum* are synonyms in this example.[90] An interpretation resembling our modern term 'Anglo-Norman', then, would seem reasonable, and would fit all the examples in the *Chronicle*, including the further example cited from the Ledger Book of Stoneleigh Abbey, with the possible exception of *ecclesia Normanglorum*.[91] However, as the *Chronicle* was produced in the same time period as the later sections of Eadmer's *Historia*, this may be a comment on ecclesiastical preferment.[92]

This interpretation would also lend credence to Short's comment that the term was 'an *ad hoc* linguistic attempt . . . to differentiate the Anglo-Normans from the Normans by signalling the formers' multiple social identity'.[93] There is, however, an important question of location if this is the case. John Gillingham has suggested that the author was a Norman writing in Normandy, but the attempt to differentiate between types of Normans seems rather at odds with Orderic's inclusionist interpretation of 'Norman', which included not only Normans in Normandy, but also those in Italy and England.[94] Equally, the suggestion that the author was based in England is difficult to reconcile – it seems unlikely that a Norman in England would want to make the strong association with the English that the term *Normananglorum*

86 Short, 'Self-Definition', 165.
87 Bates, 'Normandy and England', pp. 879–80; an example can be found at *LMH*, p. 307: '*Dum itaque rex Henricus Angliam atque Normanniam viriliter subjugatam . . .*'.
88 Bates, 'Normandy and England', 878.
89 *LMH*, 311; Bates, 'Normandy and England', 879.
90 *LMH*, 297. The use of this dating formula may indicate a relationship between the *Chronicle* and the cartulary-chronicle (*Liber de Hyda*) contained in the same manuscript, which has '*ab adventu Anglorum*' on occasion (see, for example, *LMH*, 7 & 12; also 41: '*anno secundo adventus Grimbaldi in Angliam*').
91 **Anglo-Norman**: Of or pertaining to the Normans in England after the Norman Conquest, or to their descendants, or to the variety of Norman French spoken in England after the Conquest (*Oxford English Dictionary*, vol. I, pp. 466–7). The example in the Ledger Book is noted by Bates, 'Normandy and England', 878.
92 *LMH*, 302 and see above, p. 139.
93 Short, 'Self-Definition', 165.
94 Gillingham, 'Revival', 90–1.

suggests.[95] There is, also, the possibility that the writer was of mixed parentage, as with Orderic and William; writing in England, he might perhaps have held a perspective similar to that of William regarding the two *gentes* of England, and wanted to express his perception of the attachment of the Normans in England *to* England; the hybrid term may express a push away from Normandy that foreshadows the later considerations of identity of writers such as Henry of Huntingdon. The dominance of the Norman *mores* in society may perhaps be expressing itself in the way that a term based on *Angulsaxonum* became *Normananglorum* and not *Angulnormannorum*.

Of course, much of this is speculative. The amount of evidence with which the chronicler provides us is very small, and it really comes down to this formulation alone; there is no ethnically charged dialogue beyond the comment about 'their language', no expression of the author's origins or feelings. Furthermore, there remains the possibility that all this discussion is moot. George Garnett has commented, after discussion with Elisabeth van Houts, editor of the forthcoming new edition of the *Chronicle*, that 'the contraction of the two peoples into one was probably that of a thirteenth-century scribe'.[96] If this were the case, then any attempt to understand the author based on this formulation and on twelfth-century identity trends is doomed from the outset.

Henry of Huntingdon

Henry of Huntingdon is a very different proposition. He is much more forthcoming than the Hyde chronicler, though he still provides rather less evidence of his affiliation than his predecessors, Orderic Vitalis and William of Malmesbury. The only direct insight he offers appears in his prologue, wherein he refers to his commission 'to narrate the history of this kingdom and the origins of our people'.[97] From the title of the work – *Historia Anglorum* – it is clear that the kingdom in question is that of England; the 'people' to whom he refers is a little less obvious. Though, out of context, the natural assumption is a reference to the 'English' of the work's title, with the 'our' thus indicating Henry's membership of the *gens Anglorum*, the actual comment is directed to his patron, Bishop Alexander of Lincoln. In full, Henry writes:

> With these considerations in mind, therefore, and at your command, Bishop Alexander, I have undertaken to narrate the history of this kingdom and the origins of our people, of which you are regarded as the highest and most splendid ornament,

showing that the 'our' refers to Henry himself and the bishop, and thus the *gens* in question is that to which they were both connected.[98]

While the fact that this people must be the 'English' of the title remains

---

[95] Hollister, 'Anglo-Norman *Regnum*', 231; Lewis, 'Domesday Book', 332.

[96] Garnett, '*Franci et Angli*', 112 & n. 25. The proposal that the contraction is a product of the thirteenth century is based on palaeographical work by Diana Greenway.

[97] Huntingdon, 4–6: '*Huius regni gesta et nostre gentis origines . . . decurrenda.*'

[98] *Ibid.*, 4–6: '*Hec ergo considerans. huius regni gesta et nostre gentis origines, iussu tui presul Alexander, qui flos et cacumen regni et gentis esse uideris, decurrenda suscepi.*'

unavoidable, and that Henry considered them to be 'his' people, the choice of affiliation (and corresponding definition of 'English') proves very interesting. Henry himself refers to his kinship with the family of Glanville, the English branch of which is presumed to be connected to the Norman branch, and to the village of the same name in the arrondissement of Pont l'Evêque (though we have no firm evidence to support this identification). Thus, Henry's father, Nicholas, also archdeacon of Huntingdon, had a kinsman in William de Glanville (archdeacon and dean of Lisieux), and there is every reason to suppose that Henry's family were Norman in origin; certainly, they were under the patronage of the Malet lords of Eye, who held a lordship in the Pays de Caux.[99]

However, it would seem that Henry's mother, Nicholas' wife, may have been English. Henry provides various indications that English is his mother tongue, including his use of place and personal names, and his delight in the poem on the Battle of Brunanburh; that said, he does not anywhere mention his mother, and we have no record of her identity.[100] Henry, then, like Orderic and William of Malmesbury, was of mixed race, and the fact that he lived in England and had spoken English from birth, along with the conceptual distance from Normandy created by the residence in England of at least one prior generation of his family, caused him to identify himself as English.

His consideration of Alexander of Lincoln as of the same *gens* is not something that can be explained so simply. Alexander was the nephew of Roger, bishop of Salisbury, himself originally a priest from the diocese of Avranches and bishop from 1102.[101] Roger can comfortably be described as one of the 'Norman bishops' of England, and Alexander was therefore a descendant of a Norman family.[102] Furthermore, it appears that the family was not estranged enough to cause Alexander to be ideologically different from his uncle; indeed, the family was close-knit enough for King Stephen to fear their defection to Matilda as a group.[103] It is therefore impossible to see Alexander as of anything other than Norman descent, yet Henry's inclusion of him in 'our people' suggests that this didn't matter; certainly, the Norman elements of Henry's own descent did not mark him as non-English from his own perspective.

It would appear, then, that Henry's definition of 'English' included not only those whose descent was of pure or even partial English origin, but instead included all those people who had made England their home at the time he was writing, whether they were 'true English' or, to use a modern definition, Anglo-Norman.[104]

Interestingly, while Henry's is an *Historia Anglorum*, his focus is not simply on the 'English' or England, but extends in a number of instances to Britain as a whole, and he uses the terms 'Britain' and 'Gaul' as territorial descriptions, with classical overtones, in various places in his work. It is this idea of 'Britain' with which he commences his work, drawing as he does on Bede's *Historia Æcclesiastica* to proclaim:

99   *Ibid.*, xxiii–xxv.
100   *Ibid.*, xxvi.
101   Chibnall, *Anglo-Norman England*, 128.
102   *Ibid.*, 209.
103   Barlow, *Feudal Kingdom*, 214.
104   Above, n. 91.

> That isle, blessed by its far-famed splendour, surpasses in fertile fields, milk and honey, all others which that god rules, from whose foaming mouth the ocean flows.[105]

Again, it is Britain whose pre-eminent wealth 'excites the spite and jealousy of all its neighbours. Therefore it has been frequently conquered, and even more frequently attacked.'[106] Henry also provides an origin story for the people of this island, taken from Geoffrey of Monmouth's *Historia Regum Britannie*: though not in the history itself, his account appears in a letter to 'Warin the Breton', and it is evident from the context of the letter that this was a matter that concerned him.[107]

Given this usage of Britain, and Henry's apparent definition of 'English', territories were obviously very important to the way that he understood the world. Equally important, however, were the perceptions of his own day, which he imposed on the past that he constructed. His references to Britain and Gaul seem to be intended to provide a classical veneer to his *origines gentium*, and yet he colours them with contemporary interpretations and naming traditions: thus his 'most celebrated of islands' was 'formerly called Albion, later Britain, and now England'.[108] Similarly, his 'Belgic Gaul', which lies to the south of Britain, is a province 'now evidently divided into two parts: one part is called Ponthieu and the other Normandy'.[109] This only adds to the confusion, however, as the area which became Normandy was apparently never part of either the province of *Belgica Prima* or *Belgica Secunda*, as these were provinces in the north-east of the Gallic area.[110]

The confusion aside, however, it is Henry's consideration that Britain and England are synonymous that is of greatest import here; this reveals two possibilities. Firstly, Henry may be using the term to refer to an area that equated to the Roman province of *Britannia*, and therefore England; secondly, he may be using the term inconsistently, sometimes to refer to 'Great Britain' and sometimes '*Britannia*'.

A fuller understanding of Henry's perceptions of Britain and England can be gleaned from his historical writing, in which he attempts to construct a chronology of conquest and settlement for Britain, going back to earliest times. He mentions that 'the Britons came to Britain in the third age of the world', and that five plagues were subsequently sent into Britain, by 'the divine vengeance':

> The first was through the Romans, who overcame Britain but later withdrew. The second was through the Picts and Scots, who grievously beleaguered the land with battles but did not conquer it. The third was through the English, who overcame and occupy it. The fourth was through the Danes, who conquered it by warfare,

---

[105] Huntingdon, 20: '*Illa quidem, longe celebri splendore beata, / Glebis lacte fauis supereminet insula cunctis, / Quas regit ille deus, spumanti cuius ab ore / Profluit occeanus.*'

[106] *Ibid.*, 28: '*Omniam circumadiacentium in se liuorem et inuidiam mouit. Quamobrem sepe expugnata, sepissime uero inpugnata est.*'

[107] *Ibid.*, 558ff.

[108] *Ibid.*, 12: '*Insularum nobilissima*'; '*Quondam Albion nomen fuit, postea uero Britannia, nunc autem Anglia.*'

[109] *Ibid.*, 12: '*Gallia . . . Belgica*'; '*Nunc in duas diuisa uidetur: in eam scilicet que uocatur Pontica, et in eam que uocatur Normannia.*'

[110] Henry's editor does, however, note that this may come from a source similar to the legendary *Gesta Romanorum* (*ibid.*, p. 58, n. 175).

but afterwards they perished. The fifth was through the Normans, who conquered it and have dominion over the English people at the present time.[111]

Much is revealed in this passage concerning Henry's perceptions, and those comments that qualify the information therein. Firstly, concerning the idea of Britain and England, it becomes clear that he is using the terms synonymously and, therefore, that Britain (*Britannia*) is used to describe the Roman province rather than the whole island. Had it been otherwise, the impact of the Picts and Scots would presumably be noted rather differently, and the English could not reasonably be seen as having overcome and conquered the place. Even though there is some reference to the Picts and Scots sharing the island of Britain with the Britons in the earlier parts of the island's history, they are also described as being separated from the Britons by 'two intervening frontiers of sea, which extend a long way inland'[112] (namely, the Forth and the Clyde), and what confusion remains doubtless stems from Henry's rather uncritical usage of Bede's *Historia Æcclesiastica*.[113]

Henry's historical study also reveals interesting information about his perception of the *gentes* who had invaded and inhabited Britain; most significantly, the English and the Normans. Henry's 'third plague' is that of the English, his own *gens* and the subject of his *Historia Anglorum*; this is the *gens* who 'overcame and now occupy' Britain. In his account of the first coming of this people to Britain, he refers to 'the race of Saxons, or English', who had been invited by the British king, Vortigern, to assist the Britons against the Picts and Scots.[114]

In this and his subsequent commentary on the coming of the English, Henry very closely follows Bede, discussing their origin among three powerful peoples in *Germania*, the Saxons, Angles and Jutes.[115] Yet, once again, there is a problem of interpretation: does Henry's use of *Angli* actually constitute an understanding of 'Angles' on his part, or does it represent simply 'English', as it does later? Presumably, the latter case is true, and this is perhaps reflected in Henry's comment that Mercia was 'also called "Middelengle" (that is midland England)'.[116] Certainly, Bede did not have a concept of separate 'Angles' and 'English', and the distinction is, seemingly, a modern conceit.[117] If this is indeed the case, however, then Henry is here recording an *origo* for his people that is not, surprisingly, dependent upon their Christianity; he is, in fact, quite happy to record 'the deeds of the English while they were still unbelievers', rather than maintaining Bede's usage of pagan 'Saxons' and Christian 'English'.[118]

111 *Ibid.*, 30: '*Britones namque in tercia etate mundi Britanniam, Scoti in quarta venerunt Hiberniam*'; 14: '*Diuina ultio*'; '*Primam per Romanos, qui Britanniam expugnauerunt sed postea recesserunt. Secundam per Pictos et Scotos, qui grauissime eam bellis uexauerunt, nec tamen optinuerunt. Terciam per Anglicos, qui eam debellauerunt et optinent. Quartam per Dacos, qui eam bellis optinuerunt, sed postea deperierunt. Quintam per Normannos, qui eam deiecerunt et Anglis inpresentiarum dominantur.*' Greenway's translation of '*plagas*' as plagues is informed by usage in the Vulgate Bible; see p. lix, n. 13 for references to such usage, and for the Vulgate Bible.
112 See, Huntingdon, 26–8 for examples; 70: '*Duobus finibus maris interiacentibus . . . longe irrumpunt.*'
113 *Ibid.*, p. 27, n.44: Greenway observes Henry's usage of Bede contradicts his own commentary.
114 *Ibid.*, 78: '*Gens . . . Saxonum uel Anglorum*'.
115 *Ibid.*, 80; Bede, *Ecclesiastical History*, I.15, p. 27.
116 Huntingdon, 120: '*Que etiam uocatur Middelengle, id est mediterranea Anglia*'.
117 N.P. Brooks, 'Bede and the English', Jarrow Lecture (1999), 6–7.
118 Huntingdon, 128: '*De gestis Anglorum adhuc infidelium*'.

The final plague mentioned by Henry is that of the Normans, and some examination of the relationship of *Normanni* and *Angli* in the *Historia Anglorum* has already taken place above. However, something further must be said on this subject, not least concerning the way in which Henry represents the Normans in the period before his own day. His comments regarding the conquest of England at the beginning of book VI ('on the coming of the Normans') set the stage for his subsequent accounts. He refers to the connection of the English and Normans, through the marriage of Emma and Æthelred, as 'the Normans' unexpected trick . . . since from this union of the English king with the daughter of the Norman duke, the Normans were justified according to the law of peoples, in both claiming and gaining possession of England'.[119]

As one of the five plagues, Henry also saw the Norman invasion as directed by God, and the Normans as 'His own avengers', who had been chosen 'to wipe out the English *gens*'.[120] Yet Henry also saw the Normans in a negative light, as unjust and destructive, and as a people who 'surpassed all other people in their unparalleled savagery'.[121] Clearly, the Normans, namely, those to whom Henry refers using the ethnonym *Normanni*, were the 'other' here. How then does he arrive at the inclusion of Alexander, bishop of Lincoln, among his English 'us'?

The argument that this was an ethnonym bestowed by territory (i.e. English because of residence in England) has already been advanced, but there is a need for further qualification of this statement, especially in light of the alternatives advanced by John Gillingham in 'Henry of Huntingdon and the Twelfth-Century Revival of the English Nation'.[122] One cannot, at the outset, disagree with Gillingham's statements that Henry wrote of the subjugation of the English by the Normans in the earlier parts of his history, particularly in those sections composed prior to *c.*1132 and dealing with the reign of William I. Yet his assertion that Henry 'clearly regretted this' attributes to our author a view that he did not necessarily hold.[123] True, Henry does observe of the English that 'all had been reduced to servitude and lamentation, and it was even disgraceful to be called English', but he is writing here of events that had occurred a generation previously and, indeed, before he was born.[124] It is equally true that he recorded that England, under William II, 'had been unable to breathe', but this is an indictment against an individual, not a *gens*; from Henry's *De Contemptu Mundi*, we can see that he wasn't exactly Henry I's greatest adherent either.[125]

The downtrodden English of whom Henry writes, in the period including and following the Norman conquest, are not Henry's own *gens Anglorum* but instead

---

[119] *Ibid.*, 338: '*De adventu Normannorum*'; '*Normannorum inprouisam . . . cum ex hac coniunctione regis Anglorum et filie ducis Normannorum, Angliam iuste secundum ius gentium Normanni et calumpniati sunt et adepti sunt.*'

[120] *Ibid.*, 412: '*Uindices quidem suos*'; 402: '*Ad Anglorum gentem exterminandam.*'

[121] *Ibid.*, 402: '*Prerogatiua seuicie singularis omnibus populis . . . eos preminere.*'

[122] *Concepts*, ed. Forde, et al., 75–101.

[123] *Ibid.*, 78.

[124] Huntingdon, p. 402: '*Omnes ad seruitutem et ad merorem redacti essent, ita etiam ut Anglicum uocari essent obprobrior*'; xxvii: Greenway suggests *c.*1088 for Henry's birth; the events in question occurred in 1087.

[125] Gillingham, 'Revival', 78; Huntingdon, 448: '*Nec respirare poterat Anglia miserabiliter suffocata.*' Huntingdon, 606–8.

their forerunners. Henry does not lament this defeat and subjection for the same reason that he does not bewail the attacks of the Danes in book V: the English, so Henry wrote, deserved these trials, for 'all goodness [had] so withered away in them, that no other *gens* was their equal for treachery and wickedness'.[126] In 1087, it was indeed 'disgraceful to be called English', but only because 'the Normans had fulfilled the just will of the Lord upon the English people'.[127] What we are seeing here is not the evolving perceptions of a historian concerning his own people, but rather a writer telling of the formative influences on the *gens* of which he is a member; the 'plagues' of which he writes are part of the *origo* of the English as Henry himself saw them in his own day, and follow the form of a literary *topos* far more than that of a subjective analysis.

It is here that the importance of Henry's account of the Battle of the Standard becomes evident. This is not, however, to accept that, to Henry, the Battle of the Standard 'represented the revival of the English nation'.[128] Firstly, the term 'nation' here is far too loaded to use in any useful discussion of medieval identity structures, and the debate concerning the admissibility of this term to describe medieval societies is still ongoing.[129] Secondly, the term revival is, in this instance, an inaccurate one, in the main because it implies that the nature of the *gens Anglorum*, as Henry perceived it, had remained the same between the events of 1087 and those of 1138. Did the events of 1138 simply reflect the resurgence of that *gens Anglorum* who had, only fifty years before, found themselves at their lowest ebb beneath their Norman oppressors? Or did this battle, in which we see the '*gens Normannorum et Anglorum in una acie*', indicate something else, something newer?[130]

The latter seems by far the most convincing of the two possibilities. In that fifty-year period, the *gens Anglorum* had changed, and those things that symbolised the *gens Anglorum*, their customs and so forth, had changed also. That Henry believed in a capacity for change in his people can be seen in their earlier history: he mentions that the Saxons '*were* men of tremendous physique, energy, and daring, whereas *in our own time* one or other army is forced to retreat at the first clash of arms, men nowadays having such puny physique, energy, and daring'.[131] It would therefore seem that the Battle of the Standard is the first significant event recorded by Henry in which the changed *Angli* of his own day and, indeed, his own generation stood side by side with the *Normanni* against a common enemy, the *Scoti*.

This still does not clarify the matter of exactly who constituted the *gens Anglorum*, however, how they related to the *gens Normannorum* and how such men as Alexander of Lincoln could be considered part of the group membership. There is a very

---

[126] Huntingdon, 274: '*Adeo omnis uirtus in eis emarcuit, ut gentem nullam prodicione et nequitia sibi parem esse permitterent.*'

[127] *Ibid.*, 402: '*Anglorum uocari esset obprobrior*'; '*Iam Domini iustam uoluntatem super Anglorum gentem Normanni complesent.*'

[128] Gillingham, 'Revival', 79.

[129] See, for example, Breuilly, *Nationalism* and Hastings, *Construction* for two sides of the argument, and above, pp. 7–8.

[130] Gillingham 'Revival', 79; Huntingdon, 716.

[131] Huntingdon, 104: '*Maxime stature et uigoris et audacie fuerint, quamuis nostri temporis exercitus in ipsa prima collisione statim alteruter in fugam conuertatur, uiris scilicet modo parue stature et uigoris et audacie existentibus.*'

problem of definition and translation here, concerning two sentences in Henry's account:

> *Tota namque gens Normannorum et Anglorum in una acie circum Standard conglobata persistebant inmobiles*

and

> *Nostri uero minime sanguine fuso feliciter triumpharunt.*[132]

To be more specific, exact positions, formations and amounts of bloodshed are not what concern us here; rather, it is important to understand exactly what it was that Henry meant by '*gens Normannorum et Anglorum*' and, subsequently, by '*nostri*'.

Gillingham apparently goes too far in his interpretation of these expressions, considering Henry to be bringing 'Normans and English together in a single *gens*', with which, according to Gillingham, he identified.[133] This stands in stark contrast to Greenway's translation of the 'Norman and English *host*', and the corresponding 'our men'.[134] Evidently, it is necessary to examine these two pieces of text closely in order to unravel their meaning, when two translators can arrive at such significantly different results with no suggestion (in notes or otherwise) that the author's meaning is unclear.

Firstly, our '*gens Normannorum et Anglorum*'. Gillingham's assumption is clearly that *gens* is used here as an ethnic term, Greenway's that it is not. Herwig Wolfram noted that the meaning of *gens* changed in the early middle ages, and that it came to embrace a wide spectrum of meanings, not all of which were of an ethnic nature, though referring to a community of biological descent.[135] Thus, the term *could* be ethnic, but might not be. Greenway's translation, though not a 'standard' translation of *gens*, has merit in the context, resembling closely the interpretation of the Old English word '*folc*', meaning not only a people, nation or tribe, but also a troop or army.[136] We know that English was Henry's mother tongue (see above), so it is reasonable to attempt an understanding of his Latin from this viewpoint. However, given the context of the piece, concerning as it does such a significant battle against the *Scoti*, the likelihood is that Henry intended to distinguish the two sides on the grounds of their race, and that the term is therefore to be translated as such. That *gens* is qualified by the term '*tota*' does not detract from either translation, but in the ethnic context lends a certain epic quality to Henry's prose: 'The whole of the *gens Normannorum et Anglorum* stood their ground unmoved, in one dense formation around the Standard.' Therefore, Gillingham's attribution of an ethnic meaning to *gens* is probably correct.

His proposition that Henry refers, here, to a single *gens* of Normans and English is rather less convincing. The verb, *persistebant*, is a plural, suggesting a plural sense to

---

132   *Ibid.*, 716 & 718.
133   Gillingham, 'Revival', 79.
134   Huntingdon, 717 & 719.
135   Wolfram, *History*, 5.
136   *Cassell's Latin Dictionary* (D.P. Simpson, 5th edn repr. London, 1997), 263–4 translates *gens* as: (1) a clan, a number of families connected by a common descent and the use of the same gentile name; (2) an offspring, descendant; (3) more generally, a people, tribe, nation. J.R. Clark Hall, *A Concise Anglo-Saxon Dictionary* (4th edn repr. Cambridge, 1991), 123 for *folc*.

gens, and, were the noun intended only as a singular, the Latin would require a singular verb for agreement – this does not necessarily require multiple instances of a noun to be represented in the text. Furthermore, Gillingham's observation that neither Henry nor any other writer of the time brought the *Normanni* and *Angli* together in a single *gens* anywhere else makes one suspicious of this solitary instance. It is likely, therefore, that rather than reading this as '*gens Normannorum et Anglorum*' out of context, it was intended to be read as '*gens Normannorum et [gens] Anglorum*'. Henry does not make a bid for ethnic unity here, he merely clearly delineates the sides in the battle: his use of language brings the *Normanni* and *Angli* together, but not so close that he could dispense with the separating '*et*'.

Equal concern is aroused regarding Gillingham's proposal that Henry's use of *nostri* leaves 'no doubt that Henry, although not a northerner, identified with this *gens*'.[137] There is no greater *gens* here for him to identify with, other than the *gens Anglorum* to which he has shown his affiliation throughout his work. Greenway's neutral 'our men', of classical tradition, is an entirely adequate translation here; Henry is simply observing that 'we' had defeated 'them', that his side had defeated their enemies.[138] The ethnic composition of these sides is irrelevant in this instance.

If we do not have a unified Anglo-Norman *gens* with which to work, then, how could Henry see himself and Alexander as both members of the same people, the *Angli*? Some explanation of Alexander's background and apparent *Normanitas* has been mentioned above, and the consideration of territorial affiliation has already been advanced. Gillingham admits that Henry talks of those who had 'their lands, interests and careers almost entirely based in England', but he does not explicitly consider the notion of territorial identity.[139] Rather, he considers the terms *Normanni* and *Angli*, as applied by Henry, to be representative of political interests; hence Alexander is 'English' because he is associated with the pro-English court faction. Political interests are, however, the symptom and not the disease here, in the same way as they are with simple ethnic affiliation: 'identity is an internal attitude of mind which may express itself through objects, norms or particular ways of doing things'.[140] Thus the territorial element within identity more effectively explains Henry's considerations of what it was to be English.

Elements of Wolfram's discussion of the evolution of *gentes* can be seen here: early *gentes*, *in peregrinatione*, have no *patria*, that is, no territorial element. Once the *gens* has completed the process of *Stammesbildung* (tribal formation), however, it then enters *Verfassung*, political constitution, and becomes a *populus* (a term that Henry himself uses), fulfilling one of the anthropological conditions of a functioning ethnic unit, that of historical establishment on a given territory.[141] This particular aspect of group unity is reflected in the expression of the group's ethnonym, such that *Angli* came to incorporate the concept of *Anglia* as a *patria*; the same is true of *Normanni* and *Normannia*.

What we are therefore seeing in Henry's work is not in any way a 'revival of the

---

137 Gillingham, 'Revival', 79.
138 Huntingdon, 719.
139 Gillingham, 'Revival', 89.
140 Heather, *Goths*, 309.
141 Wolfram, *History*, 11; Heather, *Goths*, 7. For Henry's use see, for example, Huntingdon, 414.

English nation'. Rather, it is the movement of the *gens Anglorum* to a new stage in the development of its identity, a step that brings it yet closer to those definitions of 'nation' that are currently so uncertain. These ideas of territory are not entirely new by the time that Henry is writing, and their appearance can be seen earlier in the century in the works of Eadmer and Baudri of Bourgueil. Henry's usage is not prompted by any political sensitivity, however, but by a real change in the way that people were perceived.

This does, however, raise a question. If territorial affiliation is a constituent part of the identity of individuals, then within Henry's work there are those who are *not* English, by reason of their involvement and affiliation with Normandy: are these 'Normans', then, the 'other'? The answer would have to be a tentative yes. They are clearly not the 'other' in the same way that the Danes were, for example: the English were not, at least in Henry's period, at war with them. They share a leader and, from the events of the time of William Rufus, one gets the sense that the kingship is very much held to be 'English'; he is, after all, *rex Anglorum* and not *rex Normannorum*. There are differences of culture and customs, but because of those who are 'English' but of Norman descent, these differences, as with those of language, are not consistent. Indeed, as the fact of territorial affiliation causes this question to be asked, it also allows it to be answered: it was territory by which the *Angli* and *Normanni* could be distinguished from one another. One's *gens* was, for the first time, defined in a way that approximated the modern interpretation: you could reasonably be said to be 'English' if you could reasonably be said to be 'of England'.

Some final comments should be made concerning the 'others' found in Henry's work, as these concepts provide further insight into Henry's definition of the English and Normans of his own day. Henry's attitude to the 'other' is one that is strongly territory-based: if a *gens* hadn't attacked or settled in 'England' at some point, then Henry wasn't overly interested in them. The only real exception to this rule concerns the First Crusade, in which the enemy have form and name, and can be distinguished from one another by their styles of fighting: 'Whereas the Turks, Persians, and Medes inflict death with arrows, the Cilicians and Agulani do so with spears, and the Saracens and Arabs with lances, but the Paulicians with maces of iron and swords.'[142] The crusaders are called by their 'traditional' name of 'Franks', though the term '*Franci*' is rarely found elsewhere in Henry's work.[143] However, Henry shows, by his provision of their *origo gentium*, that they were a distinct and separate *gens* from his own and from the Normans.[144]

As for more immediate 'others', both the Scots and the Danes make significant appearances in the *Historia Anglorum*. The involvement of the *Scoti* in the Battle of the Standard has already been mentioned; their 'otherness' is readily apparent, in their opposition by 'the whole of the *gens Normannorum et Anglorum*', and their 'ancient rallying-cry' of 'Albani! Albani!'; the terminology is so clear that the crushing defeat inflicted on the Scots is almost predictable.[145]

---

[142] Huntingdon, 426: '*Dum namque Turci et Perse et Medi mortem inmittunt sagittis, Cilicienses uero et Augulani telis, Sarraceni quidem et Arabes lanceis, sed Publicani clauis ferratis et gladiis.*'

[143] See *ibid.*, 428 & 430, for example.

[144] *Ibid.*, 478.

[145] *Ibid.*, 716: '*Tota . . . gens Normannorum et Anglorum*'; '*Insigne patrium*'.

Henry's coverage of the Danes, while less directly relevant to his lifetime, provides an interesting insight into the way that he saw the reputation of the *gens Anglorum*. The Danes, for Henry, were a *gens* who are unequalled 'for treachery and wickedness', and his discussion of them dominates book V of his history.[146] He records that England was ravaged for 230 years by 'the most cruel of peoples, who would spare neither age nor sex', and the true significance of this 'stigma' appears in Henry's account of the Battle of Hastings.[147] Before the battle, so Henry reports, William made a speech to his men, which included the following passage:

> 'Let any of the Englishmen, whom our Danish and Norwegian ancestors have conquered in a hundred battles, come forth and prove that the nation of Rou [Rollo], from his time until now, have ever been routed in the field, and I will withdraw in defeat.'[148]

Clearly, the Danes played an important role in Henry's conception of both the *gens Anglorum* and the *gens Normannorum*.

The final 'other' of note are the British, of whom Henry is widely scornful. It is clear that he did not hold the pre-Roman Britons in high esteem, as he makes comments on their 'slackness' and the fact that they had 'accustomed hiding places'.[149] In his own day, Henry also writes negatively of the Welsh, who are clearly distinct from the Normans and English in that they clearly have their own king. Further, the Welsh are shown as militarily weak – they lose in almost all instances against the English or Normans, and even when they fight alongside these other *gentes*, they break quickly.[150] The attitude that Henry displays is perhaps best represented by the speech of Baldwin Fitz Gilbert of Clare before the Battle of Lincoln of 1141:

> 'Let the Welshmen he brings with him be no more than objects of scorn to you, for they prefer unarmed boldness to battle and lacking both skill and experience in warfare, they charge like cattle towards the hunting-spears.'[151]

Henry's contemporary, Geoffrey of Monmouth, is rather more positive about the British, however. Unfortunately, his *Historia Regum Britannie* does little to advance our understanding of the state of the *gens Normannorum* and *gens Anglorum* at this time. As with Henry of Huntingdon, he makes use of Bede's *Historia Æcclesiastica* in his initial remarks on Britain, but his is not a history of events up to and including his own time; rather, as his editor comments, it is a 'pseudo-history of great imaginative power'.[152] From such a piece, it is difficult if not impossible to extract the author's

---

[146] *Ibid.*, 274: '*Gentem nullam prodicione et nequitia sibi parem esse permitterent.*'

[147] *Ibid.*, 274: '*Gentes crudelissimas, que nec etati nec sexui parcerent.*'

[148] *Ibid.*, 390–2: '*Procedat aliquis Anglorum quos centies antecessores nostri Daci et Norwagenses bellis uicerunt, demonstretque gentem Rou, ex eius tempore usque nunc, semel milicie naufragia perpessam esse, et ego uictus abscedo.*'

[149] *Ibid.*, 80: '*Segnitia Britonum*'; 76: '*Ex more . . . latebras*'.

[150] *Ibid.*, 736. In only one instance is there difficulty against the Welsh, and this is more of an indictment against William II than a significant *gens* event (*ibid.*, 444).

[151] *Ibid.*, 734: '*Walenses autem quos secum adduxit soli uobis despectui sint, qui inermem bello preferunt temeritatem, et arte et usu belli carentes quasi pecora decurrunt in uenabula.*'

[152] Monmouth, p. 2, vii; Geoffrey of Monmouth, *The History of the Kings of Britain*, tr. Lewis Thorpe (Harmondsworth, 1966), 53.

views without an in-depth analysis requiring far more space than remains here; what references there are to his own society are allegorical. His tales of King Arthur are equally inadmissible, hailing from a corpus of what William of Malmesbury called 'British nonsense', and are more relevant to a study of knightly class myth.[153]

The Liber Eliensis

Like Henry of Huntingdon, the author of the *Liber Eliensis* thought of himself as English, and made reference, in the prologue to his first book, to Bede's 'history of our *gens*'.[154] Elsewhere, he bewailed the fact that England was 'oppressed under the wretched Norman yoke and robbed of all the honour of yesteryear'.[155] The Normans are clearly depicted as the 'other', and the word *Normanni* is not used simply to describe the winning side at the Battle of Hastings. It is applied also to the Vikings, in a passage that mentions that they had 'ravaged most of the provinces of the English and the French'.[156] Indeed, in the definition of these groups, the commonalities of the *Liber Eliensis* and Henry's *Historia Anglorum* go further.

In the chapter in which he describes the Battle of Hastings and the death of Harold, our author feels compelled to define for us what he means, here, by *Normanni*:

> I speak of those who have been brought up by each parent as Normans and in Normandy.[157]

We have already seen that Henry felt something similar to be true, in his usage of 'English' as a denominator that referred to those who were 'of England'; here, we see the same treatment applied, in a far more explicit fashion, to the term 'Norman'.[158] The references to upbringing would tend to support the idea of an evolving identity that was tied more and more firmly to territory; the mention of parentage goes further again, and is a far more stringent criterion of membership.

Unfortunately, the evidence of the *Liber Eliensis* has limitations. Firstly, the author speaks no further on the definition of *gentes*, though given his clarity he conveys much in this one sentence. It is, however, hard to tell whether this applies to other *gentes* as well, or is simply a functional description of *Normanni* for his readers. It is worthy of note that, if he felt the need to make such a comment, there must have been the possibility of him being misunderstood. This may or may not connect with the second problem with the work, that of its date. The latest recorded event in book two occurs in chapter 87, which details the translation of the relics of the 'confessors' buried at Ely by Prior Alexander – this occurred in 1154.[159] As the definition of *Normanni* appears in chapter 101, it is entirely possible that it was written either very

[153] *GRA*, 26: '*Britonum nugae*'. See N.P. Brooks, 'History and Myth, Forgery and Truth', Inaugural Lecture at the University of Birmingham (23 January 1986), 5.
[154] *LE*, 6: '*Nostre gentis historia*'.
[155] *Ibid.*, 147: '*Sub Normannorum iugo misere depressa ex omni pristino spoliatur honore.*'
[156] *Ibid.*, 60: '*Anglorum plurimas atque Francorum provincias depredaverunt.*'
[157] *Ibid.*, 171: '*Eorum dico qui utroque parente Normanni et in Normannia sunt educati.*'
[158] For Henry's use, see above, pp. 155–6, 157.
[159] *LE*, xlviii & 155–7.

late in, or outside our period, and may thus be intended to clear up an ambiguity, perhaps confusion created by Angevin rulership of Normandy, or a perceived need to distinguish between Insular and Continental Normans.[160] The same problem of date applies to other elements of the work, such as the account of the deeds of Hereward the Wake.[161] However, the fact that this description of the *gens Normannorum* is, seemingly, in line with Henry of Huntingdon's description of the *gens Anglorum* suggests that it is a genuine comment on the nature of a *gens*, though perhaps the clarity is informed by its (possible) late production.

Geffrei Gaimar

Geffrei Gaimar's *Lestorie des Engles* is somewhat divergent from these formulaic histories. In the form of some 6500 lines of verse, Gaimar's work is focused on events close to his own time, though not including details from his own day; as he himself observes, 'of King Henry I will give no account'.[162] His other notable work, *Le Lai Dhaueloc le Danois*, is of similar character to Geoffrey of Monmouth's *Historia Regum Britannie*, and recounts the legend of Haveloc the Dane 'in the time when Arthur was king'; as such, it is of little use in understanding Gaimar's perceptions of the *gens Normannorum* as, at the time in question, they did not yet exist.[163] However, the *gens* with which Gaimar identified is discoverable from *Lestorie des Engles* alone. Not only was he writing in an 'Anglo-Norman' dialect, he was also clearly uncomfortable using English, as his frequent mistranslations of the *Anglo-Saxon Chronicle* show.[164] Throughout his work Gaimar appears to use the terms 'Norman' and 'French' interchangeably, quite clearly so when he records the story of Hereward the Wake, and makes reference to 'our French' and 'us' in the epilogue.[165] Thus Gaimar was probably 'a Norman, the French in which he writes being his natural tongue'.[166]

One would, therefore, expect *Lestorie des Engles* to display a very Norman perspective, yet this is not entirely true. As a 'History of the English', the events detailed in

---

[160] Short, 'Self-Definition', 164.

[161] *LE*, 177–88. The account deals with Hereward's deeds at William I's siege of Ely, and a version of this legend can also be found in Geffrei Gaimar's *Lestorie des Engles* (below). Recent work by Hugh Thomas has highlighted the pro-English elements of the *Gesta Herewardi*, as it appears in a thirteenth-century manuscript, evidencing an opposition to the appointment of French churchmen, its defence of English honour, military virtue and culture, and its caricature of the Normans, who are made to show all those attributes they criticised in the English ('The *Gesta Herewardi*, the English, and their Conquerors', *ANS* 21 (1999), 213–32). However, though the version in *Lestoire* can be dated to 1136–7 (Thomas, '*Gesta Herewardi*', 218), no reliable date can be placed on either the account in the *Liber Eliensis* or on the *Gesta Herewardi* itself, though it appears that an early version of the latter (later rewritten) was complete before 1174 (and utilised for the *Liber Eliensis*; *LE*, xxxiv–xxxvi; Thomas, '*Gesta Herewardi*', 215).

[162] Gaimar, vol. 1, 278: '*Del Rei Henri ne ferai memorie*'; vol. 2, 207.

[163] *Ibid.*, vol. 1, 290: '*En icel tens qe Arthur regna*'; vol. 2, 216.

[164] *Ibid.*, vol. 1, xliv; vol. 2, x.

[165] *Ibid.*, vol. 1, 232–42; vol. 2, 173–80. Epilogue references: vol. 1, 287: '*De noz Franceis mult vnt ocis / De noz chastels se sunt s[aisiz]; / Apertement le vont disant, / Forment nus uunt manacant*'; vol., 213–14. The epilogue in question is that specifically from MSS. D and L of the 'History'.

[166] *Ibid.*, vol. 2, x.

substantial portions of the work pre-date Norman involvement in English affairs, with the result that we see early English dealings with the Normans, as well as with the Danes, Welsh and Scots. Though initial Anglo-Norman relations seem amicable, the fact that the Normans are later 'driven / Out of the land, all in anger' is clearly the mark of some division of interests.[167] The English also 'did not love the Danes', 'punished the Norsemen' and, after some amount of war in Britain, 'there was no more care about the Welsh. / But the Scots still warred against [the English]'.[168] Finally, we see those events prompted by Tostig, who joins first with Flemings and then with Danes against the English, and is on both occasions defeated.[169] From Gaimar's perspective, therefore, all of these people constituted an 'other' for the English; significantly, the same is generally true for the Normans. Indeed, Gaimar's depiction of his own people from this perspective is highly unusual.

Yet the ongoing external influences serve to unite the Normans and English over time. Though they are on poor terms initially, a relationship that culminates with Hastings, in the accounts that follow this their estrangement seemingly ceases. Shortly after Hastings, we see *'Franceis e Engleis'* fighting together against *'Daneis, Noreis'* and, equally importantly, Flemings being used by the king to defend England.[170] The Normans and English thus fight together against two of the 'others' of the English, and only when another of these is involved is there any divide: 'The English were troubled at this, / With the Flemings they meddled'.[171] Even Hereward can be seen to be fighting both Norman and English, and he and his men 'were outlaws to king William'.[172] Regarding the other traditional enemies of the English, we see the Normans making peace with the Scots, though they continue to have problems with the Welsh.[173] Indeed, in the epilogue, Gaimar mentions that the Welsh were driven out by the French, and that they had 'avenged themselves', slaying many Frenchmen in the process: 'Fiercely they threaten us, / That in the end they will have it all back.'[174]

It is through the medium of other *gentes*, also, that Gaimar makes some of his most significant comments about Norman power, revealing a good deal of the provincial enmity occurring on the continent at the same time. During his banter with William Rufus, Gaimar has Walter Tirel comment:

> 'All are your men, subject to you,
> Bretons, men of Maine and Anjou,
> And the Flemings hold of you,
> The men of Burgundy have you for king,

---

[167] *Ibid.*, vol. 1, 174 & 213: *'chasce / Fors del pais, tut coruce'*; vol. 2, 131 & 159.

[168] *Ibid.*, vol. 1, 191: *'pas namerent les Daneis'*, vol. 2, 143; vol. 1, 221: *'des Norheis fit discipline'*, vol. 2, 165; vol. 1, 215: *'Vnc puis de Waleis nout reguard; Mes les Escoz les guerreiouent'*, vol. 2, 161. The translation given deviates slightly from that of vol. 2, replacing 'Scotch' with 'Scots'.

[169] *Ibid.*, vol. 1, 218–22; vol. 2, 163–6.

[170] *Ibid.*, vol. 1, 222–6, 229–31; vol. 2, 166–9, 171–3.

[171] *Ibid.*, vol. 1, 230: *'Mais as Engleis en ad peise, / Od les Flemenes se sunt melle'*; vol. 2, 172.

[172] *Ibid.*, vol. 1, 232: *'Son ost sumond, manda guerreiers; / Franceis, Engleis, e cheualers'* & 231: *'Vdlaghes sunt Willame as reis'*; vol. 2, 174 & 173.

[173] *Ibid.*, vol. 1, p. 243; vol. 2, p. 180.

[174] *Ibid.*, vol. 1, 287: *'Seuengerent'*, *'Forment nus uunt manacant, / Ka la parfin tute lauerunt'*; vol. 2, 213–14.

And Eustace, he of Boulogne,
You can well lead at your need.'[175]

From such a list, it is evident that the Normans saw themselves to be dominant over many of the provincial groups in France. Further comments in *Lestoire* suggest that the most significant of these were the Angevins and men of Maine, with whom the Normans can be seen fighting over Le Mans, and the Burgundians, named specifically in Tirel's retort to William's proposed 'Christmas in Poitiers': 'An ill death may they die, / The Burgundians and the French, / If they are ever subject to the English.'[176] By comparison to preceding writers of histories of the English, Gaimar clearly attached more importance to these continental affairs, doubtless owing to his stronger affiliation with the *gens Normannorum* and Normandy.

Richard of Hexham

The two remaining histories to be examined both focus entirely on the period of King Stephen's reign, these being Richard of Hexham's *De gestis regis Stephani et de bello standardii* and the anonymous *Gesta Stephani*. The work of Richard of Hexham, while very brief, provides some interesting information concerning *gens* perception at the time, though he nowhere explicitly affiliates himself to one *gens* or another. The logical assumption, from the forms of names that appear in his work, is that he was English, but he never states this, and evidence about him outside his ecclesiastical career is seemingly non-existent.[177] However, this lack of expression and, indeed, the general ethnic neutrality of the work where English and Normans are concerned is very much reminiscent of the late eleventh- / early twelfth-century works of Eadmer of Canterbury and Baudri of Bourgueil, in that he at no point distinguishes between a *gens Normannorum* and a *gens Anglorum*. In the main, though there are one or two appearances of *Normanni* and *Angli* in his work, he describes the world in terms of toponyms and not ethnonyms, and there are countless instances of *Anglia* and *Normannia*, as well as references to *Scotia*, *Alemannia* and *Francia*.[178] The suggestion is, once again, that that aspect of Richard's identity that was constituted by his membership of an ecclesiastical community (first as a canon and then, from 1141, as a prior) is dominant here, and he is therefore subject more to religious ties than to those of *gens* or territory.[179]

This perhaps explains Richard's lack of comment on his affiliation, but his perceptions of *gentes* are not fully explained by this. Fundamentally, his work is about the Battle of the Standard, and this is a battle that Richard records as being won not by a Norman force, or by English and Norman forces, but by '*Anglorum*

---

175 *Ibid.*, vol. 1, 268: '*Tuit sunt ti home a tei aclin, / Breton, Mansel e Angevin; / E li Flemene tienent de tei. / Cil de Burgoine te vnt pur rei. / E Vstace, cil de Boloigne, / Poez bien mener en ta bosoigne*'; vol. 2, 198.
176 *Ibid.*, vol. 1, 246–53 & 269: '*De male mort puissent morir / Li Burgeinon e li Franceis, / Si ia sugeste sunt a Engleis!*'; vol. 2, 183–8 & 199.
177 Hexham, 145 ('*Norþamymbrorum*') & 156 ('*Swthanglia*') for example; lvi–lvii for what we know of Richard.
178 *Ibid.*, for *Angli* and *Normannia*, *passim*; for *Scotia* and *Alemannia*, 141; for *Francia*, 167.
179 *Ibid.*, lvii for Richard's ecclesiastical career.

exercitus.[180] This echoes to some extent the charter of Henry I that he quotes – 'Henry, by grace of God king of the English, to all his vassals, both of French descent as well as of English . . .' – in that it suggests an 'English' constituted not just by descent but by some other commonality.[181] When this people faced the Scots, there were those of Norman descent present, yet they can be classified as 'English' by Richard in this most important moment of ethnic identification.

This use of *Angli* goes even beyond Henry of Huntingdon's consideration of *Angli* as being those who had made England their home: Henry saw some of those on the winning side at the Standard as *Normanni*. The suggestion is that Richard did not consider any of those fighting against the Scots to be Normans, though they may have been of Norman descent, and this in turn implies either a significant change in identity structures that did not affect Richard's contemporaries (unlikely) or, more likely, a response to the politically sensitive nature of Stephen's reign. Once again, to call someone 'English' or 'Norman' was to risk setting them on one side or another, which provides an explanation of the heightened use of toponyms in Richard's work; the fight against the Scots was part of Stephen's war to defend England, and his army was 'of England': namely, English.

Even if it is impossible to state with certainty which *gens* Richard felt himself to be a part of, his depiction of various *gentes* reveal something more concerning Richard's affiliation. Throughout the work, references are made to a variety of peoples – Scots (*Scotti*), Picts (*Picti*), Welsh (*Walani*) and Angevins (*Andegavenses*) – as well as to the territorial constructions of Germany (*Alemannia*) and France (*Francia*).[182] Yet the most revealing information appears in Richard's listing of the composition of the Scottish army of January 1138. This army included not only Picts ('who are commonly called Galwegians') and Scots, but also Normans, Germans and English, as well as some provincial groups such as Northumbrians.[183] Such a list is highly significant, both because the two *gentes* of which Richard may have been a member are included, and also because ethnic distinctions are not the only ones in use; certainly, it is difficult to know what to make of such a list. The use of *nefandus* in the description of this army is indicative of Richard's attitude towards it, but this then suggests that he saw all these groups as enemies of some sort. However, it is also clear from the subsequent text that this army faced an army under Thurstan and the northern barons at the Battle of the Standard and were defeated, therefore, by the 'English'.

With this in mind, there would seem to be two possible explanations of Richard's viewpoint on this matter. As has already been proposed, there is the possibility that his perceptions were dominated by his membership of a religious community, and that these people were therefore the 'other' because they posed a threat to this way of life. However, Richard seemingly considered Hexham to be quite safe during this

180 *Ibid.*, 164.
181 *Ibid.*, 142: '*Henricus Dei gratia Rex Anglorum, omnibus fidelibus suis, tam Francigenis quam Anglicis . . .*'.
182 *Ibid.*, 141, 146, 162, 165 & 167 for examples.
183 *Ibid.*, 152: '*Coadunatus autem erat iste nefandus exercitus de Normannis, Germanis, Anglis, de Northymbranis et Cumbris, de Teswetadala et Lodonea, de Pictis, qui vulgo Galleweienses dicuntur, et Scottis.*'

turmoil, and one cannot, therefore, easily accept this interpretation.[184] If this is not the case, though, then Richard must have been looking elsewhere for his distinctions, and a recent comment by R.R. Davies perhaps helps to show just where.

Davies observes that the figure of the *rex Anglorum* was the 'cultic unifying figure' of the *gens Anglorum*, in an apparently similar fashion to the *comes / dux Normannorum* for the *gens Normannorum*.[185] The *Angli* to which Davies refers are those of the tenth century, and it is reasonable to assume that there was some deterioration of this ideology during the conquest period.[186] However, for this concept to be important in the thirteenth and fourteenth centuries, it must have resurfaced, and it perhaps here that the signs of this resurgence can be observed. In Richard's work, those who served King Stephen, the '*rex Angliae*', were *Angli* in the truest sense; those who would not serve Stephen, while of English origin, were not part of Richard's *gens Anglorum* or, perhaps more accurately, *gens Angliae*.[187] As for Richard's own affiliation, if he did indeed think this way, his work becomes one of two sides: that of Stephen, and that of the Scots (and others). He was, quite clearly, not on the side of the Scots.

Gesta Stephani

The final work to be examined is the anonymous *Gesta Stephani*, a piece that poses a number of problems, not least of which is that of the author's affiliation. The anonymous nature of the work, and the correspondingly small amount of information the author reveals about himself do not allow for any easy judgements to be made as to his *gens* membership; his possible identification as Robert of Lewes, bishop of Bath, however, makes the situation a little clearer.[188] We know of Robert's political affiliations, that he was a staunch supporter of Stephen until some time after 1148, when he became reconciled with the future Henry II, and we are also aware of his regional particularisms, especially his interest in the area of Bath.[189] This two things suggest that Robert thought of himself as English, though the fact that he himself makes no

---

[184] *Ibid.*, 153.
[185] R.R. Davies, *The First English Empire* (Oxford, 2000), 200.
[186] Indeed, this is perhaps the reason for the tenacity of Englishness (above, pp. 121–2).
[187] *Rex angliae* is Richard's own usage: Hexham, 146 & 147 for examples. *Rex Angli(a)e* is generally considered to be a (late) twelfth-century title, though there are examples of its use in earlier charters. However, many of these usages are found in late copies or forgeries, generating some problems. *RRAN* has 13 charters of William I that incorporate *rex Angli(a)e* (nos 13, 15, 18, 109, 111, 115, 116, 247, 260, 317, 328, 333, 342), though none of these are originals, and 10 are forgeries. Of the remaining three, two are of dubious pedigree, and one may be a writ of William II. Using those charters printed in full in the *Regesta Regum Anglo-Normannorum* for William II, we find that 18 of 47 charters include *rex Angli(a)e* (*Regesta* i, pp. 132–40, nos 47–8, 52, 55, 57–9, 62, 63, 66, 75, 79, 83, 88, 89, 91), with two more utilising the abbreviation '*rex Angl'*', which could conceivably be *Anglie* or *Anglorum*. Of these, one is an original (55), one is either an original or early copy (92) and one (75) is a pretended original. The others are later copies. For Henry I, 92 of the 327 printed charters use *Angli(a)e*, with 81 more including the abbreviation (*Regesta* ii, pp. 306–63). Two or three of these are forgeries (nos. 29 and 303, with 159 suspicious) and four are originals (nos 96, 202, 253–4).
[188] *GS*, xxxviii.
[189] *Ibid.*, xxxiv–xxxv.

reference to his ethnicity means that we cannot judge this with certainty. Evidently, the issue of ethnicity has no place in his history, at least where a distinction between English and Norman is concerned, and one can only conclude that, as with Richard of Hexham, either the political climate was not conducive to the use of ethnic terminology, or that our author considered that his ethnicity was either irrelevant or obvious.

The various mentions of Normans and English in the *Gesta Stephani* do not particularly clarify matters. Robert evidences no personal attachment for either group at any point, but this is only to be expected from a man who 'cultivated an impersonal style, in what he believed to be the Roman manner'.[190] His comments concerning the English are far more negative than those concerning the Normans, depicting them as 'disorderly' and 'weakened by wantonness and drunkenness', but it is evident that these comments stem less from a wish to condemn the English than a wish to praise Stephen even when times were bad.[191] Robert's attitude to the Normans is at best indifferent, apart from one instance in which he mentions, of Wales, that the Normans 'perseveringly civilised it after they had vigorously subdued its inhabitants; to encourage peace they imposed law and statutes on them; and they made the land so productive and abounding in all kinds of resources that you would have reckoned it in no wise inferior to the most fertile part of Britain'.[192] The way in which Robert defined these two *gentes* is not even clear: only one individual is named as being a member of either *gens* during the course of the *Gesta Stephani*, and this is 'a certain Turgis, a Norman by birth, whose origin, they said, was from the town of Avranches'; whether this clarification of ethnic status is in any way related to his rebellion against the king we can only speculate.[193]

If Robert is unclear about Normans and English, however, he is perhaps less confused about other *gentes*, and through these we are able to understand something more of his own *gens* affiliation. He records the case of Robert fitz Hubert, which at first looks like one of ethnic insult: our author comments that fitz Hubert was 'a Fleming by race, deceitful in mind and deed'.[194] While his ethnicity *is* revealed at a time of treachery – 'the cunning intention of that turncoat' was, apparently, to take Devizes by stealth and keep it for himself – this deceit is not necessarily perceived by Robert as an ethnic characteristic.[195] The fact that, in an earlier reference, fitz Hubert is referred to as 'a man of great cruelty and unequalled in wickedness and crime' suggests that this may be more of a reflection of his individual character than of his *gens*.[196] Indeed, other comments in the *Gesta Stephani* add support to this interpretation: Henry de Caldret and his brother Ralph are shown to be men 'utterly steeped in craft and treachery, very ready to set pillage and strife on foot everywhere, most eager

---

[190] *Ibid.*, xxxvii.

[191] *Ibid.*, 4: '*Turbulenter*' & 84: '*Luxuria et ebrietate enruatus*'.

[192] *Ibid.*, 14: '*Propriis incolis uiriliter edomitis, constanter excoluere; ad pacem confouendam, legem et plebiscita eis indixere; adeoque terram fertilem omnibusque copiis affluentem reddidere, ut fecundissimæ Britanniæ neququam inferiorem æstimares.*'

[193] *Ibid.*, 174: '*Turgisius quidam, genere Normannus, de Aurentia, ut aiebant, ciuitate oriundus.*'

[194] *Ibid.*, 104: '*Uir genere Flandrensis, animo et actu fraudulentus.*'

[195] *Ibid.*, 106: '*Uersipellis ille uersute cogitabat.*'

[196] *Ibid.*, 92: '*Uiro crudelissimo nullique in malitia et scelere æquando.*'

to commit crime and sacrilege', and the fact that they are Flemings seems more of a coincidence than an ethnic judgement.[197]

Elsewhere in the *Gesta Stephani*, two other *gentes* are distinguished above others through Robert's criticism, these being the Welsh and Scots. Robert praises Scotland itself, as a land 'well supplied with productive forests, milk, and herds, encircled by safe harbours and rich islands'; likewise, the Scottish king was 'of gentle heart, born of religious parents and equal to them in his just ways of living', though his repeated defeats by the English could not pass 'without infamy to himself'.[198] The inhabitants of Scotland, conversely, appear as 'barbarous and filthy . . . among foreigners they surpass all in cruelty'.[199] It is evident that Robert had no liking for the Scots in general, and it is regrettable that possibly the most ethnically significant event in this time period is missing from the *Gesta Stephani* – namely the Battle of the Standard – along with the retreat of and reinvasion by the Scots earlier in the same year.[200]

As to the Welsh, Robert speaks highly of their land, 'a country of woodland and pasture, immediately bordering on England, stretching far along the coast on one side of it, abounding in deer and fish, milk and herbs', but negatively of the people.[201] The Welsh, he states, were 'men of an animal type, naturally swift-footed, accustomed to war, volatile always in breaking their word as in changing their abodes', who 'cherished a deadly hatred of their masters'.[202] Elsewhere, these *Walenses* are 'a dreadful and unendurable mass' of 'untamed savagery', and 'swarming savages'.[203] It is extremely clear that he saw both the Welsh and Scots as important 'others', very distinct in their barbaric behaviour. His particular focus on the Welsh is seemingly excessive, but this is doubtless a result of their nearness to the area around Bristol and Bath.

With these ideas in mind, it is perhaps possible to say something more of Robert. The fact that the French are not a distinctive group in his work suggests that he had little interest in continental events, and correspondingly little interest in Normandy itself. Certainly, the comment that 'the Normans and the Angevins . . . had often troubled each other with disputes' seems very bland for someone who was evidently capable of intense ethnic criticism, and this in itself suggests that Robert did not really care about Normandy or the traditional Norman enemies; if nothing else, this does not support the idea that he saw Normandy as any sort of *patria*.[204] The evident and intense dislike or, more precisely, contempt that he felt for both the Scots and the Welsh suggests that he was well-schooled in the 'English' traditional 'others', and

---

[197] *Ibid.*, 188: '*Dolo et perfidiam quam maxime imbuti ad rapinam ubique et discordiam promouendam promptissimi, ad scelus et sacrilegium inferendum audissimi.*'

[198] *Ibid.*, 54: '*Siluarum fertilium, lactis et armentorum copiosa, portubus salubribus, insulis opulentis circumcincta*'; 52: '*Pectoris mansueti, progenitoribusque religiosis exortus, et ipse iusto uiuendi tramite illlos coæquans*' & 128: '*Non sine sui flagitio*'.

[199] *Ibid.*, 54: '*Barbaros . . . et impuros . . . sed inter sibi extraneos omnes crudelitate excedentes.*'

[200] *Ibid.*, xii & 56, n.1 for comments on the damaged manuscript pages.

[201] *Ibid.*, 14: '*Terra siluestris et pascuosa, ipsi Angliæ proxima uicinitate contermina, ex uno eiusdem latere in longum iuxta mare protensa, ceruorum quidem et piscium, lactis et armentorum uberrima.*'

[202] *Ibid.*, 14: '*Hominum . . . bestialium, natura uelocium, consuetudine bellantium, fide semper et locis instabilium*'; '*in dominos suos . . . mortale . . . odium spirantes*'.

[203] *Ibid.*, 110: '*Graui . . . et intolerabili . . . multitudine*'; 172: '*Effrenemque . . . barbariem*'; 194: '*Barbara . . . multitudine*'.

[204] *Ibid.*, 10: '*Normannos et Andegauenses, se sæpius dissidendo turbarant.*'

the specifics of his reactions to these 'barbarians' fit very well with his attempted 'Roman' style: he 'was endeavouring to write a history worthy of the ancients'.[205]

Given his basic cultural and territorial biases therefore, it is probable that Robert thought of himself as English and not Norman, though whether this was a matter of heritage, homeland, or anything else is hard to tell. His Romanising style speaks of the importance to him of his membership of the religious / intellectual community, and the strength of his reaction against the Welsh, along with the foci of his work, show evidence of a strong regional particularism, which functioned along the same lines as his ethnic and territorial identifications.

Before conclusions are drawn, some comment should perhaps be made regarding the two chronicle sources mentioned previously, namely the *Anglo-Saxon Chronicle* and the *Chronicle* of John of Worcester. While both of these works do cover the events of this period, they cannot be reliably used for the study of identity within a fixed time-frame. This problem, very much specific to chronicle-type sources, and generally not encountered with standard narrative histories, is a result of the difficulties of dating the precise time at which any given set of chronicle entries were written. As the purpose of this study is to examine the changes within the identity of the *gens Normannorum* over a fixed period of time, it is not a valid approach to use a source from outside the period in question, as such a source would inevitably express identity information from a later (or, indeed, earlier) incarnation. As the dating of the later entries of both these works is problematic, and the authorship often inconsistent and uncertain, it has been decided to avoid using these sources for the twelfth-century examination, if only to avoid investigative work beyond the remit of this book. Current thinking suggests that the *Anglo-Saxon Chronicle* entries (Peterborough (E) Chronicle) for 1132–55 were the product of one scribe writing some time *after* 1155, and unable to assign events to their proper year (suggesting a fairly distant removal); the lack of the first volume of the recent edition of John of Worcester's chronicle leaves the precise dating of this work still rather uncertain.[206]

Conclusions

What, then, can be concluded about the *gens Normannorum* in the twelfth century? Were these writers in the process of becoming English? Had the *gens Normannorum* been swallowed up into the *gens Anglorum*? The answer to both these questions is no. As can be seen from the evidence presented above, all of our writers were in the process of *being* something, whether English, Norman or something of both; there was no transition occurring here. The *gens Normannorum*, equally, had not been swallowed up by the *gens Anglorum*, but there had certainly been some significant process of change. The fact that, by the end of this period, descent was no longer sufficient to indicate the ethnicity of an individual in England is indicative in itself of an important alteration in the way that people saw the world. The membership of the groups of 'English' and 'Normans' was no longer as simple as it had been previously, doubtless because of the mixing that had taken place in the aftermath of the

---

[205] *Ibid.*, xxxvii.
[206] *The Chronicle of John of Worcester*, ed. P. McGurk, vol. III, OMT (Oxford, 1998), xxi.

conquest, and it quickly becomes clear that people had come to be considered as 'English' or 'Norman' based on the land that held their allegiance and interest, which they considered a home. The precise reasons for this are better left for the General Conclusion, but it is sufficient to note that, if someone lived in England, was at home in England, and obeyed the king of England, then they are likely to have considered themselves English; whether or not such claims were legitimate is a different matter.

By 1154, however, it would be entirely untrue to say that the Normans had 'become English' or, as one often hears, 'adapted themselves out of existence'. Independent groups of 'Normans' and 'English' continued to exist, continued to have identities, and continued to write history. Indeed, the writing of histories containing ethnic sentiment is what underlies this book, and particularly this last chapter, and the developments in historical writing in the twelfth century perhaps explain what was occurring better than anything else.

In the early twelfth century, we have three historians writing as approximate contemporaries, all three producing comprehensive, large works, and yet all siding with differing ethnic affiliations. Orderic Vitalis portrayed himself as a Norman, Henry of Huntingdon as an Englishman, and William of Malmesbury held to his dual-socialisation, as part-Englishman, part-Norman. The historical tradition that produced these works was, it is fair to say, a Norman import; though all three writers apparently knew and respected the work of Bede, one cannot argue that a sudden resurgence of narrative history after more than three centuries was 'continuing a tradition'. Significantly, the 'Norman' of the three was writing from Normandy and the 'Englishman' from England, and this would seem to be the rule for their successors, such as the apparently 'English' Robert of Lewes and 'Norman' Robert de Torigni (who wrote first from Bec and later from Mont-St-Michel). William of Malmesbury, perhaps fairly, wrote in England and not in the middle of the Channel, and his status, as a member of both *gentes*, was something that was seemingly impossible by the next generation. If people were, by the end of the period, named more from their territorial bonds than from their descent, then the concept of being both Norman *and* English would no longer be sustainable.

In all this discussion of the 'English', though, it often seems the case that the Normans have become lost. In the aftermath of the conquest of England, certainly, the majority of modern, Anglophone historians focus intently on events in *England*, the effects of this on *England*, and how the Normans became *English*. Surprisingly, this proves very hard to avoid, even when one sets out with the best of intentions, if only for one simple reason: the weight of historical material favours England. Though the histories written immediately around the conquest are all Norman, the hiatus of the late eleventh century is followed by a period in which material produced by those who apparently considered themselves to be 'English' outweighs that produced by 'Normans' with relative ease. The Norman tradition continues onwards, producing (roughly) one writer per generation; the English tradition produces an abundant flow of material to inform the student of events in the British Isles.

The result of this is that the *gens Normannorum* actually becomes very difficult both to isolate and to study. Normandy repeatedly takes second place to England, both in terms of records and of ethnically significant events; it was seemingly rare for the inhabitants of Normandy to need to express their difference from their neighbours, perhaps because they lacked the 'barbarous' surroundings of England. The *status quo* that had formed in France was apparently far less volatile than that in England, and once again we see that the Normans, for all their strength and spirit, had run out of things to conquer. As with their brethren in southern Italy, the result of this was infighting and a fragmentation within the identity of the *gens Normannorum*: the fighting was over leadership (as usual), the fragmentation into distinct and separate territories. The Battle of the Standard saw Normans and English fight together against a common enemy of England, but only a few years later people could already view this as a pure English victory: England had been defended by those who lived there, namely, the English. The Normans may have conquered England, but Normandy was still the traditional *patria* of the *gens Normannorum*, and it was to Normandy that the name, and thus the concept, had in time become bound.

General Conclusion

Between 911 and 1154, *Normanitas*, the defining nature of the *gens Normannorum*, had undergone many changes. The pages above have attempted to follow the changes in this strand of identity through three cycles of conquest and settlement, as identity conflicts were triggered and resolved, and the identity was transformed. At the forefront of this process were the Norman leaders, those men who personified the values of *Normanitas* and to whom the historians of their *gens* could look with pride, even as the 'other' viewed them with scorn or, on occasion, respect. The thread of identity evolved in these years, through changes of *patria*, of language, of enemy and of religion, and though the ethnonym 'Norman' was used in Normandy, in England, and in Italy and Sicily, to do so was to assert different claims in different areas, and at different times.

The *gens Normannorum* was constituted when Scandinavian 'proto-Normans' ceased to be *in peregrinatione*, and settled in Francia.[1] Under the leadership of Rollo and his successors, this Viking group took on some of the aspects of the *gentes* around them, not least of which was their Christianity, and worked to achieve a level of acceptance. They adopted the name of *Normanni*, which, while originally a generic term used to describe Northmen, came to represent their *gens* of mixed descent, loosely connected to a *patria*, a *tellus Normannica*.[2] The following years saw the embattled *Normanni* strengthen their originally precarious hold on their lands, and evolve into a *gens* who could participate in Frankish politics with success. By the mid-eleventh century, the identity of the *gens Normannorum* in Normandy had assumed a relatively stable form; they had become 'established'.

During the early eleventh century, however, movement had begun towards southern Italy and Sicily, and the Normans that travelled this way maintained some form of *gens* unity until the end of the century. The atmosphere of battle in the south maintained the perception of difference of the *gens Normannorum* from 'others', and the histories continue to tell of a *gens* of warriors who could even be so bold as to challenge both the Roman and Byzantine emperors at the same time. Yet, at the end of the eleventh century, and at the start of the twelfth, these conquerors of Italy ceased to conquer anything at all. The completion of the conquest of Sicily in 1091 marked the beginning of a slow stagnation of the 'Norman' way of life in the south, and the perceptions of *Normanitas* were consequently affected. Though some took the cross in the continued spirit of martial achievement, there was much infighting and

---

[1] Above, p. 21.
[2] Above, pp. 30–1.

fragmentation, and a division into two groups occurred. While one group held to the *patria* of Normandy, and to 'Norman' ways, the other adopted regions of southern Italy as its new fatherland, and sought integration into a new ethnic context. Over time, the identity of the former group proved weak, and collapsed; the latter survived to an extent, though under the domination of the Sicilian kings.

Those of the southern Normans who left on crusade, however, faced different forms of challenge to their identity. The war on which they embarked not only served to reinforce the martial and religious elements of their identity, but also united the southern Normans with the Normans of Normandy, and people of other French provinces, under the banner title of *Franci*. The usage of this ethnonym as a unifier was not new, however, as it had occurred in the north in previous years, during the Norman conquest of England. Yet this connection was clearly a temporary one, and had done nothing to diminish Norman separateness in a French context. Through the conquest of England, the Norman duke became a king in his own right, creating new complications within the *gens Normannorum*. Though the conquering generation were already established in *Normanitas*, their descendants were not so, and the lack of further expansion took its toll here again. Conflict between William II and Robert Curthose caused a division of Normandy and England, which in turn created problems of definition for the *gens Normannorum*. Ethnic affiliation obtained, for a time at least, a certain political element, and though the divide was temporarily repaired under Herny I, it was reinforced again in the time of King Stephen. Perceived identity was becoming more and more strongly tied to territory and leadership, and by the mid-twelfth century, to be English could be defined as being 'of England', and in support of the king.

It is notable, from this short résumé, that there are clear commonalities between the events in the north and those in the south. As England and Normandy followed different paths of historical evolution, so the identities in these two areas differed fundamentally. It becomes abundantly clear, therefore, that the identity portrayed in twelfth-century Normandy by Orderic Vitalis was very much backward-looking, and such an attitude in the original *patria Normannorum* is unsurprising.[3] A resistance to changes that shifted the focus of power and attention away from Normandy and towards the more recently established kingdoms of England and Sicily was only to be expected. Yet he was attempting to lay claim to a wider *gens Normannorum* that was no longer reflected by this time in English or Italian sources, and this view of the *Normanni* therefore received scant support; it was an ideological definition of an identity that focused on common descent, and not on the geographical realities that appear to have proven more and more significant in English and in Italian and Sicilian identity structures.

Interestingly, though, Orderic was not the only writer in France to connect the various Norman groups. Similar views appear, at first, to exist in the works of his neighbouring Frankish contemporaries, Guibert of Nogent and Abbot Suger of St-Denis. Guibert, in his *Deeds of God through the Franks* (composed 1106–9), connected Bohemond, son of Robert Guiscard, with Normandy, but as part of an

---

[3] Above, pp. 142–7.

insistence that he was really French.[4] Indeed, Guibert implies that Bohemond was not a Norman in his own right, though 'his family was from Normandy'.[5] Elsewhere, the appearance of Bohemond (as the Lombard leader) and Tancred as heroes is starkly contrasted by Robert Curthose's 'bodily indulgences, weakness of will, prodigality with money, gourmandising, indolence, and lechery'.[6] Equally, when Suger wrote his *Deeds of Louis the Fat*, between 1139 and 1144,[7] he echoed Orderic's accusations of Norman unruliness, referring to the Normans as 'warlike descendants of the Danes' and 'ignorant of the ways of peace'.[8] Yet it is clear from Suger's treatment of the Normans elsewhere that his motive was to create a yardstick by which the greatness of the French, and more particularly Louis, could be measured; his treatment of William II of England is in a similar vein, though he apparently has much more genuine respect for Henry I.[9] Yet even if these writers do not, in fact, support Orderic's views, their works provide interesting external views of the Normans at this time.

In the north, then, it can be seen that the areas of England and Normandy, while (in the main) politically connected after 1066, became quickly separate as far as identities were concerned. In the south, equally, the frequent uprisings on the mainland suggest a divide of identification within the Sicilian kingdom, the initial phases of which are evident in the histories of William of Apulia and Geoffrey Malaterra. Yet it must be recalled, when comparing these areas, that although both England and Sicily were the home of island kingdoms ruled by monarchs of Norman descent, with connected mainland territories, the identity structures did not mirror this political reality. The kingdoms of England and Sicily evolved in different ways, and the process of identity transformation in Sicily was unparalleled elsewhere, though Orderic's reactionary identity in Normandy bears certain similarities to the work of Geoffrey Malaterra in the 1090s. In fact, the areas of greatest similarity, in terms of the evolution of identity, would appear to be the holdings in England and southern Italy.

Both Italy and England saw *Normanni* arrive from Normandy as a military force, and though the timescale was different in the two areas, the end result was conquest. The Normans initially ruled over these areas as members of a small minority, and both groups of Normans at first looked back to Normandy as their *patria*. Unsurprisingly, the reaction of the inhabitants of both England and Italy towards these conquerors was negative, and chronicles in both areas reflect this situation. Yet extensive intermarriage with the existing populations meant that the second generation

---

4   Guibert of Nogent, *The Deeds of God through the Franks*, tr. Robert Levine (Woodbridge, Suffolk, 1997), 1.

5   *Ibid.*, 11 & 39.

6   *Ibid.*, 54, 57, 98, 111, 159. Robert's poor character is in some way redeemed by his heroism and devotion, however.

7   Suger, Abbot of St-Denis, *The Deeds of Louis the Fat*, tr. Richard Cusimano and John Moorhead (Washington, DC, 1992), 1 & 5; Suger, *Vie de Louis VI le Gros*, ed. & tr. Henri Waquet (Paris, 1929), xi.

8   Suger, *Deeds*, 70; Suger, *Vie*, 100: '*Feroci Danorum propagatione*'; '*Pacis expertes*'.

9   See, in particular, Suger, *Deeds*, 69–75; Suger, *Vie*, 98–112. Notably, Suger's recent translators have observed that Suger considered Normandy to be part of Gaul, but not part of France (Suger, *Deeds*, 70 & p. 186, n. 7) – this is reminiscent of similar comments by Norman writers such as William of Poitiers. For William II, Suger, *Deeds*, 25 and note (d); Suger, *Vie*, 6. For Henry, Suger, *Deeds*, 28 & 69; Suger, *Vie*, 14 & 98.

included many who were of mixed-blood, and could affiliate themselves with either side; in both cases, division at this point from Normandy (by distance for Italy, by politics for England) was likely to have been instrumental in a change of perceptions. The absence of new conquests to reinforce their separateness created a tendency towards change, and this in turn led to naturalisation and a shift in their affiliations, from Normandy to England and Italy respectively. Over time, the Normans in England came to be perceived as English by the writers of English histories, though they remained *Franci* in legal documents; in Italy, equally, the 'Normans' occasioned few references in the twelfth century.

In fact, by 1154, the *gens Normannorum*, which had made itself so obvious for the previous century and a half, has become difficult to spot in the historical record. This is not true in a genetic sense: the historian can still, with reasonable ease, pick out various figures of Norman descent; what proves elusive is the ideology that had always previously marked out the membership of the Norman group to outsiders – whether through skill at arms or destructive greed – and, equally importantly, the focus of this ideology: the Norman leader. By 1154, the Normans had not ceased to exist, and yet they had, to an extent, disappeared. In southern Italy and Sicily, the ruling establishment had turned away from identifiably Norman values and the Norman name, and the figure who most closely resembled a Norman leader was not King Roger I but rather the rebellious Rainulf. In England, again, the leader had been the non-Norman Stephen, immediately succeeded by the equally non-Norman Henry II; the Norman duchy may have offered a 'conservative' alternative in the second quarter of the twelfth century, but it was not an enduring reality, and though charters may have still indicated a divide between *Franci* and *Angli* in England, this did not reflect any idea of *Norman* separateness.

This replacement of the Norman leadership with those who did not tie themselves to the ideology of *Normanitas* was just one aspect of those changes that caused the Normans to fade from the historical picture. In 1154, it would appear that leadership was just as important to the Normans as it had been in 911, and the impression one receives from such writers as Richard of Hexham is that obedience to the monarch or ruler was emerging as a marker of *gens* membership.[10] No longer was the leader simply the personification of the identity; rather, he was almost the 'owner' of the identity. To belong, one had not just to accept the leader, but to 'surrender' to him.

This redefinition was not limited to the role of the leader, however. The ties of leader and name to an ethnic group, a *gens*, were being directly affected by other ties; those of *gens* to *tellus* or *patria*, to territory and, more specifically, homeland. In England, we see a *rex Angliae* (not *Anglorum*), who rules *Anglia*, where the *Angli* live. It became the case that to have one's home in England and be a subject of the *rex Angliae* made one *Anglus*. Equally, *Normanni* became those who were at home in Normandy and served the *dux Normanniae*. This tightening of ties and, in essence, polarisation of identities helped to obscure the Normans in the historical record. In the first instance, though the Normans had conquered many places, they had named only one, and as ethnonyms and toponyms were becoming so interdependent, 'true Normans' were those who were 'of Normandy'. Secondly, and perhaps more importantly, there was the problem of the Norman ruler. Not only was he not the 'true'

---

[10] Above, p. 169.

ruler of Normandy, as it was a part of France and thus part of the domain of the *rex Franciae*, but he was also not a Norman. *Normanitas* had lost its traditional focus, and was not stronger for it.

Connected with this issue of rulership and territory is the issue of historical writing itself. The major histories continued, as they had before, to focus on the lives of the 'greats', in particular on kings, and the lack of a 'Norman' king now meant that the Norman people received less historical coverage. Additionally, the Normans had ceased to be conquerors, and thus their *gesta* were no longer the stuff of epic histories and great tales. The Normans had, indeed, finally achieved an obscurity in the historical record that befitted the size of their people. None of this is to say that Normans had ceased to exist in areas other than Normandy, merely to observe that the way that *Normanitas* was judged had been altered. There remained significant numbers of Normans who viewed themselves as such in both England and in southern Italy and Sicily, they were just not in control. They often continued to own land, and control a number of vassals, but identifiably 'Norman' figures (in their mannerisms and customs) are usually those seen heading up revolts and rebellions against the ordained monarch; unsurprising, perhaps, given that Orderic Valis remarked on the rebellious nature of his *gens*.[11] Evidently Normans were not comfortable under a non-Norman ruler.

As to what happened to *Normanitas* after 1154, it is dangerous to speculate without specific study. Both England and France arguably fulfilled the requirements of *natio*, whatever its contemporary meaning, in that both reflected Bishop Bernard's requirements in being distinguished 'by their language, law, habits, modes of judgement and customs'; Normandy did not, sharing language if nothing else, though it did maintain various elements of regional dialect, laws and customs.[12] In both France and England, also, the role of the ruler was reinforced: in England, his perceived 'ownership' of the identity was enforced by his actual ownership of the *patria*; in France, the divinity of the king was emphasised so successfully in the following centuries that Charles V could not be deposed even though he was insane. Normandy, conversely, lacked a ruler whose interests were rooted there. What is difficult to guess and, perhaps, even to study, is whether or not the identity of the Normans was to become relegated to the position of a regional identity, subordinate to a wider 'national' sentiment, or whether the Normans considered themselves to have ongoing separateness. Given the political events that occurred in and with reference to Normandy through the remainder of the medieval period, the latter situation suggests itself as likely.

Finally, something should be said as to the theoretical elements of identity study. There is, perhaps unsurprisingly, little modern identity work that deals with conquest scenarios; as regards state formation and the rise of nation, even less reliable material is available, to a great extent because the definitions of 'nation' and 'state' and so on have proven so elusive. Yet the identity models that are available, while primarily focused on the modern day, can (and some would argue *should*) be used to help us understand medieval societies. That, on a few occasions during the writing of this book, potential inconsistencies turned out to be either false alarms or to actually

[11] Orderic, vol. IV bk M, p. 82.
[12] For Bernard's comment, see above, p. 8.

fit the models suggests that they function in experimental conditions, at the very least. Further application of such models to other societies will help to refine them, so that they may be used to provide a greater understanding of both modern and historical societies; further application of them to the Normans will help historians to understand exactly what happened in Normandy after 1154.

Bibliography

PRIMARY SOURCES

Printed Sources

Adhemari Cabannensis Chronicon, ed. Chavanon, J. (Paris, 1897).

Aelredi Rievallensis Opera Omnia, ed. Hoste, A. and Talbot, C.H., Corpus Christianorum Continuatio Medievalis, I (Brepols, 1976).

The Alexiad of Anna Comnena, tr. Sewter, E.R.A. (Harmondsworth, 1969).

Annales Bertiniani, ed. Waitz, G., *SRG* (Hannover, 1883).

Annales Fuldenses, ed. Kurze, F., *SRG* (Hannover, 1891).

The Annals of Fulda, tr. Reuter, Timothy (Manchester, 1992).

The Annals of St-Bertin, tr. Nelson, Janet L. (Manchester, 1991).

The Anglo-Saxon Chronicle, tr. Whitelock, Dorothy, Douglas, David C. and Tucker, Susie I. (London, 1961).

The Anglo-Saxon Chronicle: A Collaborative Edition, ed. O'Brien O'Keeffe, Katherine, *vol. 5: MS. C* (Cambridge, 2001).

The Anglo-Saxon Chronicle: A Collaborative Edition, ed. Cubbin, G.P., *vol. 6: MS. D* (Cambridge, 1996).

Les Annales de Flodoard, ed. Lauer, Ph. (Paris, 1905).

The Bayeux Tapestry, Stenton, F.M. (London, 1957).

Baldricus Burgulianus Carmina, ed. Hilbert, Karlheinz (Heidelberg, 1979).

Bede, *The Ecclesiastical History of the English People*, ed. McClure, Judith and Collins, Roger (Oxford, 1994).

Bonizonis episcopi Sutrini liber ad amicum, ed. Dümmler, Ernest, *MGH LL*, Tomus I (1891, repr. 1956), pp. 568–620.

Brunonis episcopi Signini Libellus de Symoniacis, ed. Sackur, Ernest, *MGH LL*, Tomus II (1892), pp. 543–62.

The Carmen de Hastingae Proelio of Guy, bishop of Amiens, ed. & tr. Barlow, Frank, OMT (Oxford, 1999).

The Carmen de Hastingae Proelio of Guy, bishop of Amiens, ed. & tr. Morton, Catherine and Muntz, Hope, OMT (Oxford, 1972).

Chronica Monasterii Casinensis, ed. Hoffman, Harmut, *MGH SS*, Tomus XXXIV (1980).

The Chronicle of Falco of Benevento, tr. Loud, G.A. (1990).

The Chronicle of Fulcher of Chartres and other Source Materials, ed. Peters, Edward, 2nd edn (Philadelphia, 1998).

The Chronicle of John of Worcester, ed. Darlington, R.R. and McGurk, P., 3 vols, OMT (Oxford, 1995–).

The Chronicle of Richard, Prior of Hexham, ed. Howlett, R., *Chronicles of the Reigns of Stephen, Henry II, and Richard I*, vol. III, RS 1886.

The Chronicle of Robert of Torigni, ed. Howlett, R., *Chronicles of the Reigns of Stephen, Henry II, and Richard I*, vol. IV, RS 1889.

'Chronicon Monasterii de Hida iuxta Wintoniam', in *Liber Monasterii de Hyda*, ed. Edwards, Edward, RS 1866, pp. 284–321.

Complainte sur la mort de Guillaume Longue-Épée, ed. Lauer, Ph., *Le Règne de Louis IV d'Outre-Mer* (Paris, 1900), pp. 319–23.

Das Register Gregors VII, ed. Caspar, Erich, *MGH ES*, 2 vols (1920–3).

The Deeds of King Roger, by Abbot Alexander of Telese, tr. Loud, G.A.

The Deeds of the Franks and the other Pilgrims to Jerusalem, ed. & tr. Hill, Rosalind (Oxford, 1962).

De moribus et actis primorum Normanniae ducum auctore Dudone Sancti Quintini Decano, ed. Lair, Jules, Société des Antiquaires de Normandie (Caen, 1865).

De rebus gestis Rogerii Calabriae et Siciliae Comitis et Roberti Guiscardi Ducis fratris eius Gaufredo Malaterra monacho Benedictino, ed. Ernesto Pontieri, *Rerum Italicarum Scriptores* 5.1, ed. Muratori, L.A. (Milan, 1927–8).

Dialogi de miraculis sancti Benedicti auctore Desiderio abbate Casinensi, ed. Schwartz, Gerhard and Hofmeister, Adolf, *MGH SS*, Tomus XXX, Pars II (1934), pp. 1111–51.

Dudo decanus S. Quintini Veromandensis – De moribus et actis primorum Northmanniae ducum libri tres, ed. Migne, J.P., *Patrilogia Latina* (1880), cc. 607–758.

Dudo of St. Quentin, *History of the Normans*, tr. Christiansen, E. (Woodbridge, 1998).

Eadmeri historia novorum in Anglia et opuscula duo de vita santci Anselmi et quibusdam miraculis eius, ed. Rule, Martin, RS 1884.

Eadmer's History of Recent Events in England, tr. Bosanquet, Geoffrey (London, 1964).

The Ecclesiastical History of Orderic Vitalis, ed. & tr. Chibnall, M., 6 vols, OMT (Oxford, 1969–80).

Encomium Emmae Reginae, ed. & tr. Cambell, Alistair (Cambridge, 1998).

Flodoard of Reims, *Historia Remensis Ecclesiae*, ed. & tr. Lejeune, M. (Paris, 1854).

Geoffrey of Monmouth, *The History of the Kings of Britain*, tr. Thorpe, Lewis (Harmondsworth, 1966).

The Gesta Guillelmi of William of Poitiers, ed. & tr. Davis, R.H.C. and Chibnall, Marjorie, OMT (Oxford, 1998).

The Gesta Normannorum Ducum of William of Jumièges, Orderic Vitalis, and Robert of Torigni, ed. & tr. van Houts, Elisabeth M.C., 2 vols, OMT (Oxford, 1992–5).

Gesta Stephani, ed. & tr. Potter, K.R. and Davis, R.H.C., OMT (Oxford, 1976).

Guibert of Nogent, *The Deeds of God through the Franks*, tr. Levine, Robert (Woodbridge, 1997).

Henry, Archdeacon of Huntingdon, *Historia Anglorum*, ed. & tr. Greenway, Diana, OMT (Oxford, 1996).

Historia Francorum Senonensis, ed. Pertz, G.H., *MGH SS* IX (1925), pp. 364–9.

The Historia Regum Britannie of Geoffrey of Monmouth, ed. Wright, Neil, 2 vols (Bern, 1985–8).

Inventio et miracula sancti Vulfranni, ed. J. Laporte (Rouen, 1938).

Lestorie des Engles, solum la Translacion Maistre Geffrei Gaimar, ed. Hardy, T.D. and Martin, C.T., 2 vols, RS 1888–9.

The Letters of Gerbert, tr. Lattin, H.P., Records of Civilisation Sources and Studies 60 (New York, 1961), p. 15.

Liber Eliensis, ed. Blake, E.O., Camden Third Series 92 (London, 1962).

L'ystoire de li Normant, et la chronique de Robert Viscart, par Aimé, moine du Mont-Cassin, ed. Champollion-Figeac, Louis (1835, repr. New York, 1965).

Les Œuvres Poétiques de Baudri de Bourgeuil (1046–1130), ed. Abrahams, Phyllis (1926).

Orkneyinga Saga, tr. Pálsson, Hermann and Edwards, Paul (Harmondsworth, 1981).

The Peterborough Chronicle 1070–1154, ed. Clark, Cecily, 2nd edn (Oxford, 1970).

 Recueil des Actes de Charles III le Simple, Roi de France (893–923), ed. Lauer, Philippe, Chartes et Diplômes Relatifs à l'Histoire de France (Paris, 1949).

Recueil des Actes de Lothaire et de Louis V, Rois de France (954–987), ed. Halphen, Louis, Chartes et Diplômes Relatifs à l'Histoire de France (Paris, 1908).

Recueil des Actes de Louis IV, Roi de France (936–954), ed. Lauer, Philippe, Chartes et Diplômes Relatifs à l'Histoire de France (Paris, 1916).

Recueil des Actes de Robert Ier et de Raoul, Rois de France (922–936), ed. Dufour, Jean, Chartes et Diplômes Relatifs à l'Histoire de France (Paris, 1978).

Recueil des Actes des Ducs de Normandie, 911–1066, ed. Fauroux, M., Mémoires de la Société des Antiquaires de Normandie 36 (Caen, 1961).

Regesta Regum Anglo-Normannorum, i, ed. Davis, H.W.C. (Oxford, 1913); ii, ed. Johnson, C. and Cronne, H.A. (Oxford, 1956); iii, ed. Cronne, H.A. and Davis, R.H.C. (Oxford, 1968).

Regesta Regum Anglo-Normannorum: The Acta of William I (1066–1087), ed. Bates, David (Oxford, 1998).

Richer of Reims, *Historiarum libri quatuor*, ed. & tr. Guadet, J. (1845, repr. New York, 1968).

Rodulfus Glaber Opera, ed. & tr. France, J., Bulst, N. and Reynolds, P., OMT (Oxford, 1989).

Snorri Sturlason, *Heimskringla, history of the kings of Norway*, tr. Hollander, L.M. (1964).

Storia de' Normanni di Amato di Montecassino, ed. de Bartholomaeis, Vincenzo, *Fonti per la storia d'Italia* (Rome, 1935).

Suger, *Vie de Louis VI le Gros*, ed. Waquet, Henri (Paris, 1929).

Suger, Abbot of St-Denis, *The Deeds of Louis the Fat*, tr. Cusimano, Richard and Moorhead, John (Washington, D.C., 1992).

Vita Ædwardi Regis, ed. & tr. Barlow, Frank, NMT (London, 1962); 2nd edn, OMT (Oxford, 1992).

Walter Daniel, *The Life of Ailred of Rievaulx*, tr. Powicke, Maurice (Oxford, 1950, repr. 1978).

Willelmi Malmesbiriensis monachi gesta pontificum Anglorum, ed. Hamilton, N.E.S.A., RS 1870.

William of Apulia, *La Geste de Robert Guiscard*, ed. & tr. Mathieu, Marguerite (Palermo, 1961).

William of Malmesbury, *Chronicle of the Kings of England*, ed. Giles, J.A. (London, 1847).

William of Malmesbury, *Gesta Regum Anglorum*, ed. & tr. Mynors, R.A.B., Thomson, R.M. and Winterbottom, M., 2 vols, OMT (Oxford, 1998–9).

William of Malmesbury, *Historia Novella*, ed. King, Edmund, tr. Potter, K.R., OMT (Oxford, 1998).

William of Malmesbury, *Life of St Wulfstan, Bishop of Worcester*, tr. Peile, J.H.F. (Oxford, 1934).

Online Resources

The Latin Bible: http://ccat.sas.upenn.edu/jod/bible.html

SECONDARY SOURCES

Albu, Emily, 'Dudo of Saint-Quentin: the Heroic Past Imagined', *HSJ* 6 (1994), 111–18.

———, 'Bohemond and the Rooster: Byzantines, Normans, and the Artful Ruse', in Gouma-Peterson, Thalia (ed.), *Anna Komnene and her Times* (New York, 2000), 157–68.

————, *The Normans in their Histories: Propaganda, Myth and Subversion* (Woodbridge, 2001).

Amory, Patrick, 'Names, Ethnic Identity, and Community in Fifth- and Sixth-Century Burgundy', *Viator* 25 (1994), 1–30.

————, *People and Identity in Ostrogothic Italy, 489–554* (Cambridge, 1997).

Barlow, Frank, *The Feudal Kingdom of England, 1042–1216*, 4th edn (London, 1988).

Barrow, G.W.S., *Robert Bruce*, 2nd edn (Edinburgh, 1976).

Barth, Fredrik (ed.), *Ethnic Groups and Boundaries. The Social Organisation of Culture Difference* (1969, repr. Illinois, 1998).

Bartlett, Robert, *Gerald of Wales, 1146–1223* (Oxford, 1982).

Bates, David, *Normandy Before 1066* (London, 1982).

————, 'West Francia: the Northern Principalities', in *The New Cambridge Medieval History*, vol. III: *c.900–c.1024*, ed. Reuter, Timothy (Cambridge, 1999), 398–419.

————, 'Normandy and England after 1066', *EHR* 413 (1989), 851–80.

Bates, David and Curry, Anne (eds), *England and Normandy in the Middle Ages* (London, 1994).

Baylé, Maylis, 'Norman Architecture Around the Year 1000: Its Place in the Art of North-Western Europe', *ANS* 22 (2000), 1–28.

Breese, Lauren Wood, 'The Persistence of Scandinavian Connections in Normandy in the Tenth and Early Eleventh Centuries', *Viator* 8 (1977), 47–61.

Breuilly, J.J., *Nationalism and the State*, 2nd edn (Manchester, 1993).

Brooks, N.P., 'History and Myth, Forgery and Truth', Inaugural Lecture at the University of Birmingham (23 January 1986).

————, 'Bede and the English', Jarrow Lecture (1999).

Brown, R. Allen, *The Normans* (Woodbridge, 1984).

————, *The Norman Conquest of England* (London, 1984).

Brown, Shirley Ann, *The Bayeux Tapestry: History and Bibliography* (Woodbridge, 1988).

Brown, Shirley Ann and Herren, Michael W., 'The *Adelae Comitissae* of Baudri of Bourgueil and the Bayeux Tapestry', *ANS* 16 (1994), 55–73.

The Cambridge History of the English Language, ed. Blake, Norman (Cambridge, 1992).

Campbell, J., 'England, France, Flanders and Germany: some comparisons and connections', in *Ethelred the Unready*, ed. Hill, David, B.A.R. British Series 59 (1978).

Chalandon, F., *Histoire de la domination normande en Italie et en Sicile*, 2 vols (Paris, 1907).

Chibnall, Marjorie, *The World of Orderic Vitalis* (Oxford, 1984).

————, *Anglo-Norman England, 1066–1166* (Oxford, 1986).

————, *The Debate on the Norman Conquest* (Manchester, 1999).

Clark, Cecily, '*Willelmus rex? vel alius Willelmus*', in *Words, Names and History: Selected Writings of Cecily Clark*, ed. Jackson, Peter (Cambridge, 1995), 280–98.

Colley, Linda, 'Britishness and Otherness: An Argument', *Journal of British Studies* 31 (1992), 309–29.

Collins English Dictionary, 4th edn repr. (Glasgow, 1999).

Cowdrey, H.E.J., *The Age of Abbot Desiderius* (Oxford, 1983).

Cownie, Emma, *Religious Patronage in Anglo-Norman England* (London, 1998).

Crawford, Barbara E. (ed.), *Scandinavian Settlement in Northern Britain* (London, 1995).

Curta, Florin, 'Slavs in Fredegar and Paul the Deacon: medieval *gens* or "scourge of God"?', *EME* 6 (1997), 141–67.

Dauzat, Albert and Rostaing, Charles, *Dictionnaire étymologique des noms de lieux en France* (Paris, 1963).

Davies, R.R., *The First English Empire* (Oxford, 2000).

Davis, R.H.C., *The Normans and their Myth* (London, 1976).

———, 'The Carmen de Hastingae Proelio', *EHR* 93 (1978), 241–61.

———, *A History of Medieval Europe*, 2nd edn (London, 1988).

Davis, R.H.C., Engels, L.J., et al., 'The *Carmen de Hastingae Proelio*: a discussion', *ANS* 2 (1980), 1–20.

Devroey, Jean-Paul, *Etudes sur le grand domaine carolingien* (Aldershot, 1993).

Dillman, François-Xavier, 'Bibliographie: Les Vikings dans l'Empire franc', *Revue du Nord* 56 (1974), 91–9.

Douglas, David C., 'The Norman Conquest and English Feudalism', originally *Economic History Review* (May 1939), reprinted in *Time and the Hour* (London, 1977), 161–75.

———, 'Rollo of Normandy', *EHR* 57 (1942), 417–36.

———, *William the Conqueror: the Norman Impact upon England* (London, 1964).

———, *The Norman Achievement, 1050–1100* (London, 1969).

———, *Time and the Hour* (London, 1977).

Drell, Joanna, 'Cultural Syncretism and Ethnic Identity: the Norman "Conquest" of Southern Italy and Sicily', *JMH* 25 (1999), 187–202.

Dunbabin, Jean, *France in the Making, 843–1180* (Oxford, 1985).

Eames, Elizabeth, 'Mariage et concubinage légal en Norvège à l'époque des Vikings', *AN* 2 (1952), 195–208.

Ehlers, J.H., 'Die Historia Francorum Senonensis und der Aufstieg des Hauses Capet', *JMH* 4 (1978), 1–25.

Erdmann, Carl, *The Origin of the Idea of Crusade*, tr. Baldwin, Marshall W. and Goffart, Walter (Princeton, NJ, 1977).

Fichte, J.G., *Addresses to the German Nation*, tr. Jones, R.F. and Turnbull, G.H. (1922, repr. Westport, CN, 1979).

Fleischman, Suzanne, 'On the Representation of History and Fiction in the Middle Ages', *History and Theory* 22, no. 3 (1983), 278–310.

Foot, Sarah, 'The Making of *Angelcynn*: English Identity Before the Norman Conquest', *TRHS* 6 (1996), 25–49.

Forde, Simon, Johnson, Lesley and Murray, Alan V. (eds), *Concepts of National Identity in the Middle Ages*, Leeds Texts and Monographs, New Series 14 (Leeds, 1995).

Garnett, George, ' "Franci et Angli": the Legal Distinctions between Peoples after the Conquest', *ANS* 8 (1986),109–37.

Gellner, Ernest, *Encounters with Nationalism* (Oxford, 1994).

Gillingham, John, 'Henry of Huntingdon and the Twelfth-Century Revival of the English Nation', *Concepts of National Identity in the Middle Ages*, ed. Forde, Simon, Johnson, Lesley and Murray, Alan V., Leeds Texts and Monographs, New Series 14 (Leeds, 1995), 75–101.

———, *The English in the Twelfth Century* (Woodbridge, 2000).

Goetz, Hans-Werner, Jörg Jarnut and Walter Pohl (eds), *Regna and Gentes. The Relationship between Late Antique and Early Medieval Peoples and Kingdoms in the Transformation of the Roman World* (Leiden, 2003).

Graham-Campbell, J. (ed.), *Cultural Atlas of the Viking World* (New York, 1994).

Gransden, Antonia, *Historical Writing in England c.550 to c.1307* (London, 1974).

Grierson, Philip, 'The Coinages of Norman Apulia and Sicily in their International Setting', *ANS* 15 (1993), 117–32.

Grierson, Philip and Travaini, Lucia, *Medieval European Coinage – 14: Italy (III) (South Italy, Sicily, Sardinia)* (Cambridge, 1998).

Guinet, Louis, *Contribution à l'étude des Établissements Saxons en Normandie* (Caen, 1967).

Hadley, D.M., ' "And they proceeded to plough and to support themselves": the Scandinavian Settlement of England', *ANS* 19 (1997), 69–96.

Hall, J.R. Clark, *A Concise Anglo-Saxon Dictionary*, 4th edn repr. (Cambridge, 1991).

Haskins, C.H., *The Normans in European History* (New York, 1915).

———, *Norman Institutions* (Cambridge, MA, 1918, repr. 1960).

Hastings, Adrian, *The Construction of Nationhood. Ethnicity, Religion and Nationalism* (Cambridge, 1997).

Hay, D. (ed.), *The Oxford Companion to Family History* (Oxford, 1996).

Haywood, J., *The Penguin Historical Atlas of the Vikings* (Harmondsworth, 1995).

Heather, Peter, *The Goths* (Oxford, 1996).

Helmerichs, Robert, '*Princeps, Comes, Dux Normannorum*: Early Rollonid Designators and their Significance', *HSJ* 9 (2001), 57–77.

Higham, Mary C., 'Scandinavian settlement in north-west England, with a special study of *Ireby* names', *Scandinavian Settlement in Northern Britain*, ed. Crawford, Barbara E. (London, 1995), 195–205.

Hollister, C. Warren, 'Normandy, France and the Anglo-Norman *Regnum*', *Speculum* 51 (1976), 202–42.

Howorth, Henry H., 'A Criticism of the Life of Rollo, as told by Dudo de St. Quentin', *Archaeologia* 45 (1880), 235–50.

Huisman, Gerda, 'Notes on the Manuscript Tradition of Dudo of St.-Quentin's Gesta Normannorum', *ANS* 6 (1984), 122–35.

Hummer, Hans J., 'The Fluidity of Barbarian Identity: the Ethnogenesis of Alemanni and Suebi', *EME* 7 (1998), 1–27.

Hutchinson, John and Smith, Anthony D., *Nationalism* (Oxford, 1994).

Johns, Jeremy, 'The Norman Kings and the Fatimid Caliphate', *ANS* 15 (1993), 133–59.

Jones, Gwyn, *A History of the Vikings*, 2nd edn (Oxford, 1984).

Jones, P.M., '1789 and all that. Constructing Identity in Modern France', Inaugural Lecture at the University of Birmingham (9 May 1996).

Kedourie, Elie, *Nationalism*, 3rd edn (London, 1966; repr. 1979).

Keen, Maurice, *Chivalry* (London, 1984).

Lauer, Ph., *Le Règne de Louis IV d'Outre-Mer* (Paris, 1900).

Lawrence, C.H., *Medieval Monasticism. Forms of Religious Life in Western Europe in the Middle Ages*, 2nd edn (London, 1989).

Le Patourel, John, *The Norman Empire* (Oxford, 1976).

Lewis, C.P., 'The Earldom of Surrey and the Date of Domesday Book', *Historical Research* 63 (1990), 329–36.

Leyser, Karl, *Communications and Power in Medieval Europe: the Carolingian and Ottonian Centuries*, ed. Reuter, T. (London, 1994).

Lifshitz, Felice, 'Dudo's Historical Narrative and the Norman Succession of 996', *JMH* 20 (1994), 101–20.

———, *The Norman Conquest of Pious Neustria: Historic Discourse and Saintly Relics 684–1090* (Toronto, 1995).

Logan, F. Donald, *The Vikings in History* (London, 1983).

Longnon, Auguste, *Les noms de lieu de la France: leur origine, leur signification, leurs transformations* (Paris, 1920–9).

Loud, G.A., 'How "Norman" was the Norman Conquest of Southern Italy?', *Nottingham Medieval Studies* 25 (1981).

———, 'The "Gens Normannorum" – Myth or Reality?', *ANS* 4 (1982), 104–16.

———, 'The Genesis and Context of the Chronicle of Falco of Benevento', *ANS* 15 (1993), 177–98.

Mason, E., *Norman Kingship* (Bangor, 1991).

Matthew, Donald, *The Norman Conquest* (London, 1966).

———, *The Norman Kingdom of Sicily* (Cambridge, 1992).

McKitterick, R., *The Frankish Kingdoms under the Carolingians, 751–987* (London, 1983).

Melazzo, Lucio, 'The Normans through their Languages', *ANS* 15 (1993), 243–50.

Musset, Lucien, 'Influences réciproques du monde scandinave et de l'occident dans le domaine de la civilisation au moyen âge', *Journal of World History* 1 (1953), 72–90.

———, *Les Invasions: le Second Assaut Contre l'Europe Chrétienne (VIIe–Xie siècles)*, 2nd edn (Paris, 1971).

———, *Normandie Romane – 1: La Basse-Normandie*, La Nuit des Temps 25 (La Pierre-qui-Vire, 1975).

———, *Normandie Romane – 2: La Haute-Normandie*, La Nuit des Temps 41 (La Pierre-qui-Vire, 1975).

Nelson, Janet L., *Charles the Bald* (London, 1992).

Norwich, John Julius, *The Normans in Sicily: The Normans in the South 1016–1130 / The Kingdom in the Sun 1130–1194* (1967, 1970; omnibus: London, 1992).

O'Brien, Bruce R., 'From *Morðor* to *Murdrum*: the Preconquest Origin and Norman Revival of the Murder Fine', *Speculum* 71 (1996), 321–57.

———, *God's Peace and King's Peace: The Laws of Edward the Confessor* (Philadelphia, 1999).

The Oxford English Dictionary, prepared by Simpson, J.A. and Weiner, E.S.C., 2nd edn (Oxford, 1989).

Partner, Nancy F., *Serious Entertainments. The Writing of History in Twelfth-Century England* (Chicago, 1977).

Potts, Cassandra, '*Atque unum et diversis gentibus populum effecit*: Historical Tradition and the Norman Identity', *ANS* 18 (1996), 139–52.

———, *Monastic Revival and Regional Identity in Early Normandy*, Studies in the History of Medieval Religion 11 (Woodbridge, 1997).

Ray, Roger, 'Historiography', in Mantello, F.A.C. and Rigg, A.G. (eds), *Medieval Latin: an Introduction and Bibliographical Guide* (Washington, DC, 1996), 639–49.

Renoux, Annie, 'Fouilles sur le site du chateau ducal de Fécamp (Xe–XIIe siècle)', *ANS* 4 (1982), 133–52.

Rex, John and Mason, David (eds), *Theories of Race and Ethnic Relations* (Cambridge, 1986).

Reynolds, Susan, *Kingdoms and Communities in Western Europe 900–1300* (Oxford, 1984, repr. 1986).

Ridyard, S.J., 'Condigna veneratio: Post-Conquest Attitudes to the Saints of the Anglo-Saxons', *ANS* 9 (1987), 179–206.

Searle, Eleanor, 'Fact and Pattern in Heroic History: Dudo of Saint-Quentin', *Viator* 15 (1984), 119–37.

———, 'Frankish Rivalries and Norse Warriors', *ANS* 7 (1985), 198–213.

———, *Predatory Kinship and the Creation of Norman Power, 840–1066* (Berkeley, 1988).

Shepard, Jonathan, 'The Uses of the Franks in Eleventh-Century Byzantium', *ANS* 15 (1993), 275–305.

Shopkow, Leah, 'The Carolingian World of Dudo of Saint-Quentin', *JMH* 15 (1989), 19–37.

———, *History and Community. Norman Historical Writing in the Eleventh and Twelfth Centuries* (Washington, DC, 1997).

Short, Ian, '*Tam Angli quam Franci*: Self-Definition in Anglo-Norman England', *ANS* 18 (1996), 153–75.

———, 'The Language of the Bayeux Tapestry Inscription', *ANS* 23 (2001), 267–80.

Simpson, D.P., *Cassell's Latin Dictionary*, 5th edn repr. (London, 1997).

Smith, Anthony D., *National Identity* (London, 1991).

Smyth, Alfred P., *Scandinavian Kings in the British Isles, 850–880* (Oxford, 1977).

Southern, R.W., *The Making of the Middle Ages* (1953, repr. London, 1993).

———, *Saint Anselm and his Biographer* (Cambridge, 1963).

Stafford, Pauline, *Queen Emma and Queen Edith* (Oxford, 1997).

Stenton, Frank, *Anglo-Saxon England*, 3rd edn (Oxford, 1971).

Strayer, Joseph R., 'Recueil des Actes des Ducs de Normandie (Review)', *Speculum* 37 (1962), 607–10.

Stringer, Keith J., *The Reign of Stephen* (London, 1998).

Tabuteau, Emily Z., *Transfers of Property in Eleventh-Century Norman Law* (Chapel Hill, 1988).

Thomas, Hugh, 'The Gesta Herewardi, the English, and their Conquerors', *ANS* 21 (1999), 213–32.

———, *The English and the Normans. Ethnic Hostility, Assimilation, and Identity 1066–c.1220* (Oxford, 2003).

Thomson, Rodney, *William of Malmesbury* (Woodbridge, 1987).

Van Houts, Elisabeth M.C., 'The Gesta Normannorum Ducum: a History Without an End', *ANS* 3 (1981), 106–18.

———, 'Historiography and Hagiography at Saint-Wandrille: the 'Inventio et miracula sancti Vulfranni ', *ANS* 12 (1990), 233–51.

Van Houts, Elisabeth M.C., *The Normans in Europe* (Manchester, 2000).

Vaughn, Sally N., 'Eadmer's Historia Novorum: a Reinterpretation', *ANS* 10 (1988), 259–89.

Vincent, Auguste, *Toponymie de la France* (1937).

Von Feilitzen, Olof, *The Pre-Conquest Personal Names of Domesday Book*, Nomina Germanica 3 (Uppsala, 1937).

Wallace-Hadrill, J.M., 'The Vikings in Francia', The Stenton Lecture 1974 (Reading, 1975).

Ward, John O., 'Classical Rhetoric and the Writing of History in Medieval and Renaissance Culture', in McGregor, Frank and Wright, Nicholas (eds), *European History and its Historians* (Adelaide, 1977), 1–10.

Weinreich, Peter, 'The operationalisation of identity theory in racial and ethnic relations', *Theories of Race and Ethnic Relations*, ed. Rex, John and Mason, David (Cambridge, 1986), 299–320.

Werner, Karl Ferdinand, 'Quelques observations au sujet des débuts du « duché » de Normandie', *Droit Privé et Institutions Régionales: Etudes historiques offertes à Jean Yver* (Paris, 1976), 691–709.

Williams, Ann, *The English and the Norman Conquest* (Woodbridge, 1995).

Wilson, David M., 'Scandinavian Settlement in the North and West of the British Isles – an Archaeological Point-of-View', *TRHS* 5th Series 26 (1976), 95–113.

Wolf, Kenneth Baxter, *Making History: the Normans and their Historians in Eleventh-Century Italy* (Philadelphia, 1995).

Wolfram, Herwig, *History of the Goths* (Munich, 1979, tr. Dunlop, Thomas J., Berkeley, 1988).

Wormald, Francis, 'The Inscriptions with a Translation', in Stenton, F.M., *The Bayeux Tapestry* (London, 1957), 177–80.

Index